The Anxiety of Obsolescence

The Anxiety of Obsolescence

The American Novel in the Age of Television

Kathleen Fitzpatrick

Vanderbilt University Press • NASHVILLE

10 09 08 07 06 05   1 2 3 4 5

Printed on acid-free paper.
Manufactured in the United States of America

Portions of Chapter 3 of this book first appeared in different form as "The Clockwork Eye: Technology, Woman, and the Decay of the Modern in Thomas Pynchon's V.," in *Thomas Pynchon: Reading from the Margins*, ed. Niran Abbas (2002). I gratefully acknowledge the permission granted by the Associated University Presses to reprint this material.

The "schematic diagram of a general communication system" on page 156 is reprinted from *The Mathematical Theory of Communication*, copyright 1949, 1998 by Board of Trustees of the University of Illinois Press, and is used with permission of the University of Illinois Press.

The "encoding/decoding" diagram on page 157 is reprinted from *Culture, Media, Language*, copyright 1980 by Centre for Contemporary Cultural Studies, University of Birmingham, and is used with permission of Taylor & Francis.

Library of Congress Cataloging-in-Publication Data

Fitzpatrick, Kathleen, 1967–
The anxiety of obsolescence : the American novel in the age of television / Kathleen Fitzpatrick.—1st ed.
p. cm.
Includes bibliographical references (p.) and index.
ISBN 0-8265-1519-3 (acid-free paper)
ISBN 0-8265-1520-7 (pbk. : acid-free paper)
1. American fiction—History and criticism.
2. Television broadcasting—United States—Influence.
3. Literacy—United States. 4. Popular culture—United States.
I. Title.
PS371F58 2006
813'.5409—dc22

2005031076

For Rick

Contents

Acknowledgments

Any text such as this one owes its existence to countless individuals and institutions that have supported its coming into being, and any expression of gratitude seems destined for inadequacy. Such an inadequacy in what follows should be understood as a failure in the expression, rather than the absence, of sincere emotion.

This project has taken a long and often painful path to its final fruition but has been fostered at each stage by teachers, counselors, and guides who have managed through their efforts to make it something more than I could have produced on my own. At New York University, the instruction and mentorship of Cyrus Patell, Phillip Brian Harper, Josephine Hendin, Pat Hoy, and Carolyn Dever created the atmosphere of support and rigor that enabled me to take an ill-formed question about the relationship between television and the novel and develop a project that has sustained my interest through many dark moments. The material support of both the English Department and the Expository Writing Program were crucial to the speedy completion of the dissertation from which the present project developed. That dissertation also benefited from the critical input of the postmodernist dissertation support group, including Sandy Baldwin, Martin FitzPatrick, and Jae Roe, whose camaraderie and friendly challenges made the process as worthwhile as the product. I also want to thank Megan Abbott, Margaret Longbrake, and Laurie Marcus for their demanding, insightful readings of my work. For their unflagging support through the always tendentious and often exhilarating days in the doctoral program, I'd like to convey my deepest gratitude to Corinne Abate, Stephen Brauer, Joshua Gaylord, Michael Matto, Lahney Preston-Matto, James Polchin, Aaron Rosenthal, and all the members of Table 13, whose sympathy, kindness, and eternal readiness with the appropriate televisual reference made the early days of this project more fun than I could have hoped.

At Pomona College, I have been blessed with generous colleagues, both present and past members of the English Department—Martha Andresen, Daniel Birkholz, Toni Clark, Barbara Clonts, Edward Copeland, Rena Fraden, Paul Mann, Bob Mezey, Cristanne Miller, Sarah Raff, Arden Reed, Paul Saint-Amour, Valorie Thomas, Kyla Wazana Tompkins, Penny Tucker, David Foster Wallace, Meg Worley, and Steve Young—whose guidance, support, and rigorous critique have encouraged me in my exploration of the boundaries of genre and medium. Many other friends in the wider college community, including Ronald Cluett, Donna Di Grazia, Jennifer Friedlander, Stephanie Harves, Alexandra Juhasz, Kevin Platt, Frances Pohl, Ranu Samantrai, John Seery, Shasta Turner, Peggy Waller, Nicole Weekes, and Heather Williams, have contributed readings, advice, celebration, commiseration, and friendship when most needed. Noah Buhayar, Susanne Liaw, and Sandra Zito provided able research assistance at key moments. I wish, moreover, to thank the college and, in particular, the Steele Fellowship for providing the leave that made the completion of this project possible.

Numerous other colleagues have read and supported my work throughout the years. Among them, I'd like to thank Michael Joyce, N. Katherine Hayles, Michael Bérubé, Timothy Melley, Jeremy Green, Jenny Bay, and Michele White for their dedication, encouragement, and generosity of spirit; they are the models to which I aspire, and for which I am enormously grateful. I also extend my most sincere thanks to Betsy Phillips, Dariel Mayer, Sue Havlish, Bobbe Needham, and the anonymous readers of Vanderbilt University Press, whose attention and support throughout the entire publication process were invaluable.

To my parents, Connie and Dennis Carlton, and my sister, Denise Fitzpatrick, who have been unflaggingly supportive of my at times incomprehensible desires, I give my love and my gratitude. And last, my utterly inadequate thanks to Rick Blackwood, who knows all he's done for me but has had the good grace not to mention it.

"If I were a writer," Owen said, "how I would enjoy being told the novel is dead. How liberating, to work in the margins, outside a central perception. You are the ghoul of literature. Lovely."

—Don DeLillo, *The Names*

Introduction
The Anxiety of Obsolescence

> Print is undead.
>
> —Stuart Moulthrop

The world is going to hell in a handbasket, and has been since the invention of television.

So, at least, seems to be the argument made by a range of cultural critics, both from the Right and from the Left, both academics and public intellectuals, both those who publish in highbrow venues and those who publish in more popular locales, both those who write fiction and those who write nonfiction.

What all these cultural critics have in common, by and large, is print, and the belief that Gutenberg's medium and the literature that it has made possible must be saved from the twentieth-century technologies—among which they number television, of course, but also film and the Internet—that threaten to end more than five hundred years of print's dominance in Western culture and drive it into obsolescence.

One may infer that conflict between print technologies and electronic media exists from the media and pundit attention to what seems an otherwise insignificant event: In late October 2001, Oprah Winfrey withdrew the invitation she'd earlier extended to Jonathan Franzen to appear on her show as a featured book-club author. This unprecedented disinvitation rocked the literary world and produced a round of accusations, vilifications, and finger-pointing from folks on both sides of the issue. Was Franzen right to suggest his discomfort with the Oprah seal of approval on the jacket of his book, an indication of the questionable effects of corporate intervention in literary production? Was he being an elitist jerk when he bemoaned the other mainstream Oprah selections with which his book would now be lumped? Was Oprah too easily offended by Franzen's ill-thought-out comments, and too ready to flex her quite significant media muscle? Or did she respond in the only way that made any sense by releasing an author uncomfortable with the milieu into which he'd been thrust from his obligations to that milieu, in order to protect her audience from condescension? At base: Was Oprah's Book Club hopelessly middlebrow, catering as it did to an audience of Middle American television watchers, or did it perform a significant cultural service in introducing important books to people who might not otherwise have found them? Was it a monolithic mass-branding machine that tyrannized bookstores into shifting their sales priorities, fronting Oprah's choices and ignoring the unselected masses, or was it a miraculous means of getting people to go into bookstores and buy books? Finally, given the conflict's fallout—Oprah discontinued the book club altogether a few months later, while Franzen stayed on best-seller lists across the country—what, if anything, does the Oprah/Franzen flap reveal about the ongoing relationship between high art and mass culture, or about the precarious existence of publishing between literary and corporate production? Whatever conclusions one draws, the issues at stake—and particularly those that suggest an inevitable conflict between print values and the values promoted by television—cut to the heart of the serious novel's seemingly tenuous position in contemporary U.S. culture.

This book is about that seemingly tenuous position. I explore the ways the novel has been represented throughout the postmodern era as under threat in U.S. culture, driven into a state of near obsolescence by the electronic media developed during the twentieth century, most notably television. More important, however, I'll focus throughout on the cultural purposes served by the repeated proclamations of the novel's untimely demise.

As an example, take a 1997 editorial published in a Web journal called *Bold Type*. The author raises an unnerving question that many writers and scholars in the age of electronic media find themselves repeatedly confronting: "Why . . . does the book's influence over popular culture appear to be ever-waning?" Despite the hint in this quote that such a decline might be no more than mere appearance, the author takes it for verifiable fact: "The book today is the underdog; one must root for the written word" (Weissman). In this evocation of a sporting match, the editorial imagines the current media ecology to be a scene of conflict, with winners and losers, in which the book seems destined to fail and thus must rally backers to its side. A certain irony hangs about this argument, given that it appeared on the Internet. On the one hand, using the Web to make this pitch for print culture's survival only serves to call attention to the electronic sources of the book's apparent demise; on the other, the book's presumptive foe—wired, virtual, and overwhelmingly visual—is here conscripted as its champion, a service that calls the very supposition of conflict into question. The alliance between the two forms is nervous at best, as indicated by the oddness of the journal's title, *Bold Type*: though the publication may be about ink-on-paper type, it is not composed of it, and thus it serves to champion a medium that it itself eschews.[1] The purposes of the alliance, however, and further of the journal's suggestions of the book's need for cultural support in an era in which it is beset by larger, more powerful foes, become quite clear upon discovering that *Bold Type* is a publicity organ of Random House. The publisher, beset by anxieties about its own future, employs the media ostensibly arrayed against it to ensure continued support for the objects it produces; moreover, by declaring the book endangered, the publisher can rally readers to its side, encouraging them to prolong the existence of print media by purchasing the publisher's books.

The Internet is merely the latest of the competitors that print culture has been pitted against since the late nineteenth century. Threats to the book's presumed dominion over the hearts and minds of Americans have arisen at every technological turn—or so the rampant public discourse of print's obsolescence would lead one to believe. This conventional perception of the book as an endangered species among rival media rests at the heart of my investigation but is not itself the object of my inquiry. The question taken up by *The Anxiety of Obsolescence* is not whether print culture is dying at the hands of the media, but rather what purposes announcements of the death of print culture serve, and thus what all this talk about the end of the book tells us about those doing the talking. The very existence of this book, in fact, declares its author's position on the issue: the book is not dead or even dying. Rather, the growing pains of old media when confronted by new are all too easily—and sometimes purposefully—mistaken for death throes. This is perhaps especially true of the contemporary era, a "postmodern" world characterized by exponential technological acceleration. The average computer becomes obsolete in two to three years. Last year's whiz-bang cable-ready picture-in-picture television is destined to become a relic in short order, undone by the full implementation of HDTV. DVD and the DVR have all but replaced the VCR. And just when we finally finished converting that old vinyl collection to CDs, the *Los Angeles Times* announced that format's imminent death (Boucher).[2]

The purposes that these latter instances of talk about obsolescence serve are embarrassingly evident: the planned obsolescence of consumer goods is a capitalist institution worth billions annually. Talk of an old format's death will inevitably help sales of a new format. But what purpose does the discourse of the death of print serve? And, more pointedly, why has this discourse been picked up by those presumably least likely to benefit from it—contemporary novelists such as Thomas Pynchon and Don DeLillo? We are inundated with screeds from the popular, the literary, and the academic spheres that decry the debasement and replacement of the book and its attendant form of typographical literacy by something often loosely characterized as "the media." The book and its main champion, the writer, are repeatedly represented as latter-day Quixotes, tilting at the windmills of mind-numbing, dehumanizing, overpoweringly visual forms of entertainment and communication. The main locus of blame for this literary decline is, of course, television, but such metaphors of media in conflict have recurred throughout the last dozen decades. Late nineteenth-century observers imagined that the photographic image declared the realism of painting and the novel obsolete; later, film similarly fought with the novel for dominance of the narrative form. Television threatened film's position in the 1950s and 1960s; now the Internet may well be threatening television's centrality in the home.[3] New media repeatedly threaten to take the place—or the audience—of old. But none of these media, according to the popular wisdom, is more threatened than the book.

Such conventional concerns about the book's imminent demise are more than a bit specious, as a cursory look at the urban and suburban landscapes of the late 1990s and early 2000s reveals. A Borders or a Barnes and Noble has arisen (or will arise) on every corner in major metropolitan areas, as well as in most small towns. The virtual landscape gives us evidence as well: not only did amazon.com revolutionize the Internet, but it did so by selling millions of unmarketable items, if all that end-of-the-book hype were true. These merchants are not striving in some altruistic fashion to promote the Arnoldian cultural uplift of literacy against a debasing mass culture but are responding to existing markets and creating new ones. Stated most plainly, and most platitudinously, more people are buying more books than ever these days.[4] Given this growth of the market, how can one imagine the book to be an endangered species? And, not incidentally, whose interests does it serve to claim so?

Perhaps only a certain form of book is disappearing. Maybe only "high" literature is under siege, and perhaps only the serious writer need be concerned. This is the underlying contention of *Bold Type*'s editor, indicated by an oblique reference to the electronic media that are threatening typography:

> The public seems to want to devour culture as if using the high-speed dubbing feature on a VCR. It is consumption without absorption, a simultaneous informational overload and reductionism that is directly at odds with the extended narrative literature provides. (Weissman)

The literature of "extended narrative"—the serious novel—is thus the primary object of *Bold Type*'s rescue efforts. What literary fiction is being rescued from is even more enlightening: it requires protection not just from the films and television that come together in the VCR, but from the "public" that has become attuned to those newer media. In this slippage between the failings of the electronic media and the failings of its audience, an inevitable elitism begins to creep to the surface. The public, accustomed to the sound bite, is apparently incapable of reading the serious novel with the attention and care it deserves. And thus, as the editorial continues, it becomes evident that *Bold Type*'s goal is less to liberate that public from its VCRs and return it to the joys of reading than to separate the book from that public, to create in its supposed obsolescence a minority of devoted readers who are that much more devoted because they understand that they are a minority: "In this more marginal context," the author suggests, "it may be that writers will be liberated and literature as an art form will flourish anew" (Weissman). What will save the novel is thus not a return to the cultural center but an entrenchment on the edges, in which the cachet of marginality serves to create a protected space within which the novel can continue as art by restricting itself to those few readers equipped to appreciate it.

This elitism, however, is usually confined to the subtext of such discussions of the novel's obsolescence. The surface language is explicitly that of conflict, and in particular of conflict between the novel and television, in which the novelist serves on the front lines of a cultural war. Metaphors of literary production as a scene of violent conflict are not new. Harold Bloom, in *The Anxiety of Influence*, developed a theory of modern poetry as an Oedipal struggle in which the poet—always male, of course—must confront and kill his poetic "fathers" in order to bed the Muse and thus reach artistic maturity. This battle, Bloom claims, is "a battle between strong equals, father and son as mighty opposites, Laius and Oedipus at the crossroads" (11). A "strong poet" is one able to overcome his anxiety of influence by using such strategies as misreading, completion, and correction in his confrontations with the work of the precursor. However, Bloom is quick to point out that the work of this strong poet, the poem that he produces, "is not an overcoming of anxiety, but is that anxiety" (94); in fact, "[a] poem is a poet's melancholy at his lack of priority" (96). The poem is not a working-out but an embodiment of the anxiety of influence, reflecting that anxiety in its repeated engagements with the work of the precursor. Yet, as Bloom also seems to acknowledge, this anxiety, translated from the modern to the contemporary scene, is no longer focused solely upon poetic precursors. "In the contemporary poems that most move me," he admits, " . . . I can recognize a strength that battles against *the death of poetry*, yet also the exhaustions of being a latecomer" (12, emphasis mine). The contemporary poet's anxieties thus cannot revolve entirely around belatedness but must actively confront the apparent imminence of poetry's end.

The Anxiety of Obsolescence bears an obvious debt to Bloom. It is important, however—in a move that may ironically resemble the influenced poet's attempts to separate his work from a predecessor's—to suggest a number of key distinctions between Bloom's work and my own. What Bloom's theory lacks in its at times claustrophobic concern with the insular world of literary history is an exploration of the source of the poet's anxiety about the death of poetry. Given that the postmodern novel obsessively engages with the encroachments of the surrounding culture, understanding the function of its concerns about obsolescence requires a different mode of reading. The hermetic world of writers reacting with and against one another no longer exists—or worse, where it exists, it no longer seems to impact U.S. culture at large. And thus the scholarly community, as well the novelist, must give up the luxury of purely literary-historical models of creative production to confront instead the role of literature in a larger culture. It is no longer sufficient to examine the relationship of a writer to his precursors, because these precursors are no longer perceived to be anywhere near as threatening as what's coming next. As Joseph Tabbi has pointed out, "what has changed" in the age of electronic media "is not the book *per se* but the way that books can be read now. The end of books is more accurately the end of academic readings that isolate texts from the larger media ecology" ("Review"). Models of reading that are exclusively literary-historical must give way to models engaged with culture, technology, and media in an era in which these are thought to threaten literature's very existence.

It is equally important, however—and it may seem odd to need to point this out at the outset of a work that is in significant part literary criticism—to treat the novelist's perceptions of his culture, and his use of the discourses already in motion about and through that culture, as primary texts that require analysis rather than as authoritative interpretations. Too often, scholars and others take at face value the positions of critique the novelist adopts with regard to television and other forms of mass culture without exploring the ways these positions misread and misconstrue those media objects. In so doing, much recent scholarly work on postmodern fiction threatens to collapse the distinctions between the representational practices of fiction and the analytical practices of criticism and theory, treating the former as if it were doing the work of the latter. Such a treatment of fiction as theory allows the critic too easily to avoid asking difficult ideological questions about the novels. Fictions are, after all, crafted *representations* of a culture, not *explanations* of it. For this reason—much as hermeneutic modes of interpretation have been called into question in recent scholarship (due to a mistaken sense that they privilege "authoritative" readings and treat the text as though it were separable from the larger cultural sphere in which it exists)—*The Anxiety of Obsolescence* calls for a return to the critical practice of close reading. This is not a call for a return to the New Criticism, or for any form of regressive movement away from "theory." Instead, *The Anxiety of Obsolescence* models a new critical practice that pays careful attention both to cultural milieu and to textual particulars, moving between extended close readings of a number of important contemporary U.S. novels and the broader historical, cultural, and technological context for that fiction, in order to return our critical attention to representations and to the specific ideological formations with which those representations interact.

The same mode of reading is necessary in confronting other cultural representations of television, including scholarly and popular criticism of the form. Often, the positions that such writings take with regard to television conceal a critique of television's audience, as if the real problem in contemporary culture were not the media but the mindless, feminized masses that have given media texts cultural centrality. This slippage in the critical discourse, when read in conjunction with similar representations in postmodern fiction, begins to suggest that television, the apparent source of the novelist's fear of obsolescence, may in fact be a convenient screen for some other, murkier anxiety about instability in social relations. For these reasons, critics of television must likewise be read as engaging in representational practices and thus, like writers of fiction, must be observed with an eye not simply to their meanings but also to their functions.

As for my own position as cultural critic: in much of what follows, I appear to support the claims of television at the novelist's expense, given that I return repeatedly to the self-protective and potentially elitist impulses that lie beneath the anxiety of obsolescence. I do not at all intend to suggest through this critical approach that the novelists I discuss are wholly wrong, that television is blameless in contemporary culture, or that the media haven't appropriated a significant and at times troubling percentage of U.S. brain space. I intend, rather, to resist the knee-jerk vilification of television so endemic to literary culture and to explore instead the purposes that such vilification might serve. I can perhaps illuminate my own position through a brief confessional anecdote. Scholars all bear the scars of their educational histories and attempt to expunge those scars in their own work; like so many, I can trace my scars back to graduate school. Years ago, in a master's-level seminar, I inadvertently let slip my long-standing fondness for television: "I was raised by the TV set," I said, attempting to explain something or other. "I can tell," my professor responded, stunning me into silence. *What does that mean?*, I wondered. The only answer that made sense, given his tone, our surroundings, and the topic at hand, was that the pleasure I took in the medium explained my flightiness, my superficiality, my lack of serious education, my hyperactivity, my terrible vocabulary, or some other equally heinous flaw visible to the scholarly community. From that moment, I almost kept my mouth shut where television was concerned.

But not quite. Rather than take my television viewing into the academic closet, I decided to proselytize, to redeem the tube from its troublingly condescending association with the boob, to educate the visually illiterate—and to do so from within what seemed then the hushed gentility of an English department. The novel, after all, is my first love, and the joy I have taken in its pages—I am never so happy as with a novel in my lap so weighty I have difficulty standing—has been neither diminished nor tarnished by the pleasures that I've drawn from television. The entire trajectory of my work to date has had as a key goal the demonstration of the peaceable coexistence of literature and television, despite all the loud claims to the contrary. Recent academic attention to certain television series, including most notably *Buffy the Vampire Slayer* and *The Sopranos*, begins to suggest either that the academic world is catching up with me, or that it is now safe for scholarly fans of television to emerge from hiding.

In what follows, I explore the critical and novelistic representations of television and other electronic media with an eye to unpacking the complex ways in which those representations function. In Chapter 1, I survey three major areas of cultural conversation, at the nexus of which I locate the anxiety of obsolescence: the recurrent declaration of the death of the novel, the parallel assertion of the threat of new media technologies, and the postmodern condition.

The next three chapters take on, in turn, three major conceptual categories through which the postmodern novelist comes to understand and classify television: the machine, the spectacle, and the network. In Chapter 5, I return to the Oprah/Franzen conflict to expose and explore the social implications of the anxiety of obsolescence. It is no accident, I believe, that this conflict's "literary" figure is a white man, while the "televisual" position is occupied by a woman of color; the conflicts between media forms have always been about conflicts between dominant and emergent subjectivities.

It is important to remember that the anxiety of obsolescence is not new in depicting the cultural scene as one of conflict among competing media. While the bulk of this investigation is geared toward an examination of the novelist's fear of television, these same anxieties crop up whenever one form of communication or expression begins to feel threatened by a newer form. As Neil Postman argues:

> Surrounding every new technology are institutions whose organization—not to mention their reason for being—reflects the world-view promoted by the technology. Therefore, when an old technology is assaulted by a new one, institutions are threatened. When institutions are threatened, a culture finds itself in crisis. (*Technopoly* 18)

This crisis appears even where the assault is largely imaginary. The implications of the anxiety of obsolescence, then, reach well beyond the confines of traditional literary criticism. The ways we speak and write about new media—and particularly the means by which we express our concerns about the world that new media forms are eroding or leaving behind—may reveal more about our own entrenched cultural ideologies than they do about the media themselves. In paying careful attention to this discourse, we can dismantle both our technophilia and our technophobia to see what other terrors they might hide.

1

Three Discourses
on the Age of Television

Ending is a way to proceed.
—Paul Mann

"The death of the novel is here again," writes Natasha Walter in a 1996 report on the state of the British publishing industry. "It's a standing joke among newspapers' literary editors trying to find a story. Shall we commission the 'books are out' piece, or shall we commission the one that proves 'books are back'?" (Walter). This endless—and ostensibly meaningless—circulation and recirculation of the tale of the novel's demise, like the similar omnipresence of the narrative that connects technological advance with cultural decline, suggests the underlying import of such articles: rather than shedding light on the status of the book on the contemporary scene, these obituaries and rebirth announcements might serve different cultural purposes, whether merely filling column space for tired literary editors or providing ammunition in more strenuously fought culture wars. Their recurrence thus bears careful examination. This chapter situates the major conceptual formations that undergird the anxiety of obsolescence.[1] Neither technophobia nor the literary novel's obituary is new; each historical reappearance of these discourses simultaneously undercuts the gravity of our contemporary mobilizations of the notion of obsolescence and reveals the ideological work that those mobilizations perform.

In addition to the death of the novel and the threat of new technologies, the third cultural narrative this chapter confronts—the third constitutive element of the anxiety of obsolescence—is the discourse of postmodernism. Postmodernism is founded in the very concept of obsolescence—obsolescence of the modern, of the individual, of History with a capital H, of Truth with a capital T. Postmodernism is also a discourse of discourse, the very self-reflexivity of which produces the inwardness that the contemporary novelist requires for his project of self-protection.

What follows is an analysis of these three intersecting discursive formations that uncovers the "relations," as Foucault suggests, among expressions of concern about cultural change that surface in a wide range of fields.[2] The breadth of such discursive formations, in achieving the level of the commonplace, results in a quantum shift in the relationship between discourse and truth: such statements cease merely to describe reality and instead begin to create it.[3] In thinking about the "cultural discourses" of the late twentieth century, I focus not simply on the recurrence of a particular set of aesthetic or scientific or philosophical themes that surface in multiple contemporary locations but on the means by which those statements and ideas may be thought of as *doing* something—in this case, creating and perpetuating a set of hierarchical relations among cultural texts and, not incidentally, a set of power relations among cultural producers.

Such an analysis, however, must avoid the tendency toward totalization that large-scale cultural theories too often exhibit, accounting instead for the conflicts and complexities of contemporary lived experience. After all, if the discourses I examine uniformly create the reality within which I exist and the consciousness through which I understand that reality, can my discourse about them escape the epistemological structures and ideological strictures I am attempting to investigate? For instance, can I cease being postmodern long enough to critically examine postmodernism? The answer lies in the distinction theories of ideology draw between *dominance* and *hegemony*: the true significance of cultural discourse lies not in how the social world is controlled by it but in how that world is led to consent to it. Moreover, the efficacy of such discourses resides not in their univocality but rather in the negotiations among their multiple voices.

In fact, these discourses are most riven with contradictions precisely when they lay the greatest claim to totality. Stephen Connor, for instance, approaches the question of postmodernism's self-reflexive inescapability through a paradox that festers at its heart. One is repeatedly struck, he points out, by "the degree of consensus in postmodernist discourse that there is no longer any possibility of consensus, the authoritative pronouncements of the disappearance of final authority and the promotion and recirculation of a total and comprehensive narrative of a cultural condition in which totality is no longer thinkable" (10). Such a set of contradictions, inherent in many such contemporary discourses, does not undermine the significance of those discourses but instead creates the field on which paradoxical ideological concepts do battle. Statements that declare the novel dead are, as Walter pithily points out, chronically replaced by equally authoritative statements that celebrate the novel's revival—and are often embedded, as we shall see, in the very texts whose demise they announce. In the technological debates, "declinists" and "neo-Pollyannas" are present in roughly equal numbers, the voices on each side equally loud (Stephens 231). Each requires the other for the discourse to be complete; the shifting balance between the two sides works to define the cultural environment in which the discourse operates. The importance of the anxiety of obsolescence, then, lies less in revealing how these discourses about the media control contemporary notions about the postmodern novel than in exploring how contemporary use of those discourses illuminates the cultural ideologies within which we, as readers, operate.

The Novel Is Dead. Long Live the Novel.

The novel has been dead for nearly as long as it has been alive. Its very name reveals part of the problem it faces: the genre's practitioners have felt throughout its history the pressures of newness. In the words of William Hill Brown, the author of what is arguably the first U.S. novel, "What is a novel without novelty?" (qtd. in Gilmore 620). Novelty, however, while one of the genre's primary attractions, makes its downfall inevitable. One critic has in fact read the death of the novel foretold in the sequel to its originary text, Cervantes' *Don Quixote*; once the novel was no longer new, it seemingly began the long trek deathward (Reed). John Barth, in *LETTERS*, his epistolary return to the novel's origins, cites a 1758 missive in which Samuel Richardson expressed his concerns that the novel would turn out to be nothing more than a fad, and one that had likely already run its course.[4] Richardson thus becomes, in Barth's narrative, not only the first English novelist but also the first English novelist to worry about the novel's death. Just over two centuries later, Barth himself reveals a strikingly similar cluster of concerns in "The Literature of Exhaustion," a set of anxieties with which contemporary novelists continue to grapple.

But as the examples of Cervantes and Richardson indicate, the novel's death presupposes its birth, and each of the genre's origin narratives has built into it a certain fated conclusion. In Ian Watt's formulation, the novel begins with Defoe, Richardson, and Fielding, and it is irrevocably tied to the rise of a particular species of realism, as well as to the rise of the English middle class (Watt). The threat of the novel's death, in Watt's narrative, emanates from critiques of realism and carries with it the specter of the dying hegemony of the overwhelmingly white and male English bourgeoisie. In Nancy Armstrong's revision of Watt's model, however, the novel is born not simply out of the consolidation of middle-class power in England but also out of the desire to confine female influence to the domestic sphere, a relegation presented in the early novel as a fait accompli (see Armstrong). By considering the role of gender in the novel's origins, and by taking seriously the domestic fiction that predates Watt's triumvirate, Armstrong's narrative includes texts within the category of the "novel" that would, in Watt's narrative, be certain signs of its death.[5]

In fact, the novel, however defined by its origins, has always been a nervous genre, equally concerned about its present and its future, anxious about its relationships to truth and to history, apprehensive about which side of Andreas Huyssen's "great divide" between high art and mass culture it fell upon. However odd it may sound in the era of MTV and first-person shooter games, the novel was once blamed for many of the ills of youth culture that have since been charged against jazz, moving pictures, rock and roll, television, video games, and the Internet.[6] The argument that the novel corrupted the morals of women and adolescents revealed its ideological basis most clearly in the political turn such accusations took in the early United States. The novel was accused of being antirepublican, of producing solipsistic, individualistic (in the original negative, Tocquevillian sense) readers who shirked the masculine world of action and commerce for the feminine realm of domesticity and illusion.[7] This is the crux of the matter: concerns about the genre's insalubriousness mask far deeper, nearly unspeakable ideological terrors that revolve around its apparent powers of feminization.

This discourse has of course long since inverted. In his attack upon the "damn'd mob of scribbling women" who threatened his livelihood, Hawthorne began the masculinization of the novelistic form at the same time he pointedly separated his work—which he considered a form of high art—from the domestic scribbles his female competitors produced.[8] In the century and a half since, the novel has become the grand old man of popular entertainments and has acquired through its associations with the masculine and its aspirations to high art a thick veneer of respectability. The rise of serious study of the novel on the university level during the twentieth century—and the even more recent addition of the U.S. novel to the curriculum—has further transformed an object of moral opprobrium into a source of spiritual and ethical uplift. We have reserved our cultural concern and excoriation for a list of latecomers, the "popular" art forms that have at least temporarily fallen on the wrong side of Huyssen's great divide.[9] The early accusations leveled at the novel are important both as a reminder that the novel was not always considered the high-art form it is revered as today, and as an acknowledgment that the concerns about more recent media forms revealed in contemporary cultural discourses may seem equally baseless in the coming centuries.

Moreover, just as the seemingly ahistorical sense of moral uplift attributed to the novel by those who lament its passing is in fact a relatively recent development, the suggestion of such elegizers that the novel had a "day" that is now past often vastly overestimates the historical influence of the form on Western culture. Literacy, and particularly the kind of literacy that allowed for leisure-time, nonbiblical reading, has always been the province of an elite, educated few; the reading public, especially that segment of the public with the disposable time and income available to acquire a taste for printed literature as art, has always been a minority. The image many elegizers of the novel create—a moment in the past in which a people, a culture, a nation was affected as one body by the movements of literary thought—is largely mythical, a revisionist creation of a nonexistent utopia.[10]

The discourse announcing the death of the novel has served throughout the twentieth century to separate the canonical from the noncanonical, the literary from the pulp, the meritorious from the meretricious. Pronouncements of literature's death have hardly been limited to the novel, of course; in 1988, Joseph Epstein touched off a verbal avalanche in literary circles by demanding to know "who killed poetry." His contention—that university creative-writing programs were largely responsible for the genre's death by drowning in the roiling waters of hackdom—produced such an overwhelming response that two full issues of the *AWP* [Associated Writing Programs] *Chronicle* were given over to varying levels of agreement and rebuttal. Perhaps most surprising about this often vitriolic exchange was the number of practicing poets who took Epstein's salvo seriously, as though his inquest negated their continuing creative lives. As Paul Mann's *Theory-Death of the Avant-Garde* suggests, such obituaries must be read with a skeptical eye:

> Throughout the history of the avant-garde, guardians of tradition, ideologues of various parties, and a host of parasites, promoters, and dreamers have been ready with the news of the passing of this or that once-innovative movement or style; modern culture is typified by such deaths, by the death of painting, the death of the novel, the death of the author, the death of x or y movement, even the death of the new. (31)

Modern literary culture is particularly riven with these deaths; critics, readers, and writers alike seem all too ready in this turbulent era to take the bad news as gospel rather than with a grain of salt. Such death notices often look a bit different, however, when one considers what the messenger—ideologue, parasite, promoter, or dreamer—might stand to gain from the proliferation of the message.

Anxieties about the novel's role in an increasingly technological world have flourished throughout the century. In the 1920s, for instance, D. H. Lawrence felt compelled to let his readers know "why the novel matters," insisting rather airily that "[t]he novel is one bright book of life. Books are not life. They are only tremulations on the ether. But the novel as a tremulation can make the whole man alive tremble. Which is more than poetry, philosophy, science, or any other book-tremulation can do" ("Why" 105). It is intriguing to note that, while Lawrence overtly compares the novel to other "book-tremulations," the notion of "tremulations on the ether" evokes a newer, if repressed, threat: radio. Indeed, Lawrence's presumed optimism about the novel's power, which begins to ring a bit of self-conscious boosterism, is reserved for the form's potential; in "Surgery for the Novel—or a Bomb," he treats much more harshly the novel as it exists:

> How do we feel about the novel? Do we bounce with joy thinking of the wonderful novelistic days ahead? Or do we grimly shake our heads and hope the wicked creature will be spared a little longer? Is the novel on his death-bed, old sinner? Or is he just toddling round his cradle, sweet little thing? (114)

Ultimately, Lawrence hedges this question by claiming that the novel is simultaneously both dying of its own self-absorption—a reading of modernist experimentalism that might give us reason to return to Paul Mann's sense of the "guardians of tradition"—and displaying its as yet immature promise. That claim, rather than simply evading the issue, inadvertently reveals some of the subtext of all of literature's death notices: they are simultaneously birth announcements, clearing away the old to make way for the new—even when that "new" is a return to a mythologized, idealized past.

The impact of Lawrence's conviction of the derelict state of the novel appears to have been minimal; the experimentalist bent against which he railed in "Surgery for the Novel—or a Bomb" (i.e., *Ulysses*) has arguably had a more lasting effect on the literary century than has the overheated novel of tremulations (*pace* Miller and Mailer). Lawrence's contributions to the death-of-the-novel discourse nonetheless reverberate in the present. In 1987, a group of scholars connected with the journal *Novel* held a conference and in 1990 produced a volume entitled *Why the Novel Matters: A Postmodern Perplex*. Acknowledging their debt to Lawrence, the conference organizers and volume editors declared their intent to update his concerns and questions to the age of late capitalism: "Why and how do novels 'matter' in postmodern times? What kind of confidence, if any, do they inspire as literary artifacts or even as newly democratized cultural artifacts? Is the novel alive and well amid competing texts and contemporary uncertainties? Is it still empowered with some of its old socio-literary clout?" (Spilka and McCracken-Flesher 5). The scholars' projected answers to their questions are embedded, as they are for Lawrence, in the questions themselves: the novel continues to matter, though in a mode more cultural than literary; its certainty rests in its representation of uncertainties. The editors expand upon the shift they describe: "the novel continues to flourish in ethical form, and to problematize ethics throughout the world, but especially . . . wherever the problems of women and minorities are taken seriously as fictional subjects" (8)—that is, the novel is not dying but democratizing. Other critics, as we'll see, interpret this less as a change of subject matter than as a devolution of the literary into the sociological, another sign of the genre's moribundity.

The concerns about the novel's continuing role raised by the *Novel* group—Does it inspire "confidence"? Does it have "clout"?—are not only for the future status of the novelist, but also for the future status of the critic.[11] The underlying question in "Why the Novel Matters" should be interpreted not as, Will the novel survive? but as, Should we bother reading novels anymore? This question is both honorable and self-serving, asking simultaneously whether continued attention should be paid to a form historically associated with an oppressively humanist (shorthand for racist, sexist, classist) sense of the individual and whether our critical careers will suffer from such continued attention. Similarly, we see in Joseph Tabbi and Michael Wutz's more declarative *Reading Matters* the contributors' "hopeful premise" that

> as the scene of writing changes, the book will not be left behind—but neither will it be quite the same in its new context. How best to use the book in the new media ecology, and how to write about literary texts without resorting to hermeneutic modes of "interpretation," are questions that preoccupy even the most text-centered of these contributions. (2)

The concern of *Reading Matters* in demonstrating that the book lives on, even in the age of cybernetics, is thus not with how to write a novel in the age of its obsolescence, but with how to write *about* one.

This concern for the critic's integrity has long been a part of such discussions of the death of the novel and frequently takes on a pointed blame-the-victim tone. The great surge—arguably, the pinnacle—of the death-of-the-novel discourse during the late 1960s was largely created by critics of the novel who were, according to Jerome Klinkowitz, responding to a stagnation perceived in U.S. writers' steadfast refusal to give up the well-made novel (see Klinkowitz). A number of these obituarists—among them Leslie Fiedler and Susan Sontag—point to the rise of the critic as a by-product of the demise of the novel, suggesting that only the form's death could account for critics' existence (see Fiedler; Sontag). Others, including Louis Rubin, insist that reports of the novel's death have been greatly exaggerated, largely by critics who don't know where to look for the next great thing (see Rubin). But whether they argue for the novel's demise or against it, the participation of such critics in the death discourse has the inevitable effect of drawing attention to criticism itself. On the one hand, Sontag argues in "Against Interpretation" that "[i]nterpretation runs rampant here [in the United States] in those arts with a feeble and negligible avant-garde: fiction and the drama" (10). On the other, Rubin in *The Curious Death of the Novel* insists that Sontag is able to make this argument only because she is not surrounded by Faulkners, Hemingways, Joyces, Manns, and Prousts; the lull in production while the writers of the mid–twentieth century work out their issues of influence creates the space for such obituaries. Both the "hermeneutic modes of 'interpretation' " Tabbi and Wutz resist—the very focus of Sontag's ire in her famous "Against Interpretation"—and the critical eulogies Rubin derides would by this argument be unnecessary if the novel itself were in better straits.

Much of the work of the critical death discourse revolves around what Spilka and McCracken-Flesher in *Why the Novel Matters* refer to as "the new hegemony of theory itself" (4), whether striving to create this hegemony or pointing to the hegemonists as the cause of the novel's fall. Roland Barthes in "The Death of the Author" and Michel Foucault in "What Is an Author?" together famously herald the poststructuralist demotion of the writer necessary to theory's rise to dominance. For Barthes, this dominance is achieved by replacing the positivist figure of the author with the decentered "scriptor": a construct "born *at the same time* as his text, . . . he is not the subject of which his book would be the predicate" (52). In fact, this powerless scriptor is the creation of the text's true producer, the reader. Barthes argues that "in order to restore to writing its future"—a future apparently in doubt—"we must reverse the myth: the birth of the reader must be requited by the death of the Author" (55). Only in destroying the writer can writing be saved; the theorist thus kills in the medium's defense. Foucault in "What Is an Author?" similarly links writing and death, particularly as "manifested in the total effacement of the individual characteristics of the writer" (117), a destruction carried out in this case not by the critic but by the text itself: "Where a work had the duty of creating immortality, it now attains the right to kill, to become the murderer of its author" (117). Replacing the writer is the "author-function," or the figure of the author constructed through discourse, the purpose of which is "to characterize the existence, circulation, and operation of certain discourses within a society" (124); the writer is thus demoted from subject to adjective. Of course, a select few such author-functions are given extended powers as "initiators of discursive practices": the "distinctive contribution of these authors is that they produced not only their own work, but the possibility and the rules of formation of other texts" (131), a description that seems to fit the theorist best.

Theory, in the narrative of its new hegemony, thus becomes both culprit and savior, murderer and hero; theory displaces the novel from cultural centrality at the same time it "rescues" the novel by announcing new ways of reading. Theory's new dominance over the novel—or what Stephen Connor refers to as "changing relationships of priority between cultural and critical activity"—is frequently read as an element in the postmodern condition; theory becomes "the mediator and validator of this new [postmodernist] fiction (indeed, for some, began to outshine some of this primary material as evidence of the postmodern temper)" (7). I will return to consider the role of postmodernist discourse in the anxiety of obsolescence later in this chapter. For the moment, it must be noted that theory's interaction with the novel is frequently imagined to be double-edged: in mediating, theory detracts; in validating, it apparently kills. The deadly force of theory, however, is only half the equation. Paul Mann argues, in his examination of the death discourses of the avant-garde, that the very telos of the avant-garde was the production of its own death theory; theory produces the movement's death, but that death has been its theory all along and a necessary element in the movement's continuance. While the novel is of course nowhere near as self-consuming a cultural form as was the work of the avant-garde, it has arguably had its death embedded in its text since volume 2 of the *Quixote*. And while certain writers and critics lay the blame for the death of the novel on the dominance of theory, the postmodernist novel has often embraced theory as its critical counterpart. The novel both resists and requires its own theoretical death to go on.

Among those who blame theory for the novel's death is Alvin Kernan, who points in *The Death of Literature* to the much-hailed death of the author, the disintegration of the canon, and the rise of "discourse" as evidence, if not causes, of that untimely demise. "Many of our best authors," Kernan complains, numbering among them Nabokov, Mailer, Malamud, and Bellow, "have experienced and not recovered from a crisis of confidence in the traditional values of literature and a sense of its importance to humanity" (3). With such self-assured categories as "traditional values" and "humanity," however, and with his list of "our" best authors, Kernan reveals the sticky underside of such concern about theory: the problem is less the rise of the critic or the death of the author than the dismantling of the rationalist—and largely white male—individual and his centrality in the world of discourse. As Marianna Torgovnick suggests in the concluding discussion of *Why the Novel Matters*: "It may be that the question of why the novel matters only arises in economically and socially privileged cultures or in segments of such cultures free to bask in what [Charles] Newman calls 'the post-modern aura,' which depends upon an inflated rhetoric of cultural crisis" (361). Indeed, one of the conclusions toward which the present investigation is working is that the anxiety of obsolescence both requires social privilege to be mobilized as a discourse and conceals the repressed anxiety that the threatened disappearance of that privilege engenders.

In fairness to Kernan, in *The Death of Literature* he distributes the blame for the decline in literature's "authority" among the rise of theory, changes in the contemporary social structure, and a "technological revolution that is rapidly transforming a print to an electronic culture" (9). And he makes a valiant attempt at critical distance: "The death of literature looks like the twilight of the gods to conservatives or the fall of the Bastille of high culture to radicals, but my argument is, to put it simply, that we are watching the complex transformations of a social institution in a time of radical political, technological, and social change" (10). But Kernan's rhetoric is far too colored by the anxiety of obsolescence to remain this impartial; *The Death of Literature* cannot read any of this change as benign. Moreover, the bracketing of technological change by political and social change reveals their intimate connection. One of the goals of the chapters that follow is to examine the ways in which anxieties about theoretical discourse, and fears of social change even more, are repressed and replaced by a more palatable and seemingly progressive technological concern.

Surprisingly, at one moment in his study Kernan blames the overproduction of books for the medium's death, in much the same way Joseph Epstein blames the death of poetry on the existence of too many poets writing too many poems.[12] What is dying in these visions cannot be literature per se but rather some confidently asserted notion of "literary quality." Kernan draws this distinction in a telling fashion: "if *literature* has died, *literary activity* continues with unabated, if not increased, vigor" (4). Under the category of "literary activity," one can safely lump Jacques Derrida and Jacqueline Susann, poststructuralist discourse and Oprah's Book Club—all phenomena that contain or are contained by the act of reading, but that exist outside (or more frighteningly, work to undermine) the strictures of canonicity. Again, Kernan:

> This is the bizarre way that things die in a society of surplus and overproduction. The end of the age of the book, and with it the age of literature, is figured not only in the difficulties of using and storing printed material, and in the amount of printed material being piled up, but in the gradual waning of the privileged position in the world of knowledge—"what is printed is true"—that the book has held for about five hundred years. (140)

The prospect of "too many books" here is made to present a technological problem—one of information storage and retrieval—but with a problem of discernment lurking behind it, the difficulty of sorting the good from the bad, the worthwhile from the waste of time, the canonical from the non-. Louis Rubin targets this question of discernment as the key to understanding claims of the novel's death, brushing aside all the usual culprits such as social and technological change: "The truth is that the only thing that can destroy literature is *bad* books"—while quickly distancing himself from that position—"and surely these are no more common than in previous eras" (7). Kernan disagrees; the "surplus" he imagines is certainly not of good books. Kernan's mobilization of economic rhetoric in contemplating the novel's relative health suggests at the same time an oddly functionalist mode of thinking about the novel's operation in culture and a critique of that mode, in much the same way Charles Newman uses the trope of "inflation" to signify both the importance and the vacuity of the postmodern. For Newman, too, overproduction leads to meaninglessness, particularly of theoretical concepts. But for Kernan, behind the discourses of technology and economics lies a larger problem that steadily erodes the book's "privileged position": epistemological uncertainty. Once upon a time, a reader could assume what was printed to be true. Now, who knows who's writing what you're reading?

This concern with supply and demand does not, however, diminish the technological concerns that surface in much of the death-of-the-novel discourse and that characterize the anxiety of obsolescence. Kernan devotes a full chapter to those fears, entitled "Technology and Literature: Book Culture and Television Culture." Sven Birkerts likewise focuses on the technological threat to the book in *The Gutenberg Elegies: The Fate of Reading in an Electronic Age.* Birkerts, like Kernan, fears for the future of literature, but he is somewhat less apocalyptic in his approach. His concern, Birkerts claims, is to explore the ways in which literary practice registers "the shocks of the new" (3). Nonetheless, he writes in a distinctly elegiac mode, suggesting that one of the ways in which those shocks are registered is in the waning of literary authority.

> I do not anticipate a future utterly without books, or bereft of all discourse about ideas, or entirely given over to utilitarian pursuits. No, what I fear is a continued withering-away of influence, a diminution of the literary which brings about a flattened new world in which only a small coterie traffics in the matters that used to be deemed culturally central. (194)

That such literary matters once were "culturally central" is, as I suggested earlier, a suspect notion. What is important in Birkerts, however, is the degree to which he locates in new media technologies the cause of the withering away he perceives. In "The Faustian Pact," the final elegy in the volume, Birkerts claims to have met the devil—*Wired* magazine. This publication enacts for Birkerts "the argument between technology and soul" (211), the true evil of which seems to reside in *Wired*'s use of print to promote the very media that undermine Gutenberg's technologies. This complicitous arrangement reverses the situation presented by the *Bold Type* editorial discussed in the Introduction, in which new media are used to promote literature. Such an exchange of support can, for a writer like Birkerts, be valid in only one direction. The lines between good and evil have been as firmly drawn as those during World War II; while *Bold Type* may be a Schindleresque figure, saving (some) novels from certain annihilation, *Wired* is a collaborator. In fact, extending this metaphor of traitorousness, E. L. Doctorow claims that writers themselves are often coconspirators in their own demise. In a brief exchange, *New Yorker* senior editor Deborah Garrison asks Doctorow the following questions: "In our culture, in which film is the primary popular art and has sadly superseded the novel and poetry, what is the standing of reading and writing? How much are people reading? How much of the film culture crosses your mind as you are making aesthetic choices?" Doctorow responds: "Serious readership has always been the minority in this country. Novelists have always been very alert to all the enemies. Today, obviously, film is the enemy; some of us sleep with the enemy."[13] The novelist, by this logic, seems to face a difficult decision between being a marginalized cultural figure and contributing to the novel's marginality, a double-edged choice rendered particularly remarkable given Doctorow's own relationship with film.

Thus, writers and critics from across the ideological spectrum have suggested for decades that the novel is declining, has declined, should be laid to rest, is in need of revival, or some combination thereof. Some of those concerned about the novel's obsolescence blame the rise of poststructuralist theory; some blame overproduction; some blame the changing technological climate. Many, like Kernan and Doctorow, blame the novelist himself. But the most definitive statement on the novel's death, John Barth's landmark 1967 essay "The Literature of Exhaustion," takes a very different approach to the novelist's role in his form's demise. In this essay, Barth explores the novel's imminent obsolescence from the writer's perspective, claiming to see in this obsolescence no real cause for worry; in fact, Barth's ostensible fears for the end of the novel, as played out both in this essay and in his own fiction, become an overt series of poses manipulated for the novel's continuance.[14] Such an admission is made apparent in "The Literature of Exhaustion." This brief text, ostensibly a study of Borges, is most relevant and insightful when Barth uses his thoughts about Borges as a pretext for discussing "some professional concerns of my own" (29). These concerns largely revolve around the state of the novel in an era when the writer seems to be facing "the used-upness of certain forms or exhaustion of certain possibilities" (29). In one exceptionally dense paragraph, which I quote here at length, Barth sketches out both the "felt ultimacy" central to the writer's anxiety of obsolescence and the means by which that anxiety can be put to use, claiming that Borges' work perfectly illumines his subject:

> how an artist may paradoxically turn the felt ultimacies of our time into material and means for his work—*paradoxically* because by so doing he transcends what had appeared to be his refutation in the same way that the mystic who transcends finitude is said to be enabled to live, spiritually and physically, in the finite world. Suppose you're a writer by vocation—a "print-oriented bastard," as the McLuhanites call us—and you feel, for example, that the novel, if not narrative literature generally, if not the printed word altogether, has by this hour of the world just about shot its bolt, as Leslie Fiedler and others maintain. (I'm inclined to agree, with reservations and hedges. Literary forms certainly have histories and historical contingencies, and it may well be that the novel's time as a major art form is up, as the "times" of classical tragedy, grand opera, or the sonnet sequence came to be. No necessary cause for alarm in this at all, except perhaps to certain novelists, and one way to handle such a feeling might be to write a novel about it. Whether historically the novel expires or persists seems immaterial to me; if enough writers and critics *feel* apocalyptical about it, their feeling becomes a considerable cultural fact, like the *feeling* that Western civilization, or the world, is going to end rather soon. If you took a bunch of people out into the desert and the world didn't

end, you'd come home shamefaced, I imagine; but the persistence of an art form doesn't invalidate work created in the comparable apocalyptic ambience. That's one of the fringe benefits of being an artist instead of a prophet. There are others.) If you happened to be Vladimir Nabokov, you might address that felt ultimacy by writing *Pale Fire*: a fine novel by a learned pedant, in the form of a pedantic commentary on a poem invented for the purpose. If you were Borges you might write *Labyrinths*: fictions by a learned librarian in the form of footnotes, as he describes them, to imaginary or hypothetical books. And I'll add, since I believe Borges' idea is rather more interesting, that if you were the author of this paper, you'd have written something like *The Sot-Weed Factor* or *Giles Goat-Boy*: novels which imitate the form of the Novel, by an author who imitates the role of Author. (32–33)

Despite Barth's insistence on his lack of interest in the material condition of the novel, he does maintain a clear interest in the apocalyptic "feeling" that surrounds it. Unpacking the feeling that has for Barth produced the "considerable cultural fact" of the novel's demise reveals the key to the cultural function of the death-of-the-novel discourse: it is endlessly productive of more discourse.

Though Barth is clear about the apocalyptic sense many have expressed with regard to the novel, "inclined to agree" as he is that the novel may have "just about shot its bolt," he never overtly states the cause of the demise of narrative literature. Instead, Barth attempts to put off this waning of influence to the notion that "[l]iterary forms certainly have histories and historical contingencies," and thus that the novel's "time" may simply be up, a monumentally shrug-shouldered assessment of the situation.[15] But there is a hint of something further at work in those "historical contingencies," momentarily glimpsed in the use of the "McLuhanite" label "print-oriented bastard." New, nonprint artistic and communicative forms—primarily television, though it is never named within the essay—are at the root of this decentering of print and the relegation of its writers and readers to a state of cultural illegitimacy. As one of Barth's characters frames the situation:

> Nowadays the genre [of the novel] is so fallen into obscure pretension on the one hand and cynical commercialism on the other, and so undermined at its popular base by television, that to hear a young person declare his or her ambition to be a capital *W* Writer strikes me as anachronistical, quixotic, as who should aspire in 1969 to be a Barnum and Bailey acrobat, a dirigible pilot, or the Rembrandt of the stereopticon. (*LETTERS* 84)

Like the popular circus, the dirigible, and the stereopticon, the novel has become "anachronistical" not simply because its time is up, but because it has been "undermined" by newer, flashier, more technologically advanced forms of electronic communication.

But one must note that the adjective Barth uses to describe the pursuit of fiction in the age of its obsolescence derives from the text of its birth; the novel has always been "quixotic." Barth suggests in "The Literature of Exhaustion" that whether television is actually undermining the novel is beside the point; in fact, for him, whether the novel "expires or persists" is "immaterial." As another of his characters describes Barth's project, in a letter to the "Author": "A. assures me that you do not yourself take with much seriousness those Death-of-the-Novel or End-of-Letters chaps, but that you *do* take seriously the climate that takes such questions seriously; you exploit that apocalyptic climate, he maintains, to reinspect the origins of narrative fiction in the oral tradition" (*LETTERS* 438). While the belief that the novel is dying evidenced by both writers and critics is, in Barth's own words, sufficient to create the "considerable cultural fact" of its doom, this doom is itself a worthy subject of consideration. And, Barth pithily points out, unlike the prophecy whose validity is called into question when the world doesn't end, the novel's most literal continued existence does not "invalidate work created in the comparable apocalyptic ambience." Writing about the end of the novel is, after all, still writing.

Which is precisely why, unlike his characters, Barth senses "[n]o necessary cause for alarm in this at all." Perhaps "certain novelists" might worry, seeing their livelihood disappear, but there is a solution: "one way to handle such a feeling might be to write a novel about it." This is precisely the project Barth argues that writers such as Nabokov and Borges (and, with the hedge of false modesty, Barth himself) have undertaken: writing novels about the environment in which writing novels is no longer possible. Such an overcoming of apocalypse valorizes the author as one working against his time, one able "paradoxically" to "transcend what had appeared to be his refutation." The writer, in his transcendence, becomes equated with the mystic, able to escape the "finitude" of the McLuhanite age. This is Barth's impression of Borges: "His artistic victory, if you like, is that he confronts an intellectual dead end and employs it against itself to accomplish new human work" ("Exhaustion" 31). The humanness of that work is not incidental; contained within the transcendence achieved by the successful writer is a form of reversion in which the "dead end" of the contemporary is rejected in favor of a return to the values of traditional humanism.[16]

Whatever the causes of its demise—technological or theoretical, overproduction or underconsumption—the putative death of the novel forms the heart of the anxiety of obsolescence. By depicting the genre as an endangered species, critics and novelists alike have built a protected space around the novel—and, not incidentally, the novelist—in which the form and its practitioners are kept safe from the encroachments of the changing contemporary world. By carefully reading the novel of obsolescence, one can begin to uncover how the representations of the novel's "enemies" function to create that protected space, as well as how technological changes in contemporary culture serve as convenient masks for other, more threatening, social and political changes that confront the novelist. We must begin, however, by taking claims of the novel's passing with a grain of salt; as Paul Mann points out, "perhaps the avant-garde needs its death to go on living" (38). In this, the historical avant-garde, whose nominal front-lines orientation demanded a continuous rooting out of the belated, and the novel, whose claims to newness require its repeated exhaustion, are not so different. Paraphrasing Mann, we can suggest that the postmodern novel is indeed living out its death for discourse: the death of the novel is alive and well.

The Media in the Garden

As I've already indicated, the novel is hardly the sole literary form whose death has been critically mourned; one might similarly investigate the "ends" of the epic, the long poem, the sonnet, the drama in verse, the tragedy, poetry and the theatre altogether, the belletristic essay, and the literary letter. Each of these genres is "dead," and yet each lives on, albeit in altered forms. The epic has been reborn in the big novel (e.g., *Gravity's Rainbow*, *Underworld*); the popular poem flourishes in song lyrics and the spirit of the theatre in independent film; et cetera. Each form is altered by its historical circumstances of production and reception and by the forms that succeed it; this alteration does not equal death but the recombination of old forms into new. Of course, this tension between old and new is not limited to the literary sphere; each advance in communications technologies has produced a similar outcry among cultural watchdogs, mourning the loss of the trusted old form and decrying the apparent cultural decline produced by the new. Plato reports Socrates' story condemning the rise of writing in an oft-cited passage of the *Phaedrus*. In this narrative, King Thamus refuses the invention of the Egyptian god Thoth, insisting that writing "will introduce forgetfulness into the soul of those who learn it" (79), destroying the facility of memory by allowing the student to rely upon written records.[17] Whose judgment this rejection of writing ultimately represents—that of Thamus, Socrates, or Plato—is open to question, but it is important to note that the Socratic method of teaching relied upon the existence of a primarily oral culture, and that the introduction of writing to that culture could undermine the method. Similarly, Gutenberg's miraculous invention, so justly praised by critics of television, was itself accused of the same erosion of cultural standards that the boob tube has ostensibly produced.[18] Just as Mann argues that the modern era is typified by the numberless "deaths" of varying cultural forms, the era is likewise characterized by the continuous hue and cry over the cultural effects of new technologies. Much of this lamentation, however, is less interesting for its claims than for its motives; as Cecelia Tichi suggests of the battle between television and the book: "at issue here is resistance to technological change by groups perceiving their interests to be imperiled by that change" (*Electronic Hearth* 175). The lament over a new technology inevitably goes up from the quarters that house the old technology, from those who stand to lose (whether in financial terms or in less material terms of cultural status) if the old form disappears. Thus Plato's deploring the rise of writing; thus the call among Venetian abbots and scribes for banning the printing press; thus Neil Postman's concerns about television and computers. Nonetheless, these lamenters owe something to the very technology they argue against, a point that doesn't wholly disprove their critiques but does reveal something of the complexities of the media ecology. We have Plato's words today because of Thoth's invention. Alexander Pope's conviction that "the invention of Printing" was intended as "a scourge for the sins of the learned" (qtd. in Stephens 34) comes despite the connections of his fame to the printing of the *Dunciad*. And numerous sites dedicated to the work of contemporary techno-lamenter Neil Postman have sprung up on the World Wide Web.[19]

In what follows, by relying heavily on studies of the rise of individual technologies, I trace a common thread of anxiety that runs through the histories of the new communications media that have arisen since the mid–nineteenth century. The cultural discourse that surrounds such technological change has repeatedly invoked three separate yet intertwined concepts about the new forms: technologies of mechanization have produced concerns about dehumanization; technologies of image production have been greeted with concerns about illusion and ideology; and technologies of interconnection have confronted concerns about the loss of the individual. The first of these concepts, which I refer to as "the machine," posits in the increasing mechanization of U.S. culture a turn from putatively human values to those that devalue the human. The second concept, "the spectacle," reveals anxieties about the relative importance of the image and the word in its concerns about the manipulation of visuality. The third concept, "the network," relays fears about a growing web of physical interconnections through which the individual might be subjugated to the mass. Each new form of communications developed during the twentieth century interacts with at least one of these concepts, and most with more than one. Anxieties about vaudeville and other forms of popular theatre, as well as those about *USA Today* and the contemporary newspaper, connect the notions of the spectacle and the network. Anxieties about photography and film mobilize the notions both of the spectacle and of the machine. Anxieties about the railroad and other forms of transportation, as well as about the radio, link the machine and the network. And anxieties about television and the Internet terrifyingly link all three concepts.[20]

Moreover, the dual existence of these fears, manifesting both on the cultural (in the sense of aesthetic or technological) and on the social level, suggests the deep imbrication of changing modes of cultural production and changing social structures. Cultural forms develop out of and reflect their contemporary social structures, while they also affect the developing futures of those societies. Although this volume is not fundamentally concerned with unpacking the precise nature of that interconnection, it is important to note the mutual implication of the cultural and the social, and in particular to interrogate the moments at which writing that is ostensibly about one set of fears (cultural anxieties about the network's tendency to undermine individualism, for instance) reveals the latent presence of those fears' repressed other (social anxieties about the racial, ethnic, or gendered nature of the mass overtaking the unmarked "individual"). Such moments repeatedly indicate the ways that anxieties about the social, particularly in an age so concerned (at least at a surface level) with avoiding the appearance of racism, or sexism, or ethnocentrism, are often contained within and masked by more palatable discussions of the aesthetic or the technological.

The rise of the machine as a figure of literary concern during the late nineteenth and early twentieth centuries, then, signals a deep cultural ambivalence about the processes of modernization, a simultaneous fascination and revulsion. The intimate relations between writers and mechanisms throughout U.S. literature, as explored by such critics as Leo Marx and Cecelia Tichi, hint at a connection between technological and cultural production, as the dominant technology of any culture gives shape to that culture's understanding of the world. In an era dominated by the computer, the relationship between that technology and representations of virtual reality is easy to spot; such a relationship between mode of production and representational content, however, long predates the contemporary period. The U.S. identification with and anxiety about the machine can be dated, as Leo Marx's work indicates, to the introduction of steam-driven manufactures into Jefferson's pastoral ideal; as early as the late eighteenth century, the writings of manufacturing's proponents present "a prophetic vision of machine technology as the fulcrum of national power," revealing "peculiar affinities between the machine and the New World setting in its entirety: geographical, political, social, and, in our sense of the word, cultural" (Marx 155–56). These affinities between the machinic and the cultural become pronounced in the moment of modernization. The spread of mechanization, from clockworks to the steam engine to the factory production line, dramatically affected modernist cultural production, as new technologies encouraged the replacement of Romantic conceptions of being in nature with views of the human being as a form of machine.[21] This shift reflects a simultaneous cultural rejection of the Romantic dominant and a longing for the return of that dominant in response to the machine. Marx's "machine in the garden," the trope of technology's incursion into a mythologized nature, thus recurs in literary texts from the late nineteenth century onward as a continuing and intensifying—rather than momentary and localized—conflict between the Romantic ideal and a changing contemporary culture.

This conflict is due, however, not to the replacement of nature by the machine but to the protracted, if tenuous, coexistence of the two. Frederic Jameson, in one of his famous formulations of the distinction between modernism and postmodernism, points directly to that coexistence, claiming that in modernism "some residual zones of 'nature' or 'being,' of the old, the older, the archaic, still subsist; culture can still do something to that nature and work at transforming that 'referent.' Postmodernism is what you have when the modernization process is complete and nature is gone for good" (ix). Thus, for Jameson, the postmodern differs from the modern largely in terms of completion; the project of modernization, in process during the earlier era, is over in the later. This sense of completion, however, seems to suggest the perennially deferred nature of the postmodern, as the conflict between the machine and something we continue to think of as "nature" continues into the present. This suggests that, rather than indicating an authentic break between the modern and the postmodern, Jameson's gesture toward modernization creates a historical continuity across the periods it affects, an ongoing conflict between Romanticism and technology.

Modernism as an aesthetic was in part born out of the clash between the technological and the natural. Tichi argues that, in the modern period and "[u]nder the aegis of engineering, the U.S. novel of the early twentieth century conceptually changed. The lineage of narration yielded to one of construction" ("Technology" 477). By her argument, the shift from narration as the novel's key invisible element to the visibility of its processes of construction produced an "amalgamation" of technology and literature. This amalgamation, however,

> occurred with such rapidity that it often had the appearance of discontinuity. Suddenly loosed from their separate categories, technological and organic figures of speech seemed to jostle each other, suggesting the tensions that inevitably arise in times of rapid sociocultural change, when the old order seems to vanish in the onrush of the new. (*Shifting Gears* 18)

Such anxieties as here surface in the tension between the technological and the organic result whenever an old order, or an old mode of being, or an old means of making sense of the world is threatened with disappearance. The Romantic view of nature, for instance, was driven in part by a vast connotative shift in the concept of the "mechanism." Once identified with nature and "the celestial 'machine' " (Marx 162), the concept came for the Romantics to represent that *opposed to* the organic; in this shift, the machine becomes that which is specifically unnatural. Post-Romantic cultural thought has largely maintained that opposition, while gradually shifting allegiances within it, allowing the tension between the organic and the technological to intensify. In realist fiction, for instance, writers began looking equally closely at the machine and at the garden; naturalism's positivist philosophy further understood that garden as a special type of machine. Modernism thus results from the *continuing* problematic coexistence of the technological and the organic, slightly transformed by a new speed that gives rise to the "appearance of discontinuity." The formalist tendencies of the modernist writer in viewing the novel as a construction reveal an ongoing interest in the clash of technology and nature; the modern "shock of the new" arises in those writers' formal enactment of that clash in exposing what Tichi calls the "gears and girders" of their texts (*Shifting Gears* xiii).

Such conflicts between the organic and the machinic, and between the Romantic and the modern, are enacted in the technology of photography and revealed in the reception of that technology in the mid–nineteenth century. Photography in its very form implies a changing status quo; the ability to "fix" a moment in time highlights that moment's motion.[22] The technology of photography thus paradoxically communicates obsolescence through its claims to permanence. Moreover, in undermining previous notions of time and permanence, and in its seemingly objective accuracy, photography appeared at its birth to announce a direct threat to painting. This threat was famously received by French artist Paul Delaroche, who is said, upon his first viewing of a daguerreotype, to have exclaimed: "From today on, painting is dead!" (see Levinson 46). However, as Jean-François Lyotard points out, the challenge that photography posed was not to painting per se, but to one of the functions painting had been thought of as serving:

> The challenge lay essentially in that photographic and cinematographic processes can accomplish better, faster, and with a circulation a hundred thousand times larger than narrative or pictorial realism, the task which academicism had assigned to realism: to preserve various consciousnesses from doubt. Industrial photography and cinema will be superior to painting and the novel whenever the objective is to stabilize the referent, to arrange it according to a point of view which endows it with a recognizable meaning. . . . (74)

The air of obsolescence thus in the nineteenth century settled not around painting in general, but around pictorial realism; the mechanism of photography communicated more directly with realist epistemology than could the painter. Photography simultaneously threatened to displace literary realism as well, illustrating the fundamental disconnect between the ideals of realist writing and the materials at its disposal:

> Writers had been able to describe a landscape. But no writer, no matter how skilled and no matter how committed to realism, could produce a representation of a landscape—or a room or a face—as completely and exactly as a photograph. This was a major new development in the ancient competition between images and words. Nature, after all, has never been persuaded to pick up a pencil and "reproduce herself" in words. (Stephens 75)

Photography thus undermined the realism espoused by painting precisely through its technological advances and the power it wielded to represent more, faster, better. It further undermined literary realism by calling the very possibility of verbal verisimilitude into question.

But the new medium, while thus undermining literary realism, gave support to its claims about the truth value of realistic representation. In fact, the new form became a site throughout the Victorian period of the ongoing literary contest between Romanticism and realism (see Green-Lewis). Each side in this conflict saw photography as evidence of its own superiority, evidence of either the sufficiency or the insufficiency of empiricism in accounting for reality. But each position nonetheless created anxiety in the writer about his relationship to the new form. Anxieties about the photograph among Romantic writers stem not from its apparent capacity to capture reality but from two conflicting senses of its weakness as a representational form: its inability to capture the intangible, immaterial aspects of reality; and conversely, through technical "tricks," its ability to alter reality, or to lie. Where the figure of the photographer appears in the Victorian romance, he is thus largely represented as evil, the possessor of malevolent powers; these powers are "both affirmed and controlled by their relegation to the fringes of novelistic action" (Green-Lewis 7). For the realist writer, on the other hand, photography captured the tangibility of things as they are and supported his faith in the possibility of adequate knowledge of truth through the perceptions of the senses—but did so perhaps a bit too well. "Photography," Jennifer Green-Lewis points out, "promised a superior grasp of reality, a realism more real than the thing itself" (30). Through its apparent ability to capture reality, photography helped shove Romanticism out of the cultural spotlight. But by "outperforming" literary realism, photography began to call that mode's basis into question as well.

These concerns about the new medium, however, often pick up their vocabulary from the discourses of the spectacle and the machine; critics of early photography raised concerns alternately about the morally dubious nature of a form that can fool the public with realistic illusions and about the aesthetically questionable status of a picture created by an apparatus. Both concerns are aimed at writerly or painterly self-preservation. The critic who argues about photography's manipulation of illusion reveals an anxiety that "is not lest its viewers mistake a photograph for its original subject but rather that the photograph is a superior kind of painting, that painting as he knows it and painters such as he has been have been superseded by the technology of the camera" (Green-Lewis 52). Similarly, many of the concerns about the new form's status as art focused on the photograph's mechanical origin, equating the work it produced with the products of the factory or the assembly line. This discourse inevitably reveals underlying anxieties about class and gender: "Photography's frequent figuration as mechanical work and its association with menial labor were obviously in part the consequence of anxiety about the wide social range of photographers and no doubt contributed to its metaphoric evolution as a product of science rather than art between the mid and late nineteenth century" (42). Claims of aesthetic decline thus conceal more personal concerns; technological obsolescence stands in for and masks the social. Already, in this first incursion of "new media" into the territory of the old, we see in evidence many of the concerns critics will voice a century later about television.

Though not, strictly speaking, a communications medium, the railroad demands brief consideration for a number of reasons. First, as Leo Marx argues, the U.S. railroad—that quintessential machine charging through the unspoiled garden—was "*the* revolutionary machine of the age" (180). The dramatic change in transportation, both of people and materials, that its technology wrought was a necessary factor in the rapid course of industrialization that produced the modern era. Moreover, the railroad profoundly captured the U.S. imagination. "The invention of the steamboat had been exciting," claims Marx,

> but it was nothing compared to the railroad. In the 1830s the locomotive, an iron horse or fire-Titan, is becoming a kind of national obsession. It is the embodiment of the age, an instrument of power, speed, noise, fire, iron, smoke—at once a testament to the will of man rising over natural obstacles, and, yet, confined by its iron rails to a predetermined path, it suggests a new sort of fate. The "industrial revolution incarnate" one economic historian has called it. Stories about railroad projects, railroad accidents, railroad profits, railroad speed fill the press; the fascinating subject is taken up in songs, political speeches, and magazine articles, both factual and fictional. (191)

The railroad became the focus both of national pride in U.S. ingenuity and of national anxiety about the increasing power of the machine and the decreasing power of the individual. But the railroad also effected radical transformations in contemporary epistemologies. On a most basic level, the necessity of coordinating railroad schedules led to the institutional regulation of time, including the development of time zones. Furthermore, in creating new metaphors by which Americans lived, the railroad transformed the culture's notions of history, lending itself to visions of inexorable progress (see Marx 194–207).

But beyond these contemporary shifts, the railroad paved the way for future changes in communications. As Wolfgang Schivelbusch has argued, the railroad was a necessary element in bringing about the perceptual changes that prepared early twentieth-century culture for the rise of the new media that captured communications: the cinema and the radio.[23] In the railroad, argues Schivelbusch, lie the origins of the modern "annihilation of space and time" upon which twentieth-century perceptions of the real depend. This foreshortening of space—in which the train's speed caused to be "displayed in immediate succession objects and pieces of scenery that in their original spatiality belonged to separate realms" (60)—is directly connected to the filmic notion of montage, as the compression of space leads to the destruction of Walter Benjamin's "aura":

> The remote regions were made available to the masses by means of tourism: this was merely a prelude, a preparation for making any unique thing available by means of reproduction. When spatial distance is no longer experienced, the differences between original and reproduction diminish. In the filmic juxtaposition—i.e., the perception of *montage*, the juxtaposition of the most disparate images into one unit—the new reality of annihilated in-between spaces finds its clearest expression: the film brings things closer to the viewer as well as closer together. (42)

Moreover, the railroad's mechanicity allowed it to achieve what Schivelbusch calls "pure speed," which he defines as "speed perceived as an independent quality because it is divorced from the organic base of horse-power. (At the beginning of the twentieth century, the human voice was subjected to that same process of dissociation from its natural habitat, its natural condition, by the microphone and the radio)" (48). The railroad's speed, then, is achieved precisely by heightening the already extant conflict between nature and technology, dissociating perception from its "natural" origins.

Thus the mechanics of the railroad exist as the precursors to filmic montage and radio's sound projection. But a more fundamental change lay in the transformations the railroad caused in visual perception; according to Schivelbusch, the railroad

> and the motion it created became integrated into [man's] visual perception: thus he could only see things in motion. That mobility of vision—for a traditionally oriented sensorium, such as Ruskin's, an agent for the dissolution of reality—became a prerequisite for the "normality" of panoramic vision. This vision no longer experienced evanescence: evanescent reality had become the new reality. (64)

Just as photography bespoke obsolescence through its simultaneous ability and failure to "fix" an instant in time, the railroad hastened obsolescence by introducing motion into perception. Speed and motion become part of the new sensorium, which accepts change—and ever-accelerating change—as normal.[24] Contemporary anxieties surrounding this speed-up frequently connect such increases in motion—conveyed in metaphors of "unrest," of an unhealthily nervous activity—to a takeover of humans by machines (see Marx 174). Thus Emerson: "Things are in the saddle, / And ride mankind" (Emerson).[25] The machines producing the world's speed-up are perceived as controlling human direction. Many of these concerns are, as Leo Marx phrases it, "stock expressions of the widespread and largely impotent anxiety generated by mechanization; no doubt the most popular, closely akin to the 'men-will-become-machines' trope, was the Frankenstein fable: the story of the robot that destroys its heartless creator" (184). Such worries about the machine, however, whether it is transforming human nature or carrying the potential to destroy it, are securely rooted in contemporary ideologies. The "men" who require protection from the rapacious values of the machine are inevitably of a certain race, a certain class, and a certain gender; "mechanization will hardly seem a menace to those upon whom society confers little dignity of soul (or status) in the first place" (189). In fact, the democratizing power of the machine is precisely part of the problem; during the nineteenth century, the railroad partly obliterated class distinctions, for 90 percent of the railroad's passengers traveled in the same accommodations.[26] All these factors—the interconnection of the nation through the "annihilation of space and time," the increase in machinic power and authority, and the bringing together of disparate social classes—led to often violently stated antagonisms toward the railroad. Perhaps only the most extreme representation of this antagonism was the Ohio school board that declared the railroad "a device of Satan to lead immortal souls to hell."[27]

Film—once similarly described as a "primary school for criminals"—adds to such misgivings about mechanization further misgivings about illusion.[28] The very technology of film is founded in the illusion of motion, created by a rapid succession of still images, which served to heighten concerns about the still image's ability to manipulate reality and, in effect, to lie. But visible in this critic's commentary is the true source of early twentieth-century anxieties about film: not the images displayed or their motion, but the audience in attendance. It was for this reason that, in the first attempts to regulate the new medium, the rules targeted not film producers but exhibitors. That the producers (in the very early days of film, that is, before the establishment of the West Coast studios) were largely middle class and U.S. born while the exhibitors were often immigrants is not incidental. As Robert Sklar argues in *Movie-Made America*, film has its origins in working-class entertainment; the rise of film was particularly "galling" to reformers, not because of its content but because "workingmen and immigrants had found their own source of entertainment and information—a source unsupervised and unapproved by the churches and schools, the critics and professors who served as caretakers and disseminators of the official American culture" (18–19). Official culture felt itself under threat from both a new technology and a swelling working class. Much complaint about the cinema used the former threat to cover for the latter; according to Sklar, the critics of the new medium "rarely said what was on their minds," dealing instead "with symptoms rather than causes, surfaces rather than depths" (123). Thus, early calls for film censorship frequently and unsurprisingly speak of protecting women and children from depictions of licentious and otherwise immoral behavior rather than of protecting middle-class, white U.S. culture from the encroachments of values foreign to it. And thus, much early academic and writerly anxiety about film centered upon its co-optation of narrative from the novel, its manipulation of fantasy, and its use as an ideological tool, only rarely mentioning—and then in a protective, paternal fashion—those gullible masses for whom the new medium had become a primary cultural experience.

Each new technological form threatens those that have gone before. Images threaten print; photography threatens painting; film threatens the novel; television threatens film; the Internet threatens television. But, as Paul Levinson indicates, cultural jeremiads about new communications technologies, while often rightly sensing the implied loss of old forms, frequently operate under complex motives.

> Although we can sympathize with such fears on the human level of appreciating the pain attendant to any kind of cultural loss, our ethics also need to note that for most people the old way of communicating and thereby living is usually inferior to the new. Indeed, new media since the printing press have in every case served to ultimately further the democratization it engendered, with the result that critics of the new media have usually been defenders of the elite, attempting to bar the new onslaught of the masses. (56)

The onslaught of those masses—and in particular, their "otherness"—is the subtext of the anxiety of obsolescence. The masses attendant behind fears of new media come closest to the surface of texts of obsolescence as these engage with the concept of the network, but they are also visible in mobilizations of the concepts of the spectacle and the machine. In the chapters that follow, I focus in upon the contemporary novel's readings of each of these three central concepts as they revolve around television, which serves here as a metonym for something broader that might be characterized as the "electronic media." As I use this term, I mean to speak inclusively of all media forms (including photography and film) that participate in or are defined by the machine, the spectacle, and the network. "Television" should thus be read less as the historical culmination of these forms of mediation—leading to a teleological narrative of media development—than as a figure for these three concepts of mediation, the key late twentieth-century form that embodies all the complaints about the influence of the communications media on U.S. culture. As these complaints would have it, the television set itself is a machine that distances us from humanity, encouraging us to think of ourselves as machines; the televisual product is a spectacle, distracting us from the "real"; the television broadcasting system is a network of one-way connections that destroys our ability to speak back to the sources of power while providing that power with a terrifying means of control and surveillance. But by reading closely, we can uncover in diatribes about the evils of television the attempt to protect an elite and elitist culture from the incursion of the viewing masses; the true terror of television for many of these writers is not the screen or the content, but the boobs who watch it.

Internet technologies, in this model, serve as a temporary media "future," a form still in development, but one that has been much written about in relation to these three core concepts. Despite the Internet's heavy reliance on text, the new medium's adaptations of writing to the visual limitations of the computer screen (as well as the often-discussed fact that the World Wide Web only "took off" once the ability to transmit images was written into its code) firmly connect this medium to the terms of the spectacle.[29] The computer itself is often viewed as a foreign, threatening technology that has furthered our capitulation to mechanical values and heightened our sense of the human as a machine.[30] And the frequent debates about privacy, security, intellectual property, and censorship on the Internet rely upon the terms of the concept of the network. But this is not to point to the Internet as an endpoint of the media narrative. U.S. media culture has given the impression since the late 1990s of being on the cusp of some new convergence of extant technologies, a cross-fertilization whose first new shoot was seen in a short-lived hybrid technology, WebTV. In this very preliminary stab at a new integrated medium, the three concepts of spectacle, machine, and network functioned once again. As the press materials described it: "WebTV is not the Internet tacked onto your TV screen—quite the contrary. WebTV is designed to harness the power of the Internet to make watching television more involving, more entertaining, even more inspirational."[31] The contradiction embedded in these statements— WebTV is not just television plus the Internet; it's television with the Internet added!—reveals part of the reason for the ultimate failure of the technology: it wasn't new.[32] It was also far too literal an attempt to combine these two quite opposed media. Television, as McLuhan pointed out more than thirty years ago, is a "cool" medium; the viewer becomes absorbed by it. The Internet, on the contrary, is "hot"; a user (note already the important shift in terms) must take an active part in completing the communication. These two forms simply cannot be slapped together. Frankly, we don't want television to be any more "involving" than it already is. As Bruce Owen suggests: "sometimes it's nice to be passive" (10).

Worse, expecting the Internet to be a new form of television—and expecting our new convergence models to follow in the footsteps of older media—falls into the egregious fallacy that Levinson describes, following McLuhan, as "rear-view mirrorism," the determination to read new forms through the lenses of the old (see Levinson 126). Hence the "horseless carriage" and the "wireless"; hence also "interactive television," an unwitting oxymoron repeatedly perpetrated by well-meaning futurologists. This rear-view mirrorism may in part be responsible for the cultural anxieties about new media we see in the anxiety of obsolescence, as it suggests that new media can and should take over the roles of older forms, making them obsolete. But new media take unpredictable paths of development. Whatever the future of the communications media holds, we must keep in mind one key fact about all the aforementioned struggles among media: none of the forms under threat have disappeared. As Levinson demonstrates in his case study of the changes effected in radio by the rise of television, old forms often find niches within which to operate, filling demands that the new media overlook.[33] Thus impressionist (and expressionist, and cubist, et cetera) painting, which uses visuality in ways ignored by photographic realism. Moreover, many media battles are resolved not by such a division of territory but by the formation of new hybrids. Such is the argument advanced by Tabbi and Wutz in the introduction to *Reading Matters*:

> As the systems theoretician Niklas Luhmann has argued, an enlarged media environment leads not only to "differentiation"—a definition of each medium's alterity from other media—but also to a productive ecology, a reciprocity between media that ensures the continued presence of older, less advanced storage and communications technologies: "The higher complexity of a new level of development makes it possible to reinvest the old [in this case, print] with new meaning, as far as it lets itself be integrated. New technological developments do not necessarily mean the forceful negation of older media, but rather their recombination." (9; bracketed insert in original)

In this notion of media recombination, we can see the importance of cable television, pay per view, and the VCR, all of which recouped an audience for film just when television threatened to kill it off.

Given these models, there is no reason to suspect that print generally, or the book in particular, or the novel most specifically, will die. The medium, or the genre, might instead come to fill a particular cultural role ignored by film, television, and the Internet. Or print and the electronic media might produce a new hybrid. This hybrid might look something like the e-book, or it might look like hypertext on the Web. It is more likely, however, that it will take a form we cannot yet imagine; "e-book" and "hypertext" both smack of the rear-view mirrorism we should work to avoid. We might instead consider Stuart Moulthrop's vision of the future of print:

> It is part of the paradoxical nature of postmodernism that old categories do not die; instead they stick around, generating influence anxiety. While certain media ecologists once thought print might be dead, we now find ourselves in what Jay David Bolter calls "the late age of print." The culture of writing did not vanish apocalyptically in a flash of cathode rays; it has persisted, stubbornly mutating, reappearing on what Donna Haraway calls "etched surfaces of the late twentieth century"—silicon chips and digital displays. Print is undead. (269)

It is curious, of course, to think of print as "undead," existing in a vampire state of sorts—until we remember that Haraway intended the cyborg body itself as the quintessential contemporary "etched surface" (see Haraway 176). Just as the cyborg, by being both human and machine, is in Haraway's view able to escape the oppressive binaries of gender and race, so text—in a future that will be both print and electronic, both tangible and intangible, both dead and alive—may find a path out of the ideological quandaries in which it is bound.

Postmodernism Is (What Postmodernism Is)

In the meantime, there is postmodernism to contend with. In certain arguably suspect ways, the foregoing sections of this chapter, as well as the remainder of this volume, refer to "postmodernism" as if it were an already-defined, well-established, universally agreed-upon thing. Which, from one perspective, it is: in its popular usages, which are numerous and widespread, the term has taken on an almost prosaic regularity. "Postmodern," the root term, seems to indicate a chronological period that begins with the Holocaust, or the dropping of the first nuclear weapons on Hiroshima and Nagasaki, or the Kennedy assassination, or the election of Ronald Reagan, or some other moment of cultural trauma, but that is in any case witnessed in its fullest flowering in the 1970s and 1980s and is generally considered still to be in evidence. "Postmodernity," its first cognate term, seems likewise to indicate the specific cultural and material conditions of existence during this chronological period, circumstances that include but are by no means limited to a shift from monopoly capitalism to multinational capitalism, a decline in industrialism and concomitant rise of some "third-wave" electronic business culture, and a transformation of the primary arena of political economy from the nation-state to the "global village" (see Toffler; McLuhan). Finally, "postmodernism" seems to indicate a loosely defined and yet recurrent set of cultural manifestations of or responses to the conditions of postmodernity, styles that are evidenced in fragmentation, pastiche, parody, self-referentiality, and other highly ironized modes of discourse.

Of course, the three terms are used far more interchangeably than I suggest here. To be certain, the discourse of postmodernism is laden with contradictions: as a phenomenon, postmodernism is either specifically aesthetic or more generally cultural; it is either revolutionary or reactionary; it is either the end of ideology or the inescapable conclusion of ideology. It is, as Stephen Connor has pointed out, the authoritative pronouncement of the death of all authority, the totalizing vision of the impossibility of totality, the master narrative of the end of all master narratives. It is expressed in architecture, art, literature, the media, science, religion, and fashion, and at the same time it is equivalent to none of these. It is both a continuation and intensification of what has gone before and a radical break with all traces of the past. It is, above all, simultaneously critical and complicit (see Hutcheon). This swarming contradiction and complexity, however, rather than confusing the issue of what, precisely, postmodernism is, may make it more comprehensible. That all conversations about postmodernism seem to degenerate into a debate about whether it is a good thing or a bad thing, whether one is "for" it or "against" it, is the most postmodern gesture of all: for, among the many things that postmodernism is, it is none more than the discourse of itself. A welter of the self-referential, postmodernism is more or less precisely what postmodernism is.

Moreover, it is a discourse determined by the concept of obsolescence, even as obsolescence is conversely determined by the discourse of postmodernism. Postmodernism, like the anxiety of obsolescence, is a reality created by its own discourse; as John Barth might have it, all this talk about postmodernism has been enough to create "the considerable cultural fact" of its existence. Like the death of the novel, whether it exists or not is beside the point; that so many critics and writers seem to agree that it exists—even without agreeing on what it is—is the more interesting phenomenon. Charles Newman refers to postmodernism as "a terminological fiction" (16), a notion I like, invoking as it does both fictitious terms and fictitious terminations. Both postmodernism and the anxiety of obsolescence are informed by a rhetoric of postness, the sense of a culture that has suffered a radical break. And in both cases, the cultural sense of terminus evoked by the discourse serves not to illuminate but to obscure a kind of social reality.

Postmodernism has fed within the academy what David Simpson calls "an industry of definition and sub-definition" (1); this industry is not an offshoot or a by-product of the concept but the concept itself. While this volume thus resists the notion that "postmodernism" itself can be precisely defined, such definitions are de rigueur for any text that employs the term. This ritual generally involves a look back through the history of the term's usage in the interests of uncovering either an originary meaning truer to the critic's interests or a new, evolving meaning that shifts the term to its current employment. In what follows, I similarly explore that history, but not with the intent of discovering what "postmodernism" means. Defining the term in this sense presupposes its existence as a sign, however unstable, for some real referent that exists in the world as we know it. On the contrary, postmodernism is not a *thing* but a discursive function; my interest in the history of postmodernist discourse is not in what "postmodernism" means but in what it does (see Connor 10). One thing it does, according to Connor, is provide a common language for an academy in crisis. As the study of "high culture" has, throughout the modern period, become steadily less revered as a focus of intellectual pursuit, institutions previously dedicated to studying such high culture have begun to protect themselves with theories that describe what has "gone wrong" with the contemporary. Yet as Connor suggests, if the reorganization of cultural priorities "produces a sense of resentment at being pushed from the centers of power and influence, it can also offer the customary consolations of life at the margins" (12). The terms of this discourse begin to sound a bit familiar: as with the anxiety of obsolescence, a predatory popular culture has presumably shoved an older cultural institution from a position of centrality to a position of marginality. And as with the anxiety of obsolescence, both claims are dubious: the utopian vision of a past in which the intellectual pursuits of the "high" represented by the traditional academy were central to cultural life is a revisionist history; blaming changes in contemporary culture for the marginalization of academic pursuits is equally questionable. But the discourse of postmodernism and its attendant theorizations of the contemporary create a protected space within which the academy can function. Hence the importance of defining that so-slippery term; the debates about its meaning *are* its meaning.[34]

This is not, however, to endorse the cynical view Charles Newman promotes of postmodernism as a wholly vacant concept caught up in cycles of academic self-validation, postmodernism as a theory that, like many such intellectual concepts in the age of inflation, possesses solely exchange value and is devoid of use value. Rather, as Connor suggests, examining the critical discourses of postmodernism reveals how they themselves function as responses (and hoped-for solutions) to Jurgen Habermas's "legitimation crisis," providing new "criteria of value" under which choices can be made (Connor 8). The problem rests in the frequent lack of engagement of those criteria with what one might think of as political or social reality. This lack of engagement is read by Christopher Norris (following Perry Anderson, in that endless chain of academic citations) as a result of the fall of Marxism: "a recourse to theory is typically the response of any marginalized fraction of dissident intellectuals, excluded from the mainstream of political life and left little choice but to cultivate a range of more or less hopeful alternative visions" (Norris 1). Here again, postmodernism becomes a protective measure, one of the consolations of life on the margins.

This sense of postmodernism as a replacement for a failed Marxist vision is arguably the case for that most influential of postmodernists, Fredric Jameson. Jameson entered a debate already in play, of course. As most histories indicate, the first real theorization of the term (which had begun cropping up significantly earlier) began in the late 1970s with the exchange between Jean-François Lyotard and Jurgen Habermas.[35] Already the rhetoric of the histories becomes deceptive, however, as the "exchange" was in appearance (and follow-up) only; Habermas probably was not aware of the publication of *La Condition postmoderne* at the time he was working on "Modernity—An Incomplete Project." Thus, the only "exchange" rests in Lyotard's response to Habermas, "Answering the Question: What Is Postmodernism?" (see Anderson 37). Nevertheless, despite the radical differences between these two perspectives—for Lyotard, postmodernism is anarchic, an aesthetic recuperation of the sublime; for Habermas, it is a reactionary perversion of the Enlightenment project—their conjunctions say far more about the nature of postmodernism. As Perry Anderson suggests, their interventions were

> strangely indecisive. The original background of both thinkers was Marxist, but it is striking how little of it they brought to their accounts of postmodernity. Neither attempted any real historical interpretation of the postmodern,

capable of determining it in time or space. Instead, they offered more or less floating or vacant signifiers as the mark of its appearance: the delegitimation of grand narratives (dateless) for Lyotard, the colonization of the lifeworld (when was it not colonized?) for Habermas. Paradoxically, a concept by definition temporal lacks periodic weight in either. . . . The net effect was a discursive dispersion: on the one hand, philosophical overview without significant aesthetic content, on the other aesthetic insight without theoretical horizon. (45)

These oddly hollow theories highlight the difficulty of accommodating postmodernism to a socially engaged criticism. As Anderson notes, the concept is "by definition temporal" and yet is impossible to historicize. (Does it really come after? After what?) The problem, of course, is that dogged "post" and the hyphen that frequently follows it. Despite Newman's contention that the hyphen is the term's "most distinctive feature" (17), the atemporality of the concept and the vacancy of its signifiers lead one to suspect that the hyphen, when used, is misplaced: "post-modernism" might better be conceived of as "postmodern-ism," an almost metaphysical belief in a thing called the postmodern.

Into this muddle, enter Jameson, who quickly complicated the issues in this debate with the 1984 publication of his essay "Postmodernism, or the Cultural Logic of Late Capitalism," and the 1991 publication of the volume bearing the same name. Jameson's postmodernism accedes to many of the formulas already employed by Lyotard and Habermas in their initial offerings, pointing to, among the "constitutive elements" of postmodernism, a "depthlessness" that has resulted from the destruction of the depth models or master narratives that had previously informed and structured cultural life, including the hermeneutic model of inside and outside, the dialectical model of essence and appearance, the Freudian model of latent and manifest, the existential model of authenticity and inauthenticity, and the semiotic model of signifier and signified (see Jameson 12). Jameson further links postmodernism to the rise of the simulacrum and the weakening of historicity, notions that both draw from earlier models. However, Perry Anderson, in *The Origins of Postmodernity*, argues that in five decisive moves Jameson redrew the entire map of postmodernism, creating, in a sense, the territory over which subsequent postmodernist battles would rage (see Anderson 49). First, and most importantly, Jameson linked postmodernism to the economic order of late capital; by locating postmodernism through an already existing framework of cultural materialism, Jameson situated it historically—in both the small- and large-*H* senses. Second, Jameson focused much of his discussion of postmodernism on contemporary changes in the lived experience of the subject, a subject now "decentered" and "fragmented" beyond repair. Third, Jameson furthered one of the constituent impulses of Lyotard's *La Condition postmoderne* by expanding postmodernism as a concept to describe the whole spectrum of the arts, as well as the discourse flanking it, seeing an "immense dilation" of the sphere of culture and the "effacement" of the "frontier between high culture and so called mass or commercial culture" (Jameson x, 2). Fourth (though fifth in Anderson's enumeration), Jameson manages to explore postmodernism without falling into the sort of good thing/bad thing position taking that nearly all variants on this debate degenerate into, insisting on the one hand that "every position on postmodernism in culture—whether apologia or stigmatization—is also at one and the same time, and necessarily, an implicitly or explicitly political stance on the nature of multinational capitalism today" (3), and on the other that postmodernism as a "cultural dominant" subsumes all positions both for and against within its protean ooze.

Throughout Anderson's description of Jameson's significant contributions to the debate, however, in which Jameson's additions to the discourse seem to have far greater life than that discourse's ostensible object, we can see what Steven Connor refers to as "the self-conscious density of the debate itself, which began to cast a progressively longer and longer shadow over its alleged object of analysis" (6). That shadow produced some notable blind spots. Given Jameson's own insistence that every position on postmodernism is inherently a political position, I want to spend some time considering Anderson's reading of Jameson's fourth decisive move on this new postmodernist front. Anderson claims that Jameson explores, where Habermas and Lyotard before him had not, the social bases and geopolitical patterns of postmodernism. While it is unquestionably true that Jameson lays out the *cultural* bases and geopolitical patterns of postmodernism—pointing, for instance, to "the deep constitutive relationships of [the features of postmodernism] to a whole new technology, which is itself a figure for a whole new economic world system" (6)—Anderson's claim for genuine consideration of the *social* order on Jameson's part is questionable. Phillip Brian Harper, in *Framing the Margins*—which is revealingly subtitled *The Social Logic of Postmodernism*, a pointed contrast with Jameson's "cultural logic"—indicates the shortcomings of the Jamesonian project, along with those of Habermas and Lyotard:

> However differently they might interpret the political meaning of subjective fragmentation, though, all our theorists conceive of that meaning in terms of macro-level social and economic structures, leaving aside considerations of more contingent political phenomena, in particular those having to do with

the social identities of the various subjects who manifest fragmentation in the postmodern context. (9)

What Harper refers to as "macro-level social and economic structures"—such as that globalizing technology that Jameson reads as a figure for the economic world order—might best be subsumed within the category of the cultural, given Jameson's sense of that sphere's dilation to both accept and self-identify with commodity production generally. Jameson's location of postmodernism within the economic structures of late capital functions, then, as a specifically *cultural* postmodernism, taking its politics wholly on the macro level, from a post-Marxist perspective.

This cultural postmodernism can be contrasted, with Harper's help, with a more properly social postmodernism that genuinely attempts to account for those "more contingent political phenomena" that occur on the level of the subject. Taking again the example of postmodernism's much-hailed "decentered subject," Harper explores Jameson's thinking about the implications of this subject. As Jameson indicates, the existence in the postmodern of a decentered subject suggests either that a shift has occurred, and a once-centered subject has been decentered by the postmodernist forces at play, or that a veil has been lifted, and we postmoderns can now see the centered subject for the fiction that it always was. Unfortunately, this reading of the past and present status of the subject excludes a key social consideration:

> It appears logical enough to juxtapose the atemporal quality of the poststructuralist position against the contextual specificity dictated by the historicist one, but when we consider the case of a number of socially marginalized and politically disenfranchised groups in the United States, it becomes clear that a sort of timelessness is actually inscribed within the historicist analysis: Granting the historicist claim for a "once existing centered subject," it must also be acknowledged that, for certain groups in the United States—people of African descent, for instance—the historical status of such a subjectivity is precisely that of *never having existed*, due to the historical distribution of the power to conceive of oneself as a centered, whole entity. Jameson's positing of the historicist perspective as fundamentally opposed to a conception of the centered subject as never having existed indicates a deep fault in the theory of the postmodern subject, an oblivion into which the experiences of marginalized populations have been cast, effectively untheorized. (Harper 11)

By failing to consider the importance of social positionalities in arguing for the historically specific state of the postmodernist subject, Jamesonian postmodernism ignores the social construction of that subject. A truly social postmodernism, such as that explored in Harper's text, heightens the political stakes involved in postmodernist discourse by acknowledging within its theories the effects of race, class, gender, and sexuality. Harper again:

> Rather than conceiving that fragmentation as deriving solely from the various technological, economic, and philosophical developments that I cite above as reorienting our idea of human subjectivity in the late twentieth century, I would like to suggest that postmodern decenteredness may actually be a function of the increasing implication in the "general" culture of what are usually thought of as socially marginal or "minority" experiences. (11–12)

Insofar as the discourse of postmodernism tells us anything useful about the life-world or has any real political efficacy, it is thus less in confronting a totalizing set of technological and economic obstacles to centered subjectivity than in interrogating the manner in which social relations, and changes within those relations, contribute to the experiences of the contemporary subject.

I suggest that the choice on the part of the postmodernists to consider the former and not the latter, while perhaps not conscious, was also not innocent.[36] The failure on the part of the major players in the postmodern debate to consider those socially marginal experiences in the formation of their predominantly cultural discourse highlights the function of the discourse of postmodernism, particularly in its position within the framework of the discourse of obsolescence. The political shifts in contemporary critical thought—particularly those since the late 1960s—highlight "difference" as a site of progressive activity. This often-disparaged turn to "identity politics," exacerbated by the seeming collapse of Marxism in the 1980s, threatened to close a number of largely white male critics out of the vanguard of contemporary discourse. These critics' turn, in response, to a cultural postmodernism obsessed with shifts in the structures of technology and of economics, is a self-protective gesture, an attempt to find prolonged political relevance in a radically changing social structure.[37] Thus we turn again to Christopher Norris's comment, with a slightly different emphasis: "a recourse to theory is typically the response of any marginalized fraction of dissident intellectuals, excluded from the mainstream of political life and left little choice but to cultivate a range of more or less hopeful alternative visions" (1). In this context, the self-diagnosis of the ills of marginalization on the part of a group of theorists overwhelmingly both white and male becomes quite politically charged. It also becomes increasingly clear that the discourse of postmodernism is cultural criticism's expression of the anxiety of obsolescence.

The Postmodernist Writer

So, to recap: The anxiety of obsolescence, a cultural pose struck by the beleaguered postmodern novelist, has at its root three discourses with which it is mutually constitutive. These discourses—the death of the novel, the threat of new technologies, and the rise of postmodernism—all bespeak obsolescence in the interest of creating a protected space within which a threatened form might continue to flourish, but do so in highly suspect ways, ways that reveal a certain desire to submerge questions of social hierarchy within a more comfortable cultural framework. All that remains, before setting out to examine the anxiety of obsolescence in its primary texts, is to consider just who that postmodern novelist is.

My investigation into the novel of obsolescence takes the work of Thomas Pynchon and Don DeLillo as a metonym of sorts for the work of a larger cluster of postmodern U.S. writers concerned with the relationship between the novel and television. While other authors and texts enter my analysis at key moments, I focus on these two novelists in no small part for practical purposes; fully examining the instances of this discourse as it recurs across the literature of the period (much less across multiple genres and national literatures) would no doubt require a multivolume set. To analyze this discourse in sufficient detail, the field must of necessity be narrowed. However, the choice of these two novelists is significant—as, arguably, the two most important U.S. literary novelists of the late twentieth century, their work has wielded huge influence over the development of the contemporary U.S. literary scene. Many other novelists have written many other very important novels, and yet Pynchon and DeLillo remain, arguably, the Hemingway and Faulkner of the postwar period; no understanding of the era can be complete without a full accounting of their influence.

I hope, however, that my focus on these two novelists might be understood in contradistinction from what has come to form a second-order postmodern debate, a constant wrangling among critics and writers over which practitioners and texts can be properly considered "postmodernist." Within the debate that revolves around the novel, one finds numerous articles that have defined a core set of writers who together are considered the postmodern "canon," insofar as such a thing can be said to exist. Among others, and in no order but the alphabetical, these writers include, in addition to Pynchon and DeLillo, John Barth, Donald Barthelme, William S. Burroughs, Robert Coover, William Gaddis, William Gass, John Hawkes, Norman Mailer, and Kurt Vonnegut (see, e.g., Hassan; Barth, "Replenishment"). Further complicating matters is the work of more recent critics whose revisionist investigations of the postmodernist novel explore the writers left off the canon-forming lists but whose stylistic and thematic concerns warrant their inclusion, such as Kathy Acker, Joan Didion, Maxine Hong Kingston, Toni Morrison, Ishmael Reed, Leslie Marmon Silko, and so on (see Harper; also Hite and W. Steiner). Given the very size and diversity of these lists, it appears evident that, despite the presumed death of the novel, despite the depredations of technology, and despite the hopelessness of the postmodern, novelists have not stopped writing, nor have they stopped making an impression on contemporary culture. As the editor of *Bold Type* suggests, the novelist's supposedly precarious existence on the edge of contemporary culture might actually be a benefit: "In this more marginal context, it may be that writers will be liberated and literature as an art form will flourish anew" (Weissman). Indeed, as we have seen, life at the margins has its consolations.

It is particularly to the point, then, that the *Bold Type* editorial begins with Don DeLillo's claim that we live in "a period of empty millennial frenzy" ("The Power of History" 62, qtd. in Weissman). John Barth, as we have seen, distinguishes the novelist's millennialism from that more frequently associated with mystics, pointing out that "if you took a bunch of people out into the desert and the world didn't end, you'd come home shamefaced, I imagine; but the persistence of an art form doesn't invalidate work created in the comparable apocalyptic ambience" ("Exhaustion," 32). The novelist is not immune from his own millennialism; his sense of his imminent demise and disappearance is of a piece with the querulous cries of that prophet in the desert that the world—or at least the "Western civilization" part of it—is coming to an end. But he has the luxury of putting his "empty millennial frenzy" to creative use. In 1997, the literary world saw the release of huge new novels—huge in both size and reception—by both DeLillo and Pynchon, while also watching the launch of WebTV. This was a significant coincidence. This study confronts the uncomfortable coexistence of these two writers and the electronic media, exploring through the connected discourses of television as machine, television as spectacle, and television as network, these writers' engagement with their own anxiety of obsolescence.

It is because this study draws primarily from the work of Pynchon and DeLillo that the novelist of obsolescence as I have described him thus far has been so relentlessly masculine. In addition to this pragmatism of signification, however, there are larger, more theoretical reasons for suggesting that the novelist confronting the anxiety of obsolescence is male. First, this novelist is following in the tradition of Bloom's always-male poet, confronting, doing battle, and engaging in other such masculinist metaphors of contest and conquest. But more importantly, many of these readings of DeLillo and Pynchon should be extrapolated outward to connect with other members of that "canonical" group of white male writers whose texts form the core of what has, until recently, been considered the "postmodern." One critic of the postmodern novel, in attempting to delineate this canon, has posited two contrary forms of postmodernist fiction: the aesthetic and the oppositional (see Francese). This distinction casts into opposing camps formal experimentalists such as John Barth and politically motivated writers such as Toni Morrison. The flaw in this model is most clearly revealed when considering Pynchon and DeLillo, two novelists who significantly cross the line, as both combine late-modernist experimentalism with pointed commentary on the condition of postmodernity.

There nonetheless remains reason to separate these writers from a novelist such as Toni Morrison, whom I consider in the final chapter of this volume. This separation is based not on an essentialized authorial identity (white men versus a woman of color) but on the socially situated subject positions that their narratives construct. Moreover, such a separation cannot be made contingent upon a split between a false dichotomy of aesthetic postmodernism and oppositional postmodernism, as each set of writers clearly interacts with both categories. Rather, we might best be served by returning to my characterization of the split between cultural postmodernism and social postmodernism. Pynchon and DeLillo, like Jameson, repeatedly demonstrate in their highly formalist novels an obsession with the macro level systems of technology and economics, the movement of politics on a national and international scale, the global sweep of war—systems that engulf the individual and render him powerless. Morrison, by contrast, puts very similar techniques to work in exploring the local and familial effects of systems of domination that function to construct the marginalized subject in its contingent specificity, systems that do not obliterate but create the individual. Simply put, writers operating within a socially oriented postmodernist perspective, like Morrison, do not, by and large, show evidence of the anxiety of obsolescence in their texts. Such writers' interactions with and representations of television have much in common with Harper's description of the African American subject and its decenteredness; rather than a once-centered self now decentered, the "historical status of such a subjectivity is precisely that of *never having existed*" (11, emphasis in original). So with the electronic media: rather than once having had a voice and now finding themselves silenced in the cultural realm by these new technologies, such voices' historical status is that of never having existed. And just as Marianna Torgovnick suggests that the death-of-the-novel discourse requires economic and social privilege to make any sense, so the anxiety of obsolescence requires cultural privilege (see Spilka and McCracken-Flesher 361).

This does not mean that postmodernist critiques, whether theoretical, critical, or fictional, bear no import for the writers I describe as social post-modernists; as bell hooks suggests, such critiques can "open up new possibilities for the construction of the self and the assertion of agency" (par. 10). However, where such critiques are used to undermine the notion of agency, and where they appropriate the language of marginalization, these critiques have the (perhaps unintentional) effect of closing down the possibilities for radical liberation on the part of previously disenfranchised subjects. Harper argues that "the subjective disorientation entailed by social marginality is implicated in dominant conceptions of the generalized postmodern condition, with the political consequence that its specific sociopolitical import is obscured in discourse in and about contemporary culture" (28). I suggest something slightly but crucially different: Pynchon and DeLillo deploy the discourses of cultural postmodernism with the effect not simply of appropriating the experience of marginality to the writer's cultural position, and not simply of obscuring the specific sociopolitical import of social marginality, but with the further effect of camouflaging an at times troubling set of sociopolitical concerns. In this paradoxical fashion, the return of the anxiety of obsolescence's repressed winds up not obscuring but rather highlighting questions of social marginality. In the end, the novel of obsolescence functions as a contemporary version of the "melodrama of beset [white] manhood" defined by Nina Baym, in which the threat that television poses to the novelist functions as an acceptable cultural scapegoat for what is a much stickier social issue: the perceived dominance on the contemporary literary scene of fiction by women and racial and ethnic minorities (see Baym).

For the moment, I'd like to look at two key instances in which Pynchon and DeLillo figure most clearly the altogether circumscribed spaces they imagine remaining to the writer in the age of television. Writers still abound in the postmodern novel—in fact, for many of the novelists of obsolescence, the writer is the quintessential postmodern figure, postmodern precisely in his presumed decenteredness. Thus one encounters repeatedly in the novel of obsolescence the presence of the novelist as a character within his own text—"John Barth" in *LETTERS*, "Richard S. Powers" in *Galatea 2.2*, "Paul

Auster" in *The New York Trilogy*—suggesting both the author's reduction to the mere creation of his work, on the one hand, and his attempts to keep that work under control through his presence, on the other. This decenteredness becomes not only a danger to the author but also a badge of honor that marks his cultural marginalization; in fact, as we shall see in thinking about Don DeLillo's *Mao II,* the most "successful" postmodern novelist is ironically the one who does not publish.

Pynchon's view of the role of the writer is confronted most directly in *V.,* particularly in the Confessions of Fausto Maijstral:

> while others may look on the laws of physics as legislation and God as a human form with beard measured in light-years and nebulae for sandals, Fausto's kind [poets, that is] are alone with the task of living in a universe of things which simply are, and cloaking that innate mindlessness with comfortable and pious metaphor so that the "practical" half of humanity may continue in the Great Lie, confident that their machines, dwellings, streets and weather share the same human motives, personal traits and fits of contrariness as they.
>
> Poets have been at this for centuries. It is the only useful purpose they do serve in society: and if every poet were to vanish tomorrow, society would live no longer than the quick memories and dead books of their poetry. (326)

Thus the job of the poet—and by extension, the novelist, who works with the same metaphors on a larger canvas—is to clothe what is essentially inhuman in the trappings of the human, to keep the world convinced that it runs on a human principle, without which deluded conviction all culture would fall into utter ruin. Writers are, in this view, the only members of society able to see beyond that veil of "comfortable" metaphor, and thus have been charged with the responsibility for upholding it. One might well ask two questions here, however. First, who is living the necessary lie? Arguably, Fausto's delusions of grandeur regarding the importance of poetry in a dying world are what keep him moving forward; it may be his own conviction of his importance to the world that is deluded. Second, if the job of the writer is the maintenance of the illusions of metaphor, has Pynchon himself not violated the code by giving us all this blurred peek behind the curtain?

In fact, Pynchon's writerly strategy across his career has been an absolute inversion of Fausto's insistence on allowing humanity to "continue in the Great Lie" so that poetry itself may live on. Pynchon pulls back the cloak of metaphor, pointing out the determination of the twentieth century by the machine and the image, declaring at every opportunity that those things that made us human—including poetry, and potentially the novel—are at an end. The responsibility of the writer, in Pynchon's estimation, is not making society comfortable with its delusions, but rather maintaining a profoundly political opposition to the dominant culture. The response of that culture to the writer's work only reveals the necessity of his continued opposition. Take, for instance, Winthrop Tremaine, army-surplus dealer, in *The Crying of Lot 49*: " 'Books.' You had the feeling that it was only his good breeding that kept him from spitting. 'You want to sell something used,' he advised Oedipa, 'find out what there's a demand for.' " (149). The demand for books, according to this representation, is gone from the world, though Tremaine's pleasure in the surge in demand for surplus rifles and swastika armbands gestures toward the lingering need for the novel's political work.

In *Mao II,* DeLillo creates an extended portrait of the contemporary writer as prophetic voice in the desert. *Mao II*'s writer-protagonist is Bill Gray, a novelist whose retreat from the world has augmented his status as cult figure. In fact, an argument can be made that this status has actually been created by his reclusiveness; as Scott Martineau, his creepily obsessive but nonetheless brilliant assistant, insists:

> Bill is at the height of his fame. Ask me why. Because he hasn't published in years and years and years. When his books first came out, and people forget this or they never knew it, they made a slight sort of curio impression. . . . It's the years since that have made him big. (52)

This is the paradox that the contemporary writer must face, a world in which a writer gains fame by not publishing, by refusing to interact with the surrounding culture. Years earlier, in DeLillo's *Ratner's Star*, the tortured novelist Jean Venable explicates the conundrum:

> There's a whole class of writers who don't want their books to be read. This to some extent explains their crazed prose. To express what is expressible isn't why you write if you're in this class of writers. To be understood is faintly embarrassing. What you want to express is the violence of your desire not to be read. The friction of an audience is what drives writers crazy. These people are going to read what you write. The more they understand, the crazier you get. You can't let them know what you're writing about. Once they know, you're finished. If you're in this class, what you have to do is either not publish or make absolutely sure your work leaves readers strewn along the margins. This not only causes literature to happen but is indispensable to your mental health as well. (410–11)

This friction between author and audience, between author and culture, becomes literalized in *Mao II*. Bill Gray, in his reclusiveness, in his cult status, in his long silences between novels, but also in his desire to have an impact on the wider culture, is arguably DeLillo's portrait of Pynchon—but also perhaps an idealized portrait of himself, that writer who reportedly circulated at the 1998 National Book Awards dinner while handing out cards that read "I don't want to talk about it" (see Atlas).

Scott works actively to keep Gray in hiding, to discourage him from publishing his latest novel. But Gray manages, in the course of the book, to elude Scott's watchful protection, emerge from his seclusion, and enter the electronic culture, a world for which he is utterly unprepared. This world doesn't conform to the romantic images he holds of it; as his editor says, during their first meeting in decades:

> "You have a twisted sense of the writer's place in society. You think the writer belongs at the far margin, doing dangerous things. In Central America, writers carry guns. They have to. And this has always been your idea of the way it ought to be. The state should want to kill all writers. Every government, every group that holds power or aspires to power should feel so threatened by writers that they hunt them down, everywhere."
>   "I've done no dangerous things."
>   "No. But you've lived out the vision anyway." (*Mao II* 97)

Gray's regret—that there isn't, in this image-based, media-driven culture, a real threat attached to the person of the writer—suggests the contemporary locus of such a threat. It is Brita, the photographer, who must travel under assumed names, who is in mortal danger; it is the terrorists who pose the threat to society that Gray feels should come from writers.

> For some time now I've had the feeling that novelists and terrorists are playing a zero-sum game. . . . What terrorists gain, novelists lose. The degree to which they influence mass consciousness is the extent of our decline as shapers of sensibility and thought. The danger they represent equals our own failure to be dangerous. (156–57)

Gray, in his determination to "live out the vision," to find a way of evening the score in this "zero-sum game," seeks a place where writers are in danger, where he, as a writer, can ride forth and save one held captive by a fundamentalist sect determined to punish what it sees as blasphemy. We follow Gray on his delirious reenactment of the Quixotic quest, stepping into the light of day in a world he has not lived in for thirty years, attempting to save a political prisoner, and the connections in our minds are almost laughably absurd: Thomas Pynchon riding to the rescue of Salman Rushdie.[38]

But ridiculous as this quest may sound, translated into the terms of our own literary figures, it appears to be the only way for Gray, and thus for the novelist as novelist, to reassert his own preeminence in the age of television. The need to engage with contemporary culture in *Mao II* is inextricably linked to a need for renewed masculine potency, for engagement with the threat of violence. This attempted return of the writer to action is also, for Bill, a return of the writer to writing. There is some ambiguity within the novel, at least at first, as to whether the passages that record the thoughts of the tortured poet-prisoner are in fact the novel's observations in free indirect discourse, or whether these are the creations of Bill Gray, the novelist. When finally we recognize that these passages are Gray's work, we discover the true purpose of his foray into this world; these passages represent the first new writing he has produced aside from his third novel, which he has worked and reworked for the last twenty-three years.[39] He is able to write again, able to be a writer, only by emerging from his solipsism and confronting the bomb makers and gunmen. "There was something at stake," he acknowledges, "in these sentences he wrote about the basement room. They held a pause, an anxious space he began to recognize. There's a danger in a sentence when it comes out right" (*MII* 167). As Hawthorne sought to masculinize the profession of writing by separating it from those "scribbling women," so Gray, in entering the world of terrorist violence, attempts to restore not just pertinence but danger to writing. While DeLillo arguably levels a critique at Gray via the novel's satire, this critical effect is minimized by the inevitable connections drawn by the reader between the writer *inside* and the writer *outside* the text; the glorification of one, struggling against his age, cannot help but reflect upon the other. Moreover, though this move is not tainted by the overt misogyny of Hawthorne's denunciation, by seeking the danger in writing, the text makes it once again part of the specifically masculine tradition of rugged individualism.

Gray succeeds only insofar as he is able, temporarily, to think writing dangerous again. Ultimately, however, Gray's literary helplessness in coping with the electronic, visual world leads him to his own destruction. Early on in his journey, in London, Gray marvels over the logic of the pavement signs on the street corners: "It was so perfectly damn sensible they ought to make it the law in every city, long-lettered words in white paint that tell you which way to look if you want to live." Later, in Athens, we realize that Gray's reliance upon the word as a form of communication is near total, and deadly, as he is unable to interpret—does not even look for—the visual clues that would enable him on his own to keep from getting killed. He blithely walks off the unlabeled curb and is promptly hit by a car. He is helpless without the words to guide him, and even the words are not much help, when given visual, material form: He has to "[remind] himself" to read the signs when they do exist (*MII* 120).

Then again, after the accident, his reliance upon the literary and his inability to interpret visual clues worsen the situation; the outward signs of his injury are slight, so he assumes no damage has been done. Finally, in Cyprus, he is able to discover the true extent of his injuries only by approaching a group of British veterinarians with a textual question: "See, I'm doing a passage in a book that requires specialized medical knowledge and as I need a little guidance I wonder if I could trouble you for a minute or two" (*MII* 205). The veterinarians, a bit puzzled at first by the human/animal category mistake that Gray has apparently made, nonetheless comply, finding the entire thing somewhat amusing. Gray, for his part, must lead them through the events of his accident and his subsequent symptoms, but must treat his symptoms as textual choices that he, as writer, has made, thus attributing to himself a much greater degree of agency than the situation—or the age—would warrant.

"But the spleen is on the left side," Bill said. "My character feels pain on the right side."

"Did you tell us this?" the woman said.

"Maybe I forgot."

"Why not change it to the left side and do the spleen?" the bearded vet said. "It would actually bleed nonstop, I expect. Might be a nice little bit you could do with that."

The waiter came with the brandy and Bill held up a hand to request a formal pause while he drank the thing down.

"But, see, I need the right side. It's essential to my theme."

He sensed they were pausing to take this in.

"Can it be the upper right side?" the second man said.

"I think we can do that."

"Can we give him some pain when he takes a deep breath?"

"Pain on breathing. Don't see why not."

"Can we make his right shoulder hurt?"

"Yes, I think we can."

"Then it's absolutely solved," the woman said.

> The bearded vet poured the wine.
> "Lacerated liver."
> "Hematoma."
> "Local swelling filled with blood."
> "Doesn't show externally." (208)

Gray, the obstinate writer, still awash in the belief in his own omnipotence in a world he stubbornly insists on imagining to be text based, ignores the advice of the veterinarians to get his character to a doctor and instead sails for Lebanon, convinced that he can create for himself a new ending. Instead, in his last moments, he comes to realize that "it was writing that caused his life to disappear" (215). Doomed by his inability to view the world or his life outside the boundaries of the textual, doomed by his attempts to become a writer who writes, rather than a writer famous for not writing, Bill Gray dies alone in a cabin on the boat, his passport and identification stolen, his disappearance from the world complete. No one will ever be certain whether he is really dead.

DeLillo's vision of the doomed writer coupled with Pynchon's portrait of the novelist as the marginalized voice of reason forms the backbone of the anxiety of obsolescence. For both Pynchon and DeLillo, the most apparent strategy for contending with this anxiety is its novelistic reproduction, thematizing the anxiety in the very works in which the electronic media seem to have destroyed their faith. Each rejoices in his putative marginality, claiming that, contrary to our expectations, "the writer is working against the age . . . and so he feels some satisfaction in not being widely read. He is diminished by an audience" (DeLillo, qtd. in Aaron 73). There is, of course, a level of disingenuousness to this depiction of the novelist's joy in being ignored, much less in his inevitable demise; Pynchon's and DeLillo's very successes give the lie to that death.[40] But perhaps the novel, in thematizing this anxiety, serves a talismanic purpose, magical thinking that both valorizes the novelist's marginalization and creates the conditions for his return to the center. Or, as Bill Gray tells Brita during their photo session,

> It's the self-important fool that keeps the writer going. I exaggerate the pain of writing, the pain of solitude, the failure, the rage, the confusion, the helplessness, the fear, the humiliation. The narrower the boundaries of my life, the more I exaggerate myself. If the pain is real, why do I inflate it? Maybe this is the only pleasure I'm allowed. (*MII* 37)

Thus, as John Barth suggested, writing about the novel's end paves the way for a new beginning. But while Paul Mann argues that "death-theory" is used within the avant-garde to "terrorize" writers into finding the new within the conditions of its own impossibility, the novel of obsolescence's manipulations of "the pain of writing" seem to indicate a certain joy in anxiety, made possible by the knowledge of a much deeper safety.[41] Perhaps an exaggeration of the novelist's anxieties, the depiction of a world in which we all have much to fear from the writer's cultural displacement is indeed one of his last pleasures, and one that makes it safe for him to keep writing.

2

Machine

> Our machines are disturbingly lively,
> and we ourselves frighteningly inert.
> —Donna Haraway

At an early moment in Thomas Pynchon's *V.*, the reader is introduced to the members of the Whole Sick Crew, a loose coalition of alienated youth cavorting about 1955 Manhattan. As the narration emphasizes, each member of the Crew participates in an "exhausted impersonation" of bohemian artiness, a kind of Beat-lite, in which aesthetic and social rebellion fail to find either a stable position to revolt against or a sufficiently shocking "new." Slab, for instance, is the Catatonic Expressionist painter who hopes that his work will be "the ultimate in non-communication"; Melvin plays an endless stream of dull liberal folk songs; and Raoul writes for television while "keeping carefully in mind, and complaining bitterly about, all the sponsor-fetishes of that industry" (56). Thoroughly bourgeois revolutionaries all, the Crew's self-declared Sick-ness mostly manifests in excessive alcohol intake and painfully hip name-dropping, thus bearing in common with the much later Generation X slackerdom a premature sense of exhaustion, an absence of the critical potential once thought to be inherent in ironic alienation. The cause of both the alienation and the impotence from which this group suffers (and from which, by extension, an entire culture may be said to suffer) is most explicitly announced in the figure of Fergus Mixolydian, a fringe member of the Crew. Fergus, described as the self-proclaimed laziest person in New York, is more-or-less comatose throughout the novel; his projects, complex as they are, aim at nothing more than furthering his slothfulness. Fergus produces, for instance, through a careful and rigorous adherence to scientific procedure, a series of chemical reactions that inflate a balloon marked with a giant "Z," which he ties to his bedpost as a marker of his lethargy. This bizarre admixture of the uselessly productive culminates in Fergus's invention of "an ingenious sleep-switch, receiving its signal from two electrodes placed on the inner skin of his forearm. When Fergus dropped below a certain level of awareness, the skin resistance increased over a preset value to operate the switch. Fergus thus became an extension of the TV set" (56). Much like the other members of the Whole Sick Crew, who strive ambitiously for the appearance of alienation, Fergus's labors are aimed at their own undoing. In this regard, Fergus's literal interface with the television set is not that different from Raoul's: each maintains a careful connection to the medium while feigning disdain; each becomes a willing functionary of the machine. Understood in this way, Fergus's transformation into a human remote control merely exaggerates the Crew's disaffected torpor.

The inclusion of the technology of television in this particular circuit is no accident, however. The alienation figured throughout *V.* in literally dozens of references to "decadence" and "inanimation" is specifically a response to the omnipresence of machines, and the troubled relationships between those machines and the humans with whom they interact. In Fergus's case, the relationship between man and machine is a direct wiring-in, but this physical connection and the torpor it makes possible—signified by the "Z" thought-balloon, lifted directly from cartoons—are only a literal rendering of the general couch-potato syndrome into which so many intellectuals have imagined the United States sinking. While Fergus may, through his sleep-switch, become an extension of the TV set, the relationship of the average viewer to the set in the popular imaginary is not much different. Like Fergus, like Raoul, those who connect themselves to the television set become inescapably part of its workings. Thus, one of the dangers represented by the tube in the novel of obsolescence, made strikingly visible in Fergus's sleep-switch, is this much-too-literal bringing together of human and machine, a coupling destined to confuse one category with the other.

Despite the reminders of numerous critics—Donna Haraway, Anne Balsamo, Judith Halberstam, and Ira Livingston, to name but a few—that we are all already cyborgs reliant upon pacemakers, contact lenses, Cochlear implants, and e-mail accounts for our day-to-day existence, the literal linkage of Fergus's connection to the machine remains predominantly the stuff of fiction. Recently, however, scientists have begun exploring the neuromotor possibilities presented by such interfaces. In June 2000, for instance, the *New York Times* reported on a wiring together of the organic and the mechanical that resulted in what it termed an "artificial animal" (see Sorid). Dr. Sandro Mussa-Ivaldi, working with a team of scientists from the United States and Italy, succeeded in connecting part of the brain of a lamprey with a small robot, resulting in two-way communication between the organic and mechanical halves of this "animal." "The aim of the research," according to the *Times*, "is to untangle the mysteries of brain signals and to see how the brain's circuits change and adapt to different stimuli." The newspaper of record was unable to avoid commenting on the "eerie" nature of the experiment, however, despite its own assessment of the researchers' ostensibly reasonable purposes. In seeking a justification for this test's weirdness, the article turns to Steve Grand, CEO of Cyberlife Research, a company described as "trying to create forms of synthetic life." Says Grand: "People are sometimes fearful that artificial life research will reduce us all to machines and explain away our souls. . . . On the contrary, I believe it will give us a new understanding and a new respect for ourselves, as the most sublime machines in the known universe."

Regardless of the contradiction inherent in Grand's assessment (humans are more than machines—we're the best machines), his sense of the anxiety produced by a technology that encroaches upon life is strikingly accurate. As is Mussa-Ivaldi's own response to concerns about the creepy nature of his work: "It has echoes of a literary kind," he acknowledges (Sorid). Indeed, as the Western cultural obsession with technology has grown over the last two centuries, so has a parallel cultural terror; machines of all varieties, of all levels of complexity, have long troubled the literary imagination. Television of course introduces another dimension to this novelistic technophobia; when the machine to which humans seem to be so drawn is a representing machine, one that performs the narrative function of fiction while ostensibly encouraging passivity in its audience, the threat of dehumanization inherent in the machine becomes a direct threat to the existence of a reading public.[1] Thus the importance of Fergus's self-invention as remote control: this literal manifestation of the television watcher's lassitude underscores a perceived decadence in U.S. culture, a decay directly responsible for the novel's—and not incidentally, the novelist's—marginalization.

Representations of technology in the novel of obsolescence are thus unavoidably imbricated with concerns about the contemporary state of the act of reading. Moreover, the danger implied in the technologized decline of reading is imagined to be a specifically political danger. A reading public, as critics including Neil Postman and Sven Birkerts argue, is an active, involved, invested public, a true democratic citizenry taking serious part in public discourse.[2] As the textual forms of such public life come to be replaced by televisuality, the give-and-take of discourse yields to the one-way stream of representation, inducing passivity in a once-active public sphere. And as such representing machines further expand their influence over the work of communication, mediating all forms of political knowledge, the individual is led to identify not with the ideas expressed or with the people expressing them, but with the machines themselves. This technologized political life, in undermining the act of reading, creates a precondition necessary for fascism not only by naturalizing a mechanical control over public discourse, but also by alienating the individual from his own humanity, leaving him manipulable, impotent.

My use of the masculine, both in pronoun form and in the metaphor of impotence, in conjunction with this amorphous notion of "humanity" is no accident. While there is an unquestionable link between masculinity and the development of technology, in these representations the humanity that is alienated through its dealings with technology is inescapably masculinist, bound up in centuries-old tropes of the liberal subject as both rugged individualist and committed citizen. Through the decadence it ostensibly produces in that liberal subject, technology becomes one among many social forces that threaten the subject with feminization; anxieties about mechanical alienation thus participate in the same line of historical discourses as the frontier myth and the "genteel tradition" that disrupted it.[3] Representations of technology in the novel of obsolescence, then, indicate at once anxieties about the current state of reading and anxieties about the current state of masculinity. To borrow Timothy Melley's useful phrase from *Empire of Conspiracy*, the "agency panic" induced by such "influencing machines" as television is inevitably gendered, as the agency imagined to be draining away is always masculine, and the vacuum that it leaves behind is likewise imagined to be feminine (see Melley, esp. 32–37). In this manner, the question of an alienated "humanity" serves as a foil for concerns about a decentered, fragmented masculinity.

In this chapter, I approach these questions of the interrelationship of the anxiety of obsolescence and cultural technophobia in the novels of Thomas Pynchon, with particular attention to the implications these representations bear for our understanding of gender and sexuality. These novels, most particularly *V.*, *Gravity's Rainbow*, and *Vineland*, are engaged in the progressive business of reanimating a too-passive reading public by means of a thoroughgoing critique of the political couch-potatodom into which the United States has gradually declined. This activism comes at the expense of the feminine, however, which is too easily conflated with the technologies that threaten human agency.

Border War

Since Mary Shelley's *Frankenstein*, writers have repeatedly warned that our scientific reach may exceed our philosophical grasp. In fact, dozens of literary, filmic, and pop-cultural texts represent the dangers that out-of-control technologies present to human existence. By momentarily focusing on such representations in film, we can see that these out-of-control technologies generally pose the greatest threat to human survival when they themselves take on characteristics of the human. Such appropriations of humanlike qualities can be thought of in two categories: first, technologies that take on the bodily form of the human, as in the killer robots of *Metropolis*, *Eve of Destruction*, and the *Terminator* films; second, technologies that take on the sentience associated with the human, as in the computer-based artificial intelligences of *War Games* and *The Matrix*. These artificial intelligences seem at first to present a danger that is both more widespread and more deadly than the bodily forms—universal nuclear annihilation. Moreover, the threat imagined from such computers has increased as their intelligences have grown; while a computer glitch early in the cold war produces accidental nuclear destruction in *Fail Safe*, and a computer's inability to distinguish between the real and the virtual almost triggers a nuclear holocaust in *War Games*, the fully conscious, wholly self-aware computers of both *The Matrix* and the *Terminator* films intentionally begin a nuclear war with the hope of exterminating human life. This interweaving of the computer and nuclear threats indicates the cold war's influence over popular visions of technology; at such a moment of ultimacy, as Don DeLillo suggests in *Underworld*, it appears that "all technology refers to the bomb" (467).

However, while the other category of humanoid machines—those that appropriate the physical form of the human—may be imagined to pose a threat less global in its implications, they often prove more insidiously dangerous. In fact, as Martin Heidegger suggests in "The Question Concerning Technology," the cold war's obsessive focus on the threat of literal annihilation posed by nuclear technologies risks ignoring a more subtle kind of danger. "The threat to man does not come in the first instance from the potentially lethal machines and apparatus of technology," he argues. "The actual threat has already afflicted man in his essence" (333). In Heidegger's analysis, technology's "enframing" character has damaged humans by irreversibly altering their understanding of the nature of being: "Enframing does not simply endanger man in his relationship to himself and to everything that is. As a destining, it banishes man into the kind of revealing that is an ordering. Where this ordering holds sway, it drives out every other possibility of revealing" (332). Technology, in other words, promotes a functionalist epistemology that makes it impossible to read the world—or to read the self—except through technology's own framework. Thus Cyberlife Research CEO Steve Grand, while attempting to explain that his research into synthetic life will not "reduce us all to machines," is none-theless forced to use a technological metaphor to describe his concept of the human, as quoted earlier : "the most sublime machines in the known universe" (Sorid).

This epistemological shift underlies the representations of danger in ma-chines that appropriate the bodily form of the human: when confronted with the Terminator, or with the evil robot Maria of *Metropolis*, or with Eve in *Eve of Destruction*, the human characters at first fail to distinguish human from machine. This inability to tell the difference not only allows the destructive machine to physically harm human beings but also encourages a kind of self-identification with the machine and its values that further weakens human resistance to dangerous technologies. It is of course absolutely to the point that each of these humanoid machines wields a hypersexualized form of self-presentation as a key weapon. The Terminator's threat arises equally from his overdeveloped steroidal musculature and from his indestructible endoskeleton; Maria and Eve each lead men to their destruction through displays of active feminine erotics. These machines threaten through their too-accurate appro-priation of the human form and their too-knowing manipulation of stereo-typically gendered sexualities—mimetics that imply intimate bonds among human self-perception, human consciousness, and conventional understand-ings of sex and gender.

In what follows, I focus on the concept of the machine as it is mobilized within the novel of obsolescence, examining the literal fears of technology's destructive powers, as well as the more epistemological anxieties suggested by Heidegger. Technology may, in this discourse, destroy the human by killing human beings, or it may destroy the essence of the human at its root by alter-ing human understanding of the nature of being. Whether the destruction the machines wreak is physical or metaphorical, the novel of obsolescence posits again and again through its representations that the relationship between hu-man subjects and their machines is threatening to invert; that humans have long since been demoted, as Edward Tenner suggests, from tool users to tool managers (see Tenner 17); and that we may in fact be precariously close to becoming the tools used by machines.

This potential inversion implies a relationship between human and ma-chine founded simultaneously in separation and proximity. Philosophers have, since Descartes, drawn lines between humans and machines, whether those lines have been based on the faculty of language, or reason, or the more amor-phous existence of the "soul." As N. Katherine Hayles argues, however, these attempts at separation draw the ostensibly opposed terms together: "If I say a chicken is not like a tractor, I have characterized the chicken in terms of the tractor, no less than when I assert the two are alike. In the same way, whether they are understood as like or unlike, ranging human intelligence alongside an intelligent machine puts the two into a relay system that constitutes the human as a special kind of information machine and the information machine as a special kind of human" (64–65). As with all interfaces, that between human and machine is both boundary and connection, both line of demarcation and shared surface. The connective aspect of the human/machine interface, and the implication that the two entities must be understood in relationship to one another, is a source of technological anxiety for many writers and critics.

It is no accident that many of these writers reveal, in their anxiety, an interest in maintaining the structures of Enlightenment thought represented by Descartes. As Donna Haraway writes in her classic "A Cyborg Manifesto": "In the traditions of 'Western' science and politics—the tradition of racist, male-dominated capitalism; the tradition of progress; the tradition of the appropriation of nature as resource for the productions of culture; the tradition of reproduction of the self from the reflections of the other—the relationship between organism and machine has been a border war" (150). By describing the human/machine conflict as a "border war," Haraway calls our attention first to the shared boundary that exists between the two categories, and second to the fact that the struggle is itself about definition, about the power to safely determine what—or who—is and is not human. The blurrier that boundary becomes, the more the privileged category of the human, and the hierarchies that category has for centuries been used to support, come under threat.

Such anxieties about the proximity of human and machine, and about the eroding boundary between them, frequently surface in representations of communications technologies in the contemporary novel. Film, radio, and particularly Fergus Mixolydian's television are all depicted as responsible for creating humans in complicity with the ethics and aesthetics of the machine. Film fascinated its audiences by capturing the human form in mechanical fashion, presenting a reproduction of the actor rather than her live performance; radio and television furthered this project by bringing the mechanized human voice and image into the home. These machines' power to project believable representations of the human, these novels suggest, has led human subjects to identify increasingly with the machines themselves, privileging machine values over human values. However, the gendered nature of both the images that these technologies project and the spaces into which they are projected is inextricably bound up with the "machine values" these technologies are said to promote. Film allowed female spectators access to traditionally male public spaces, and television brought the public realm into the female-controlled domestic space; both technologies thus created possibilities for rupture and subversion of conventional gender roles.[4] The "human" values that these technologies are represented as eroding, then, must be interrogated for their gendered specificity, and for the hierarchies that they seek to reinstate.[5]

This erosion, whether of the human or the masculine, is most frequently imagined to originate at the level of language. Taking the computer as an example: the computer is by far the most advanced of the technologies imagined to threaten human existence, given its flexibility as a metamachine to replicate the functioning of any number of other machines; some researchers in fact believe that the computer will one day replicate the processes of human thought.[6] Popular representations of sentient killer machines aside, however, the danger in the computer resides, according to Neil Postman, less in anything the machine can actually do than in the metaphors it introduces, metaphors we retroactively apply to the other machines by which we are surrounded: "what we have here is a case of metaphor gone mad. From the proposition that humans are in some respects like machines, we move to the proposition that humans are little else but machines and, finally, that human beings *are* machines. And then, inevitably . . . to the proposition that machines are human beings" (*Technopoly* 112). The danger in these metaphors lies in their power to correlate our understanding of what it is to be human with our understanding of technology, thereby threatening not only to open the category "human" to beings that do not belong but also to radically alter our ways of understanding ourselves and our place in the world. This correlation thus risks, in Postman's view, diminishing both the human and humanist epistemologies.

The machine/human conflict is thus conceived of on both sides of this discourse—both by the so-called cyborgologists, as represented by Haraway, and by those labeled Luddites, as represented by Postman—as largely epistemological in nature, in which one way of understanding the world slips, or threatens to slip, into another. But to suggest that this conflict is largely epistemological is not to say that it is *merely* epistemological; critics as vastly different as Neil Postman and Michel Foucault insist that ways of knowing are intimately tied to the ordering of the universe, and thus have significant material resonance.[7] The distinction between these two positions on new technologies and new epistemologies lies in that boundary between human and machine, and whether it is a line primarily of separation or connection, whether it is to be shored up or undermined. Those on the Luddite side of this discourse display an interest in maintaining a clear distinction between the values of technology and the values of humanism in order that the values of humanism survive; those on the side of the cyborg hope that a movement into the posthuman, in which human and machine are radically interconnected categories, might similarly initiate a movement into posthumanism, in which new, progressive, nonhierarchical values might prevail.[8]

All this relentless binarizing, however—human/machine; technophobe/ technophile; humanism/posthumanism—in which one category must be maligned to support the other, does not begin with the late twentieth-century cyborg but has its origins forty years earlier.[9] The founding document of the contemporary conflict between technology and humanism is C. P. Snow's 1959 Rede lecture, "The Two Cultures and the Scientific Revolution" (republished in 1963 as *The Two Cultures: And a Second Look*). This lecture, infamous now for the endurance of its central metaphor, as well as for the nastiness of the debate that it provoked, argues that "the intellectual life of the whole of western society is increasingly being split into two polar groups" (10), literary intellectuals and scientists. The crisis in this polarization, as Snow sees it, results from the inability of these two groups to communicate adequately; the two must reestablish ties, he claims, if intellectual progress is to continue. But because he defines "progress" in "Two Cultures" entirely in terms of production and material gain, this reconnection, as Snow imagines it, wholly entails work on the part of the literary intellectuals to understand the scientists, rather than the other way around. This one-sidedness seems not to have disturbed Snow—he remained unapologetic even in his "Second Look" at the subject— but unsurprisingly produced a significant backlash among those relegated to the apparently backward realm of the literary. While Snow equates science with rigor, progress, and morality—this last perhaps a bit surprising fifteen years after World War II's nuclear end—critics like F. R. Leavis bridle in their responses to Snow's assumption that literary intellectuals are "natural Luddites" (Snow 27): "The upshot," Leavis retorts, "is that if you insist on the need for any other kind of concern, entailing forethought, action, and provision, about the human future—any other kind of misgiving—than that which talks in terms of productivity, material standards of living, hygienic and technological progress, then you are a Luddite" (38).

Given the fundamental nature of this conflict, and the power of the scientific/literary binary in the popular imagination, it is little wonder that this kind of dichotomizing persists in contemporary discussions of technology. It is also perhaps unsurprising that both Neil Postman, in his book about the dangers of the dominance of the technological epistemology in contemporary U.S. culture, and Thomas Pynchon, in his brief article reclaiming a revolutionary political position for the Luddite, open their texts with reference to

Snow and "Two Cultures."[10] They do so to significantly different ends, however. Postman introduces the dichotomy in order to widen it, broadening the schism to reflect the one he sees operative today: "the argument is not between humanists and scientists but between technology and everybody else" (*Technopoly* xii)—thus both suggesting that technology has developed a "body" and indicating its all-pervasive danger. Pynchon begins with this scientific/literary binary in order to explode it: "the two-cultures quarrel can no longer be sustained. As a visit to any library or magazine rack will easily confirm, there are now so many more than two cultures that the problem has really become how to find the time to read anything outside one's specialty" ("Is It OK," 1). While Postman goes on to a fairly stereotypical argument on behalf of the Luddite perspective,[11] Pynchon attempts to interrogate the history and meaning of "Luddite" itself, reclaiming the term from its Snovian reactionary associations and instead claiming for it radical possibilities.

Pynchon traces the history of Luddism through the figure of the "Badass," most notable for being both "Bad" and "Big," employing a "controlled martial-arts type anger" for the purposes of resistance ("Is It OK," 40). And, as seen in the frame-breaking Ned Lud himself, this anger is largely directed at the machines, both technological and corporate in nature, that enslave the majority of human beings. Pynchon follows the course of literary representations of the Badass from Shelley's *Frankenstein* through the eighteenth-century flood of gothic novels to *King Kong* and the science fiction of the 1950s, noting that in each case, though the Badass owes his power to extrahuman forces, those forces are distinctly nonmechanical. They celebrate rather a belief in the supernatural that makes human transcendence seem possible: "To insist on the miraculous," Pynchon argues, "is to deny the machine at least some of its claims on us, to assert the limited wish that living things, earthly and otherwise, may on occasion become Bad and Big enough to take part in transcendent doings" (41). Luddism, in this rendering, is transformed from a reactionary antitechnological stance into one concerned with the kind of amelioration of human existence that Snow imagined was the basis of science's moral high ground. This reclamation of political possibility for "living things, earthly and otherwise," however, requires an overt refusal of the machine and its claims on human existence.

There is thus a contradictory purpose at work in "Is It OK to Be a Luddite?": Pynchon attempts to explode the easy dichotomy between the scientific and literary communities while he opposes the realm of the "living" to that of the machine. Such an ambiguous motive can be read most significantly in Pynchon's description of the ultimate Badass, the one that he projects will finally catch "even the biggest of the brass" off guard. This Badass is both transcendent living creature and technological nightmare, to be produced "when the curves of research and development in artificial intelligence, molecular biology and robotics all converge." The product of these three fields, which will represent both the world's "next great challenge" and the redemption of Luddite hopes, a simultaneous destroyer and savior, is as yet only imaginable in cyberpunk. The fictionality of this Badass is to be separated from the concerns of earlier science fiction in two important regards. First, midcentury science fiction relied heavily, Pynchon reminds us, on "a definition of 'human' as particularly distinguished from 'machine,' " a distinction that will no longer be tenable should computer and genetic engineering merge. Second, and perhaps more importantly, is the introduction of the computer into the writing process itself. "Writers of all descriptions are stampeding to buy word processors," Pynchon tells us. "Machines have already become so user-friendly that even the most unreconstructed of Luddites can be charmed into laying down the old sledgehammer and stroking a few keys instead" (41). The computer thus becomes, in the hands of the writer, one instrument of Luddite revenge, the agent of the machine world's undoing. Of those "transcendent doings" in which the human being can currently involve himself, then, the greatest may be the writing of fiction.

In this regard, it seems, Pynchon's position may not be terribly far from that of Donna Haraway, who argues in "A Cyborg Manifesto" that while, in the past, progressivist analytical resources were used to argue for the need to overcome technology with a return to the organic, in the cybernetic age, a merger of the two may be more in order. The cyborg produced in this merger is, like Pynchon's Badass, not simply a creature of the literary, but a factor in literary production: "The silicon chip is a surface for writing" (153), Haraway reminds us. In fact, not only is the cyborg available for writing *on*, it is the agent that makes writing possible; where the human and the computer come together, writing results: "writing is pre-eminently the technology of cyborgs, etched surfaces of the late twentieth century" (176). The cyborganized subject, in its relationship to writing, is thus that subject most able to participate in the "transcendent doings" Pynchon seeks in fiction. The crucial distinction between Pynchon's position and Haraway's arises from both what is being transcended, and what the manner of the transcendence will be. For Pynchon, the merger of the human and the machinic realms enables an escape from domination by machines, both the technological and capitalist, an escape made possible by the human manipulation of technology's own out-of-control tendency to bite the hand that feeds it. For Haraway, by contrast, this merger allows for a breakdown in the structures of domination associated with humanism, the oppressive hierarchies of race, gender, nationality, and sexuality. Haraway's cyborg, unlike Pynchon's redeemer-destroyer Badass, functions not through the physical danger it poses but the epistemological categories it shatters.[12]

The crisis that the cyborg has produced in humanism has led, for both the novelist and the critic of obsolescence, to a second locus of machine anxiety, one substantively different from technology: "theory." This mode of critical discourse has, as we saw in the last chapter, been widely held responsible for the purported demise of literature, in no small part because theory is interpreted as promoting machine, rather than human, aesthetics. Catherine Liu, in *Copying Machines: Taking Notes for the Automaton*, interrogates the discourse of mechanicity as it has been used to contain and manage poststructuralist theory: "The Cartesian prejudice against the machine is difficult to overcome, but most recently, this particular myth of the Enlightenment (based on the idea that the human being and the machine were to be differentiated in a radical way) has been redeployed by critics of literary theory who defend literature in the name of its singularly nonmechanical qualities" (2). Paul de Man and other deconstructionists have thus been demonized for their radical formalism, for arguing that the structure of a text functions "like a machine." Even such a machinic simile is dangerous, the critics of theory argue, as the language of the technical steers literature that much farther away from the values of humanism.[13] Beyond the problem of metaphor, however, anxiety about theory often stems from its penchant for models and systems, structures that apparently mechanize the reading process itself. For critics such as Gerald Graff, theory has become a machine for reading with (and, not incidentally, writing with): "Ever since the New Critical discovery that almost any work of literature could be read as a complex of paradoxes and ironies, critical 'methodology,' whatever other purposes it has served, has been an instrument for generating new 'readings'—and thus new publications" (97). Moreover, many critics understand the instrumentality of this critical apparatus to be directly connected to the technological age itself. Cecelia Tichi, for instance, in *Shifting Gears*, argues that early twentieth-century authors' appropriation and emulation of mechanical structures evidenced a deep instability in the relationship between machine and organic orders of being. "In imaginative literature and criticism," Tichi writes, such destabilized modernist "presumptions have conceptually dislocated the word and the text in a crisis continuing from the late Victorians to the deconstructionists" (xv). Poststructuralist theorists, then, in their progressive subversions of textual stability, operate in a feedback loop with a technology-obsessed culture, creating a deepening sense of crisis for the contemporary author.

Literary representations of the machine in the novel of obsolescence thus frequently comment on the practice of reading itself. While for Mark Seltzer, the shift explored in the naturalist novel from the logic of the market to the logic of the machine finds its "most explicit and most radical rewriting" in scenes that "[make] visible the technology of writing itself" (8), that "scene of writing" has dramatically changed in contemporary fiction. While writers abound as the subjects of such fiction, the writing they do is most often fractured, incomplete, unread. The scene of writing has been displaced in the postmodern novel to the margins of the text; foregrounded instead is a scene of reading that explicitly highlights the technological mediation of most such textual encounters in contemporary culture. The machines of representation—machines for producing, distributing, and viewing film, television, and other technologized texts—are in many ways depicted as being responsible for writing's marginalization, having mechanized the reading process, both through the literal encounter with the machine required for reading and through the theoretical systematizing of interpretation, as well as having mechanized the reading subject, in encouraging the reader's own identification with a technologized epistemology. In encountering the machine-mediated text, all readers are imagined to become Ferguslike: comatose, wired in, reduced to a mode of control for the machine.

The machine thus becomes a figure of novelistic anxiety in an era in which the core values of humanism—and particularly the Cartesian cogito, which indicates linguistic representation itself as the basis of the human—come into question. Machines—theoretical, representational, and technological—interfere, for the novelist of obsolescence, with the processes of communication so vital to human existence. Such anxieties produce a number of key questions in Pynchon's fiction, as the reader confronts in a figure such as Fergus the interface between humans and machines. As the boundary between human and machine narrows, these representations ask, will humans begin to lose the thing in which "humanity" consists, becoming somehow dehumanized? If, however, as the many examples from popular culture lead us to suspect, this putatively universal "humanity" is in fact bound up with masculinity—if it is not the human principle but the masculine principle that the machine threatens—we must question how the machine is imagined to interfere in the processes of human sexuality, and how that sexuality is imagined to be constitutive of the human. And finally, once that sexuality has been machinically altered, what kinds of alienated humans do we encounter—and what kinds of monstrous machines?

Desiring Machines

Early in Pynchon's *V.*, during a brief flashback to the previous summer, while Benny Profane is working as the assistant salad man at a resort in the Catskills, he meets Rachel Owlglass—"meets" quite literally, as their introduction results from her nearly running over him with her MG. At the time, Benny is only able to make sense of their encounter by comparing Rachel with his boss, Da Conho, who appears to be in love with a machine gun: "Love for an object, this was new to him. When he found out not long after this that the same thing was with Rachel and her MG, he had his first intelligence that something had been going on under the rose, maybe for longer and with more people than he would care to think about" (23). Benny thus begins in a flailing way to understand that something in contemporary culture has produced a deep shift in the functioning of human desire, resulting in its redirection onto objects of a distinctly inanimate, and indeed mechanical, nature. In this we see that one of the key sites of anxiety about the relationship between humans and machines—in particular, the future disposition of the human body—is desire.

In fact, for many contemporary thinkers, Benny's perception of this sub-rosa shift may not be far off. "Everywhere *it* is machines," Deleuze and Guattari famously claim at the opening of *Anti-Oedipus*; "real ones, not figurative ones: machines driving other machines, machines being driven by other machines, with all the necessary couplings and connections" (1).[14] It is certainly machines with Fergus: a chemistry-machine plugged into a sleep-machine, a sleep-machine plugged into a television-machine. And it is machines with Benny, though as seen in the murderous MG, machines far less benign in their function. Such machines are, like all Deleuzian machines, double-edged in their implications: they redirect, break into, and stem flows, but they also produce and conduct flows, particularly of desire. There are machines that free and machines that capture, but everywhere in contemporary culture we find interconnections, links, couplings, assemblages.

For Deleuze and Guattari, replacing the Freudo-Marxist "subject" with the notion of machines provides the possibility of escape from the oppressive cycles of deterritorialization and reterritorialization inherent both in capitalism and in its critiques, as well as an alternative to "molar" or totalizing thought, allowing for an unleashing of desire as a revolutionary force. In this shift from the humanist notion of subjectivity to the posthumanist machine, desire is freed from the Oedipal yoke, transformed from the Platonic expression of lack into a positive, productive flow. The machine in Deleuze and Guattari takes on many forms—desiring machines, organic machines, technical machines, social machines, abstract machines, and so on—but each use of the notion of the machine is intended to indicate that the barrier has fallen between the human and nature, between the human and the not-human, between the subject and the object, emphasizing instead their intimate and functional interconnection. Desire, that most ostensibly human quality, is in this view inseparable from these assemblages: "Desire and its object are one and the same thing: the machine, as a machine of a machine. Desire is a machine, and the object of desire is another machine connected to it" (*Anti-Oedipus* 26). Human desire is in this view dependent upon the existence of machines in the broad sense: "Desiring-machines are the nonhuman sex, the molecular machinic elements, their arrangements and syntheses, without which there would be neither a human sex specifically determined in the large aggregates, nor a human sexuality capable of investing these aggregates" (294). Human desire is thus always already a machine, requiring interconnection with other such machines in order to function; without machines, there can be no desire.

This posthumanist perspective on the nature of the machine is by no means comforting, however, for a largely still-humanist culture. The relationship between the machine and desire, in a culture still determined to define the human in opposition to the machinic, is far more antagonistic, far more dangerous, than for Deleuze and Guattari, who spend relatively little time considering the ruptures and failures of interconnection. Even where such coupling succeeds, however, the machine in its humanist renderings produces, as with Fergus, not unleashed desire but the eradication of desire in a creeping inanimateness. That television is the particular source of Fergus's inanimateness reflects the deep social anxieties that the new communications medium produced in the U.S. home. By 1955, the year of *V.*'s present, television had found its way into two-thirds of U.S. homes, and anxieties about its role in those homes had begun spreading (see Spigel 1–2). As Lynn Spigel indicates, the popular magazines of the late 1950s reveal multiple anxieties about television's effect on the family, including the fear that the medium would contaminate the female members of the household through its representations of the public world and contaminate the male members of the household by subjugating them within the domestic sphere: "Television was depicted as the new patriarch, a threatening machine that had robbed men of their dominion in the home" (60). Moreover, Spigel demonstrates, these magazines played upon their readers' fears that the machine was inappropriately interfering with matters conjugal, "show[ing] people how television's libidinal imagery, and in particular its invocation of male desire, would disrupt the sexual relationship between man and wife" (119).[15] The threat of television thus rests in part in its ability to "invoke" male desire, disrupting the Oedipal channeling of that desire within the safe confines of the family. In this sense, television couples directly with the Deleuzian desiring machine of the unconscious, freeing desire from its societal regulation.[16] In its popular representations, however, television's danger is more often imagined less as a revolutionary unleashing of desire than as a redirection of that desire onto unacceptable objects.

Desire in fact functions in the popular imaginary as one of those characteristics—like language, reason, and "soul"—that separates humans from machines. Thus in Pynchon's *V.* Benny Profane imagines it, after the better part of a case of beer: "Inanimate objects could do what they wanted. Not what they wanted. Not what they wanted because things do not want; only men. But things do what they do, and this is why Benny was pissing at the sun" (26). Things do not want, and thus remain things. On the other hand, if inanimate objects "do what they do," and if this serves as the justification for Benny's urinary attempt to put out the sun, one begins to suspect the ultimate frustration of human desire. Only "men" want, only humans feel desire, and yet, unlike things, they apparently cannot do what they want. Human desire is thus cathected onto the machine as a substitute for a lost human agency, an agency that has been forfeited, it increasingly appears in *V.,* to the machine itself. In the mechanical age, as Marshall McLuhan famously suggested, "man becomes, as it were, the sex organs of the machine world" (46), agent not of his own destiny, but of the devices to which he is so intimately bound.

Though both Pynchon and McLuhan here ostensibly intend "man" in its prefeminist "universal" sense, this unselfconscious norming of the masculine position with regard to the machine may in fact reveal precisely the kind of conservative attempt to regroup behind the humanist boundary I suggested earlier, here manifested as an attempt to reclaim masculine agency. Each case, while attempting to account for women under the umbrella of the male universal, instead unconsciously suggests that women may bear a different relationship therein. For Donna Haraway, this relationship between woman and machine may be developed into an affinity of political interests aimed at transgressing and dismantling the boundaries thrown up by Western, masculinist, capitalist culture. Similarly, in Deleuze and Guattari, for whom "becoming-woman" is a politically and personally radicalized position, the desiring interface with the machine may evade the constraints placed upon the self by a fully territorialized, Oedipalized society, constraints that include gender itself.[17] In Pynchon, however, as we shall see most clearly in the character of V., the implication is by no means such a progressive one; women, it is to be understood, are in substantive part responsible for the culture's increasing mechanization. Whether, finally, Pynchon and McLuhan intend here to single out the masculine position as a means of separating out the feminine, or whether the invocation of "man" is an unthinking generalization, the point remains the same: the loss of agency thus feared in a machinic world is a masculine agency.

The relay created between this loss of agency and the rise of a mechanized desire raises two interlocked issues throughout Pynchon's fiction, though perhaps most explicitly in *V.* and *Gravity's Rainbow*: first, whether the dissociation from the powers of human agency implied when the body becomes or is treated as a machine will interfere with that body's production and flow of desire, both sexual and otherwise; and second, whether mechanical desire is itself an objectifying force capable of transforming other human bodies into machines. To return to Benny Profane, for starters: as our observer of the Whole Sick Crew's decadent meanderings toward inanimateness, Benny stands outside the object lust revealed in Da Conho's relationship with his machine gun and Rachel's love for her MG. Rachel attempts to explain this desire to him as strictly akin to masturbation: "a young girl has to take her virginity out on something, a pet parakeet, a car—though most of the time on herself." But Benny doesn't buy it: "There's more. Don't try to get out of it that way" (*V.* 384). He finds himself bewildered by this attempt to escape the animate, in part because of the hostility he believes objects hold toward him as a "schlemihl," something "he'd known about for years. Inanimate objects and he could not live in peace" (37). But far from creating for Benny a privileged position outside the Crew's decadence, his schlemihlhood is an inverted image of machinic desire; by imagining things being persistently "out to get" him, Benny attributes to those hostile objects surrounding him far greater agency than he does to himself. Thus, while his desire may still take a human object, his relationship to machines is in fact more troubled than either Da Conho's or Rachel's.

Moreover, as he reveals in his getting-laid theory of history, the flow of Benny's own desires suffers from a different kind of encounter with the mechanical. He imagines his theory to be a further outgrowth of the traditional Marxist notion that "history unfolds according to economic forces," the new development in Benny's idea being that "the only reason anybody wants to get rich is so he can get laid steadily, with whomever he chooses [. . .] anybody who worked for inanimate money so he could buy more inanimate objects was out of his head. Inanimate money was to get animate warmth, dead fingernails in the living shoulderblades, quick cries against the pillow, tangled hair, lidded eyes, twisting loins . . ." (*V.* 214). Benny's drive toward the animate rather than the inanimate is clear, and yet this "animate warmth" is deceptive. Without realizing it, both through his equation of desire and economics and through his segmentation of the desired body, he has recast the object of his desire as an object, a living fetish.[18] The lover, once purchased with one's inanimate paycheck, takes on the mechanical form of the commodity, no longer human but an amalgamation of parts, beginning, as in Benny's litany, with "dead fingernails," the inanimate outgrowth of life.[19] Though unable to articulate precisely what the problem is—and thus unaware that his desire has become just as mechanized as that of those around him—Benny is at least dimly cognizant of the result of this objectification, the absence of real human interaction in sexual encounters. It is for this reason that he resists getting sexually involved with Rachel, finding himself

> unwilling to see her proved as inanimate as the rest.
>
> Why that last? Only a general desire to find somebody for once on the right or real side of the TV screen? What made her hold any promise of being any more human? (359)

Benny's desire for Rachel may in fact be a desire for the machine, in a loose sense, if television's mechanicity has drawn her too far into its orbit. The medium thus, as argued by the popular magazines of the age, corrupts human desire by channeling it toward inappropriate objects, and by objectifying the more appropriate human subjects.

In Pynchon's *Gravity's Rainbow*, we encounter a more extreme version of this mechanical corruption of human sexuality and desire. Tyrone Slothrop finds himself at the center of what appears to be a vast technological conspiracy in which humans exist only to reproduce and guide machines, in which the most basic responses and behaviors associated with the human are in fact mechanically contrived, ending finally in a complete disposition of "man" by machine. Slothrop has himself been engineered in a most literal sense, the subject of some only partly explained scientific experiment. This experiment echoes Kurt Mondaugen's comment to Lieutenant Weissman in *V.*: "Politics is a kind of engineering, isn't it. With people as your raw material" (242). Slothrop in fact serves as the raw material of a project that appears political in nature, one bound up with World War II and Germany's quest for dominance over Europe. But, as we discover late in the novel, the question remains whether technology, not politics, has actually been running the show, including the war, including Slothrop's engineering. The war, we are told by one narrative voice, "was never political at all, the politics was all just theatre, all just to keep the people distracted . . . secretly, it was being dictated by the needs of technology . . . by a conspiracy between human beings and techniques" (521). This conspiracy, if in fact it exists, has served as the driving force for a series of self-justifying experiments conducted with an utter disregard for their human ends. The development of the V-2 is only the most prominent of those projects; we are similarly told, with regard to Slothrop's engineering, that "back around 1920, Dr. Laszlo Jamf opined that if Watson and Rayner could successfully condition their 'Infant Albert' into a reflex horror of everything furry, even of his own Mother in a boa, then Jamf could certainly do the same thing for his Infant Tyrone and the baby's sexual response" (84). To what end, of course, we are never told. We are, rather, left with Jamf performing this conditioning because he "could," serving the technology of human engineering.

Of course, technology has a response to this accusation: "All very well to talk about having a monster by the tail, but do you think we'd've had the Rocket if someone, some specific somebody with a name and a penis hadn't *wanted* to chuck a ton of Amatol 300 miles and blow up a block of civilians? Go ahead, capitalize the T on technology, deify it if it'll make you feel less responsible—but it puts you in with the neutered, brother" (*GR* 521). Remembering that the war has been described as a conspiracy between humans and technology, the voice of technology here has a point; each party must assume some responsibility, and human responsibility in this case rests squarely in desire. Any less an admission than full human partnership in this enterprise reproduces what Neil Postman refers to as the "agentic shift," whereby human responsibility is foisted off onto more abstract, less human agents.[20] "When this happens," Postman warns, "we have relinquished control, which in the case of the computer means that we may, without excessive remorse, pursue ill-advised or even inhuman goals because the computer can accomplish them or be imagined to accomplish them" (*Technopoly* 114). Thus, as with Jamf's experimentation on the Infant Tyrone, carried out because he "could," the displacement of desire into mere ability contributes to the loss of agency experienced throughout the culture.

Given this vacuum of human agency, the reader of *Gravity's Rainbow* should recognize the precise nature of the danger in technology's relegation of its addressee to the realm of the "neutered." The sexual function, the sexual response, and the force of desire provide the loci of the novel's clearest representations of human engineering. Just as Pointsman manipulates Brigadier

Pudding's psychosexual aberrations into a profound despair to keep him out of the way of Pointsman's other experiments (see 231–36), Weissman's cruelty has conditioned Gottfried's sexual responses to bind Gottfried more closely to him and to the rocket, as Gottfried himself is all too aware: "the word *bitch*, spoken now in a certain tone of voice, will give him an erection he cannot will down" (103). As Gottfried's stimulus itself indicates, of course, this "neutering" may more accurately be described as feminizing; the masculine sexual function is throughout the novel diverted from its "proper" expression of dominance and self-control into passivity and masochism. In each case, the conditioning of the self, the technologizing of the human, produces not only a destruction of individual agency but also specifically a perversion of masculine desire into a feminized lack. It is of course no accident that Katje Borgesius is implicated in both men's "neutering," the tool of Their machinations. Just as Weissman wields Katje's role as Gretel to push Gottfried's Hansel into the oven, the rocket, and just as Pointsman uses Katje as Domina Nocturna to neutralize Pudding, so Katje is finally used as one of the last instruments in Slothrop's own conditioning, which begins with Jamf and the Infant Tyrone and works inexorably toward the ultimate rocket, the 00000.

The connection between Slothrop and the rocket has lingered in the novel's background all along, from the first stirrings of Slothrop's erection at "6:43:16 British Double Summer Time" (*GR* 26), the moment of the falling of the first V-2 on London, to the revelation of the significance of Slothrop's sexual map of London and Roger Mexico's V-2 Poisson distribution:

> It's the map that spooks them all, the map Slothrop's been keeping on his girls. The stars fall in a Poisson distribution, just like the rocket strikes on Roger Mexico's map of the Robot Blitz.
> But, well, it's a bit more than the distribution. The two patterns also happen to be identical. They match up square for square. (85)[21]

But it is not until the beginning of book three that Slothrop comes to a dawning awareness of his machinic state. He has obtained documents that detail a business transaction between Jamf and Lyle Bland, a former board member of the Slothrop Paper Company. As Slothrop reads, he notices:

> He is also getting a hardon, for no immediate reason. And there's that *smell* again, a smell from before his conscious memory begins, a soft and chemical smell, threatening, haunting, not a smell to be found out in the world—*it is the breath of the Forbidden Wing* . . . essence of all the still figures waiting for him inside, daring him to enter and find a secret he cannot survive.

> Once something was done to him, in a room, while he lay helpless . . .
> His erection hums from a certain distance, like an instrument installed, wired by Them into his body. . . . (285)

The image of the wiring of his penis is all too appropriate: Slothrop was sold as a baby to IG Farben; the haunting smell, he begins to suspect, is Imipolex G, described as "nothing more—or less—sinister than a new plastic, an aromatic heterocyclic polymer, developed in 1939, years before its time, by one L. Jamf for IG Farben" (*GR* 249). The purposes behind this particular plastic, somehow connected to the V-2, remain unknown for some time, but the material does conform to "plasticity's central canon: that chemists were no longer to be at the mercy of Nature" (249). Certainly Laszlo Jamf was not; nor, for that matter, is Tyrone Slothrop, who appears instead to be at the mercy of Imipolex G.

What is curious about Imipolex G, however, particularly given this relationship with Slothrop, is that it is "the first plastic that is actually *erectile*. Under suitable stimuli, the chains grow cross-links which stiffen the molecule and increase intermolecular attraction" (*GR* 699). In fact, given the "conditioned" nature of these chemical erections, the plastic itself appears to be a polymerized, if not to say cyborganized, Slothrop—Slothrop recreated as plastic. This suggestion has the potential to stand the relationship between Slothrop and Imipolex G on its head, inverting cause and effect much as deconditioning "beyond the zero" would. Was Slothrop conditioned into infantile erections not as a reaction to the presence of Imipolex G, but rather so that Jamf might study the erectile phenomenon and thereby create the plastic in question? The relation of conditioning and plastic is never fully clarified; in any case, having been engineered by Laszlo Jamf into evidencing an erection in the presence of this "conditioned stimulus," and then having been "deconditioned," whether accidentally or intentionally, to a point "beyond the zero" (85) at which the stimulus-response pattern happens in reverse—having been so deeply engineered, Slothrop's penis seems his "own" in only the most attenuated sense.[22]

In both *V.*'s Benny Profane and *Gravity's Rainbow*'s Tyrone Slothrop, then, the reader encounters a represented falling off of human agency in the face of contemporary technologies, a dehumanization that results directly in a misdirection or deterioration of the "natural" functioning of sexuality and desire—most particularly masculine sexuality and desire. This relationship is complicated, however, by a further outgrowth of the relationship between humans and machines: the individual longing to efface all traces of human agency, to achieve a more machinelike state. This desire for a dehumanized, inanimate equilibrium, seen most pointedly in Fergus's transformation into a remote control, is repeatedly represented in both Pynchon and DeLillo as a consequence of the too-close relationship between "man" and machine, leading not simply to the objectification of man by machine, or of the human individual in his encounters with dehumanized others, but instead to a kind of self-objectification in which the subject comes to understand itself and desire a deeper existence as a machine.

Mechanical Alienation

In Pynchon's *V.*, the title character is of course the primary reference point for exploring this longed-for transformation of self into object. She is moreover, the narrator tells us, the ultimate signifier of female sexuality: "As spread thighs are to the libertine, flights of migratory birds to the ornithologist, the working part of his tool bit to the production machinist, so was the letter V to young Stencil" (62). V., in taking on the very shape of the parted thighs, becomes the ultimate coupling/uncoupling machine. For "young Stencil," that is; before turning to V. herself, it is important to note the textual means by which the reader is led to her discovery. Our first introduction to the character arises from Sidney Stencil's journal entry, the same entry that spurs his son Herbert on his mad pursuit of V. across history: "There is of course more behind and inside V. than any of us had suspected. Not who, but what: what is she" (53). As punctuated in the text, this sentence (like many other such sentences throughout) is not a question, but a statement, betraying both flatness of affect and the presence of conviction: V. is a what, a thing, that seems to produce a deep "thingification" in the culture around her. Stencil *fils* for instance, in his pursuit of the "what" behind and inside V., practices a form of self-denial designed to let himself slip in and out of personas and temporalities: the "forcible dislocation of personality" (62), which includes perpetually speaking about himself in the third person. Stencil thus intentionally joins V., on some level, in the realm of whatness.

Stencil's excursions into the past—his self-insertion into the past as narrative—should be considered in connection to Fredric Jameson's conception of Pynchon's project in the novel, in which

> a semblance of historical verisimilitude is vibrated into multiple alternate patterns, as though the form or genre of historiography was retained (at least in its archaic versions) but now for some reason, far from projecting the constraints of the formulaic, seems to offer postmodern writers the most remark-

able and untrammeled movement of invention. In this peculiar form and content—real sewer systems with imaginary crocodiles in them—the wildest Pynchonesque fantasies are somehow felt to be thought experiments of all the epistemological power and falsifiable authority of Einstein's fables, and in any case to convey the feel of the real past better than any of the "facts" themselves. (368)

This "fantastic historiography" is as much Herbert Stencil's project as it is Pynchon's; his dislocation into alternate historical personae is imagined within the context of the novel to be just this kind of "thought experiment," producing a more accurate rendering of V. than any of the "facts" would permit. History itself thus becomes an object to be manipulated, a technology of reading. Stencil's portrait of V. is built, he admits, of "a nacreous mass of inference, poetic license, forcible dislocation of personality into a past he didn't remember and had no right in, save the right of imaginative anxiety or historical care" (62), thus aligning the imaginative and the historical in one technology of reading. Through this simultaneously personalized and mechanized history, Stencil conducts a peculiarly postmodern investigation, looking backward for that "telltale instant" when it all changed.[23] This same historical project is at the heart of *Gravity's Rainbow*, whose "present" may be thought of more accurately as "the future-shocked American landscape of the 1960s and 1970s" (Slade 72) than as the immediate postwar period that appears to occupy most of the novel. This representation of events surrounding World War II can be more deeply understood precisely as a representation, a speculative, causal reading of history much like Stencil's forays into the past, a reading that attempts to find the origins of the Nixon era in the development and firing of the V-2. Given the foregrounding of history as technology, however, we should begin to find this drive toward causality suspicious. *Gravity's Rainbow* is ultimately, like *V.*, less about the events of the past than about the technologies in the present through which we read those events, and the tendency of all systems of historical "facts" toward conspiracy when read by postmodern sensibilities. These are Jameson's "shifts and irrevocable changes in the *representation* of things and the way they change" (ix, emphasis mine); it is less true, in this sense, that from the firing of the 00000 comes Richard Nixon than it is that from Richard Nixon comes the firing of the 00000.

And similarly, via Stencil's "forcible dislocation" of self, the novel begins to suggest that V. is the driving force at the heart of twentieth-century decadence; if she is not strictly responsible, she is nonetheless a prime mover in what Stencil *père* refers to as "The Situation." This hopelessly confused and explosive set of persons and intelligences and events that structure the hidden center of twentieth-century political life—the Fashoda crisis, the Vhiessu affair, the June Disturbances on Malta—is, it seems, wrapped up in progressive self-mechanization. The first glimmers of this human drive toward the functionality of the machine appear during the Fashoda crisis, as Victoria Wren (the first presumed incarnation of V.) is caught up with several members of the intelligence community, including Porpentine and Bongo-Shaftsbury, with whom Victoria's sister Mildred later sits on a train. As Stencil, in the projected persona of Waldetar the conductor, watches from outside the compartment, Bongo-Shaftsbury torments Mildred, asking her if she'd like to see an "electro-mechanical doll." When she at last relents, Bongo-Shaftsbury rolls up his sleeve, revealing that "shiny and black, sewn into the flesh, was a miniature electric switch. Single-pole, double-throw. . . . Thin silver wires ran from its terminals up the arm, disappearing under the sleeve" (*V.* 80). At least some of the operators in the "human engineering" of politics, it is thus suggested, may have so firmly committed to their view of the human other as a manipulable mechanical object that they have begun a similar transformation of the self.

This commitment, while literalized in Bongo-Shaftsbury's arm switch, is equally operative in the appalled Porpentine, if on an emotional level. Mildred flees in horror into the next compartment, as Porpentine demands that Bongo-Shaftsbury stop—not out of concern for Mildred, but because "one doesn't frighten a child." Bongo-Shaftsbury responds:

> "Hurrah. General principles again." Corpse fingers jabbed in the air. "But someday, Porpentine, I, or another, will catch you off guard. Loving, hating, even showing some absent-minded sympathy. I'll watch you. The moment you forget yourself enough to admit another's humanity, see him as a person and not a symbol—then perhaps—"
>
> "What is humanity."
>
> "You ask the obvious, ha, ha. Humanity is something to destroy." (*V.* 81)

In the end, this hinted plan comes to fruition: Porpentine, distracted from his machinelike "general principles" by his unrequited love for Victoria, is killed by Bongo-Shaftsbury. But in this passage, the players in The Situation reveal the purpose of twentieth-century political intrigue: Politics is not here a game played on behalf of human society, or even a social manipulation undertaken with some vague concept of "humanity" in mind. It is rather a project of engineering, one steering, as Mondaugen suggests, toward a fully mechanized society, in the service of which humanity must be destroyed.[24]

This trope of the destructive, mechanizing force of politics returns in Herbert's reading of the back story of Schoenmaker, the plastic surgeon. As a youth during World War I, Schoenmaker worked as a grease monkey on airplanes that flew missions out of France. In the midst of this story, the reader is suddenly informed that "since those days as we know democracy has made its inroads and those crude flying machines have evolved into 'weapons systems' of a then undreamed-of complexity" (*V.* 97). The intimate correlation of the spread of democracy and the development of technologies of destruction suggests a relay system between the two: democracy as technologized politics; weapons systems as democratic machines; each aimed at parallel forms of human destruction.[25] Given these ties, Mondaugen's comment to Weissman becomes all the more potent; the two are of course destined to meet once again, in *Gravity's Rainbow*, over the development of the V-2. Politics as human engineering thus gives way to weapons engineering with ease, and both are revealed to have the same goal in mind: a mechanized, if not yet properly cybernetic, social control.

But Schoenmaker's story also reveals—as does Bongo-Shaftsbury's arm switch—the levels on which this transformation of human into machine is not simply metaphorical or ideological but very physical. Schoenmaker, working on the airplanes and watching the heroic figures of the pilots, develops a crush on the dashing young flyer Evan Godolphin (son of Hugh Godolphin, one of the players in The Situation). This crush reveals another negative-feedback loop at work between technology and male sexuality; Schoenmaker's work as a mechanic redirects his desire onto "improper," nonheterosexual objects, a redirection that has the effect of intensifying his involvement in the mechanical. This intensification begins when Godolphin's plane, crippled in a dogfight, misses the runway and crash-lands. Godolphin miraculously survives, though he limps away from the wreckage as "the worst possible travesty of a human face lolling atop an animate corpse" (*V.* 98–99). A young plastic surgeon named Halidom attempts reconstructive surgery on Godolphin, using a controversial procedure known as "allografts: the introduction of inert substances into the living face" (99). This melding of the human and the inanimate, put into practice during the exigencies of the war, has two practical effects. The first is the destruction of the human element of this cyborg body: Godolphin's face is ravaged by a "foreign-body reaction" that causes his immune system to attack the "inert substances" implanted in his flesh. The second, of course, is the rise of modern cosmetic surgery. Schoenmaker ("beauty maker"), in his outrage, determines to become a plastic surgeon, dedicated to "prevent[ing] a takeover of the profession by its unnatural and traitorous Halidoms." In this fashion, the narratorial voice informs, Schoenmaker imagined he would promote the natural, the human: "If alignment with the inanimate is the mark of a Bad Guy," the reader is told, "Schoenmaker at least made a sympathetic beginning" (101).

This beginning does not last, however, as the technologies of plastic surgery, the subordination of the human form to a kind of fleshly engineering, lead Schoenmaker further and further down the road toward the inanimate. He is ultimately inspired not to fight such implantations as Godolphin suffered but to find ways of ensuring their acceptance by the body, of subduing the body's responses to such technological infiltrations. By the time of the novel's present, and Esther's nose job, he has suffered a clear "deterioration of purpose; a decay" (*V.* 101) that unmistakably connects him to the Whole Sick Crew's decadent alienation. His desire for Esther becomes a desire to continue operating on her, which he attempts to rationalize as creating, rather than destroying, her humanity:

> Did she want him so shallow he should only love her body? It was her soul he loved. What was the matter with her, didn't every girl want a man to love the soul, the true them? Sure, they did. Well, what is the soul. It is the idea of the body, the abstraction behind the reality: what Esther really was, shown to the senses with certain imperfections there in the bone and tissue. Schoenmaker could bring out the true, perfect Esther which dwelled inside the imperfect one. Her soul would be there on the outside, radiant, unutterably beautiful. (296–97)

But clearly, as even Esther recognizes through Schoenmaker's sophistry, the "plastic" in plastic surgery signifies not merely malleability, but also artificiality; he wants to create of her, like Bongo-Shaftsbury, like V., a living doll.

It is interesting to note, given her resistance to him in this instance, Esther's quasi-ecstatic response to her initial surgery. "It was almost a mystical experience," she recalls. "What religion is it—one of the Eastern ones—where the highest condition we can attain is that of an object—a rock. It was like that; I felt myself drifting down, this delicious loss of Estherhood, becoming more and more a blob, with no worries, traumas, nothing: only Being. . . ." (*V.* 106). But Being and such a rocklike state do not wholly correlate; as Heidegger argues, individual coming to Being (*Dasein*) requires self-awareness, and particularly an awareness of death. This acceptance of Being's vulnerability, which Heidegger calls *Sorge*, or "care," is at the root of human freedom. And techniques—or technics—are "radically dishonest" when used to escape "care."[26] If, as Don DeLillo suggests in *White Noise*, "it's a mistake to lose one's sense of death, even one's fear of death," it is precisely because death represents "the boundary we need," giving life "a sense of definition" (228).

Death is the boundary that defines being exactly because it separates life from its true opposite: not death, but inanimateness. Death gives life its separateness from technology; thus the danger in attempting to escape death, or even an awareness of death, through technics lies in the power of those technics to mechanize being, to transform the living into the inanimate.

This, then, is the significance of Esther's nose-job dissociation in *V.*: not a discovery of a higher level of being but an escape from being, a self-objectification. The desire Esther reveals runs rampant through the Whole Sick Crew; even Benny, whose schlemihldom should cause him to resist the object world, succumbs to its pressures. Were he an object, he fantasizes, he would not be responsible for acting or reacting, for he would be subject to outside control. Thus the many games he plays with himself, including his aleatory choice of employment agency: his erection having created a "crosswise fold" in the newspaper on his lap, and that fold running through a list of employment agencies, Benny decides that "just for the heck of it I will close my eyes, count three, and open them and whatever agency listing that fold is on I will go to them. It will be like flipping a coin: inanimate schmuck, inanimate paper, pure chance" (*V.* 215). Inanimate schmuck with involuntary erection—desire thus becomes no more than a tool of the random, a means of escaping responsibility for one's choices. And thus, upon rediscovering Rachel in the agency his erection selected, his longing to give up all control:

> Any sovereign or broken yo-yo must feel like this after a short time of lying inert, rolling, falling: suddenly to have its own umbilical string reconnected, and know the other end is in hands it cannot escape. Hands it doesn't want to escape. Know that the simple clockwork of itself has no more need for symptoms of inutility, lonesomeness, directionlessness, because now it has a path marked out for it over which it has no control. That's what the feeling would be, if there were such things as animate yo-yos. Pending any such warp in the world Profane felt like the closest thing to one and above her eyes began to doubt his own animateness. (217)

Benny's desire for complete passivity within the comfort of external control is metaphorized as a longing to be a mechanical object twice over: first, of course, the yo-yo, which Benny has imitated throughout the novel; but second, and more importantly, the "simple clockwork" of self, the ego captured within the automaton, the human freed from all desire.

This fantasized "simple clockwork" of self—as well as the clockmaker-run universe it suggests—in which desire, death, and language can all be evaded through technology reaches its crux in V. and her intimate, libidinal couplings with objects. The first of these objects is an ivory comb, "whose shape was that of five crucified, all sharing at least one common arm. None of them was a religious figure: they were soldiers of the British Army." This secularized and politicized religious imagery has its origins in Victoria Wren's desire for a world ordered according to semi-religious principles. In "her private, outré brand of Roman Catholicism," we are told, Victoria has "crystallized into a nun-like temperament pushed to its most dangerous extreme." Her variant on this nun-like temperament is of a decidedly different physical character; feeling herself "married" to Christ, she believes that "the marriage's physical consummation must be achieved through imperfect, mortal versions of himself—of which there had been, to date, four. And he would continue to perform his husband's duties through as many more such agents as he deemed fit" (*V.* 167). In this apparent abdication of responsibility for her desires, in her willingness—in fact, her longing—to submit to the greater desire of a force outside her control, Victoria, like Benny, enters into a kind of collusion with the object world, readily giving up agency over her own desires to submissive abandon.

In the episode entitled "V. in love," the relationship between V. and the young dancer Mélanie l'Heuremaudit ("cursed hour") is similarly both sensualized and dehumanized, both passionate and objectifying.[27] V. defines the relationship for Mélanie: "Do you know what a fetish is? Something of a woman which gives pleasure but is not a woman. A shoe, a locket . . . une jarretière. You are the same, not real but an object of pleasure" (*V.* 404). Mélanie is apparently for V. no more than such an unreal object; in fact, the narrator insists, lesbianism, "we are prone to think in this Freudian period of history" (407), arises precisely from a narcissistic longing to experience the self as an object and a projection of that longing onto another, similar object. Mélanie, for instance, in her many mirrors, becomes the object of her own aggressive gaze, wishing to "fragment herself into an audience" (410) but unable to achieve such self-objectification on her own. V. is able to provide the audience: "she recognized—perhaps aware of her own progression toward inanimateness—the fetish of Mélanie and the fetish of herself to be one" (410). This longing for the decadent pleasures of the object world finally leads to Mélanie's death, however, during the sadistic ballet in which she dances, "The Rape of the Chinese Virgins." Having grown accustomed to thinking of herself as an automaton, like the mechanical dolls that also appear in the ballet, Mélanie fails to wear the chastity belt designed to protect her and so is viciously impaled: "Adorned with so many combs, bracelets, sequins, she might have become confused in this fetish-world and neglected to add to herself the one inanimate object that would have saved her" (414). Unable to distinguish between herself as object and the objects by which she is surrounded, and, the suggestion goes, unwilling to protect the chastity her culture suggests she ought to value, Mélanie dies. Finally, with this destruction of her human fetish, V. turns wholly to an objectification of herself, transforming herself into the clockwork automaton Mélanie impersonated.

V.'s replacement of her human parts with artificial ones continues until, like *Gravity's Rainbow*'s Tchitcherine, V. is "more metal than anything else" (*GR* 337). When Sidney Stencil meets V. (as Veronica Manganese) on Malta during the June Disturbances of 1919—the crux moment for which Stencil *fils* appears to be searching—she expresses her desire for further self-objectification:

> "See my lovely shoes," as half an hour before he'd knelt to remove them. "I would so like to have an entire foot that way, a foot of amber and gold, with the veins, perhaps, in intaglio instead of bas-relief. How tiresome to have the same feet: one can only change one's shoes. But if a girl could have, oh, a lovely rainbow or wardrobe of different-hued, different-sized and -shaped feet." (*V.* 488)

By the time of her final appearance, chronologically speaking, V. has achieved just such an accessorized self. The last persona she assumes in the novel is that of the Bad Priest, in which she has cast away even the confining roles of sex and gender and returned to her own "outré" theology. As the Bad Priest, the reader is told through Fausto's memoir, V.

> taught no consistent philosophy that anyone could piece together from the fragments borne back to us by the children. The girls he advised to become nuns, avoid the sensual extremes—pleasure of intercourse, pain of childbirth. The boys he told to find strength in—and be like—the rock of their island. He returned . . . often to the rock: preaching that the object of male existence was to be like a crystal: beautiful and soulless. (340)

The object of existence for V., then, in both her gendered and genderless manifestations, is to achieve the same sort of objecthood Esther finds in her nose job: to be deadened to all sensation, to be a rock. But as we have seen, such an escape from the "care" that goes hand-in-hand with Being is inextricably tied to a fundamental dishonesty, a soullessness, which makes itself evident in the "bad"ness of her priestdom.

It is important to remember at this juncture, however, the technologies of reading through which V. is constructed in the novel. Not simply a product of the mechanical parts with which she couples, she is a product of Herbert Stencil's mechanized reading process. As Stencil dislocates himself into alternate historical personalities, he gathers the textual pieces of which V. is composed. V., in fact, exists outside of Stencil's consciousness in only one section of the novel, the epilogue on Malta. Aside from this passage, V. is wholly constructed by Herbert himself. The significance of this work of historical construction becomes most clear at precisely the moment at which we at last see the inert, technological substances with which Sidney Stencil had noted V.'s "obsession with bodily incorporating" laid out before us: the "disassembly of the Bad Priest" (*V.* 488, 343). First, of course, there are her inanimate component parts: an ivory comb, a long white wig, a tattoo of the Crucifixion on her bare scalp; prosthetic feet with attached golden slippers; a star sapphire sewn into her navel; a set of false teeth; a glass eye. The key to this scene, and in fact to Stencil's production of V., lies less in the parts than in this "disassembly" itself, which replaces any conception of V. as a coherent individual with a fragmented jumble. Phillip Brian Harper has explored the implications of the distinction between "dismemberment" and, in his term, "dismantling," and its implication for the fragmentation of the subject in the postmodern novel, pointing out that

> [if] "dismemberment" connotes the destruction, through fragmentation, of an organically integrated physical whole, "dismantling" suggests the division of an *assembled* entity into its constituent parts. The very form of "dismantling" suggests its origin as a designation for the removal of a person's outer garment, or mantle. Insofar as a garment and its wearer's body are not organically united, "dismantling" suggests the demonstration of essential discontinuities rather than the disintegration of essentially integrated wholes. (48)

However, while "dismantling" connotes the removal of an outer garment from an essentially human body, "disassembly" suggests the taking apart of a machine into components that not only are not organically united, but also are not human in the first place. V., as the product of Herbert Stencil's mechanical reading process, has never been allowed human integrity, human unity, but has always been a technological assemblage. V., the signifier of parted thighs, the ultimate coupling-uncoupling machine, the lesbian fetish best able to "stack" with its like, is prevented throughout the novel from achieving genuine subjectivity, instead remaining trapped within the realm of objects. Furthermore, in Stencil's construction, several of V.'s "parts," though not living elements of her body, are sutured in. Her connections of self to machine take place at so fundamental a level that, separated from her inorganic parts and literally crushed by a collapsing church, the two mechanical means by which her life has been kept running, V. dies.

The most central, most focal (if you can pardon the pun) of those technological components that finally comprise the assemblage V. is the glass eye. In the Südwest, in 1922, Kurt Mondaugen meets Vera Meroving, the sadomasochistic partner of Lieutenant Weissman. As he approaches, he notices that her left eye is artificial. This replacement of V.'s own eye with the manmade, particularly after Mélanie's death by fetishizing, calls to mind the biblical dictum, "If thine eye offend thee, pluck it out" (Mark 9:47). However, V., as always carrying religion forward into her own realm of the earthly, has replaced her eye not simply with an artificial, inanimate eye, but with a mechanical one. In this mechanical eye, V. echoes Andreas Huyssen's thoughts on the fundamental problem of the dominance of vision in contemporary culture: "Vision as pleasure and desire has to be subdued and manipulated so that vision as technical and social control can emerge triumphant" (76). V. has in fact replaced her own gaze with the mechanism of that technical control, the regularity of clockwork:

> A bubble blown translucent, its "white" would show up when in the socket as a half-lit sea green. A fine network of nearly microscopic fractures covered its surface. Inside were the delicately-wrought wheels, springs, ratchets of a watch, wound by a gold key which Fräulein Meroving wore on a slender chain around her neck. Darker green and flecks of gold had been fused into twelve vaguely zodiacal shapes, placed annular on the surface of the bubble to represent the iris and also the face of the watch. (*V.* 237)

This replacement of the "natural" processes and materials of vision—a vision already transformed in V.'s relationship with Mélanie into a cruel, objectifying gaze—with those of clockwork produces a complex relation among visuality, the mechanical, the passage of time, and the structure of the universe, all of which homes in on V. as its center; in this construction, Vera is literally "a Hand to Turn the Time" (*GR* 760), the driving force behind the clockwork universe. Stencil's quest has sought all along to place V. at the heart of The Situation, to lay at her feet all responsibility for the decadence of midcentury culture, and this determination to connect herself with clockwork is a strong indictment indeed of V. and her effect on the century, given the novel's insistence that "alignment with the inanimate is the mark of a Bad Guy" (*V.* 101). We can see this indictment even more clearly when read in connection with Norbert Wiener's *The Human Use of Human Beings*: "When human atoms are knit into an organization in which they are used, not in their full right as responsible human beings, but as cogs and levers and rods, it matters little that their raw material is flesh and blood. *What is used as an element in a machine, is in fact an element in the machine*" (185). V.'s transformation of her body into a clockwork assemblage, and her mechanical relationships with those around her, reduces all of what remains of the human to mere elements in a machine. Or, more accurately, Stencil's construction of V.'s body as a clockwork assemblage reveals his mechanized desire to localize the responsibility for the twentieth century's mechanical alienation.

That Stencil traces V.'s history across the twentieth century—that V. is in fact a product of the technology of history itself—suggests a key difference between the representations of the contemporary mechanical alienation of the human in Pynchon and DeLillo. Where Pynchon historicizes this development, drawing parallels among many disparate technologies—including television, plastic surgery, clockwork automata, and the rocket—DeLillo, as I explore more fully in the next chapter, focuses on the present machinic ecology and its tendency toward technologies of simulation. Thus, while television, for Pynchon, represents a new and particularly effective mode of technological engagement, the specific engagement with the medium is merely a symptom of the movement of the human toward mechanicity begun long before. For DeLillo, by contrast, television itself, as part of an expansion of the mediation of experience in contemporary culture, is responsible for this movement into mechanicity. Thus, in DeLillo's *Running Dog*, Lightborne holds film's mechanicity responsible for the shifts in contemporary libido that render traditional erotica dull: "Movement, action, frames per second. This is the era we're in, for better or worse," he argues. "Sure, a thing isn't fully erotic unless it has the capacity to move" (15). Similarly, David Bell's literal movement toward the machine in DeLillo's *Americana*:

> I looked at the TV screen for a moment and then found myself in a chair about a foot away from the set, watching intently. I could not tell what was happening on the screen and it didn't seem to matter. Sitting that close, all I could perceive was that meshed effect, those stormy motes, but it drew me in and held me as if I were an integral part of the act, my molecules mating with those millions of dots. (43)

A mere glance at the machine seems to induce a catatonic state, a complete loss of consciousness of the self, as David "finds" himself before the television seeking a kind of metaphysical union with the machine, a "mating" destined to produce a new hybrid culture, inhuman and yet alive. Fergus's coupling with the machine, by contrast, produces nothing but stasis, product itself of the culture's pre-existing drive toward self-destruction.

The mating of self to the television set must draw us, finally, back to

Pynchon's *Gravity's Rainbow*. Recalling for a moment the peculiarly "erectile" nature of Imipolex G "under suitable stimuli," we might question precisely what those "suitable stimuli" are. The stimulus, we are told, "would have had to be electronic," though why remains unclear (699). However, the three possibilities outlined for this sort of electronic stimulus are themselves interesting. The first, "a thin matrix of wires" that sends "commands" to the surface evokes printed circuits, transistors, and computer chips (699–700). The third, even more interesting, is described as "the projection, *onto* the Surface, of an electronic 'image,' analogous to a motion picture," suggesting film's power to produce an erectile response. The second possibility, however, is the most peculiar of all:

> a beam-scanning system—or several—analogous to the well-known video electron stream, modulated with grids and deflection plates as needed on the Surface (or even below the outer layer of Imipolex, down at the interface with What lies just beneath: with What has been inserted or What has actually *grown itself a skin of Imipolex G . . .*). (700)

A beam-scanning system: television. What lies just beneath, in his skin of Imipolex G: Gottfried. In addition to the erectile system of Imipolex G, however, we find Gottfried at blastoff encased within the rocket with a small green window through which he can watch, and "in one of his ears, a tiny speaker [that] has been surgically implanted" (*GR* 751). Gottfried has, as the culmination of Weissman's rocket plan, thus completed Fergus Mixolydian's project in advance of Fergus himself; he has become wired into a television set. This intimate coupling of human and machine does something more than simply mechanize (and destroy) Gottfried; it creates a living television set, an animate machine that approaches life faster than the speed of sound.

Synthetic Human Object

What Fergus Mixolydian achieves, then, in his connection of self to television set—and that the wider culture considers this assemblage an achievement can be inferred from his receipt, later in the novel, of a grant from the Ford Foundation—is the creation of a synthetic human object (see *V.* 355). The television, as the mechanical heart of this object, obtains via its connection to Fergus some facsimile of consciousness, waking and sleeping. Similarly, the televisual rocket, with Gottfried wired in, lives and breathes, sees and hears, up to the moment of its impact. Like the lamprey-robot, these two assemblages take on, in their interconnections of living tissue and mechanical components, the characteristics of artificial life. This is the other side of the writer's anxieties about the machine; as the chapter epigraph from Donna Haraway's "A Cyborg Manifesto" suggests, the problem for the humanist who confronts the cyborg is not simply that we have become "frighteningly inert" in the interface, but that machines themselves are now "disturbingly lively" (152). Thus the nervous ambiguities of Fergus's sleep switch: Is he operating the television set, or is the television set operating him?

The animate robot is largely the stuff of science fiction and techno-prophecy. Nonfiction writers such as Ray Kurzweil and Hans Moravec predict a future populated by conscious machines; novelists such as William Gibson, Bruce Sterling, and Rudy Rucker narrate similar futures.[28] In Pynchon and DeLillo, we find mere inklings of this future, including early examples such as Vaucanson's mechanical duck, which appears in Pynchon's *Mason & Dixon*, and more recent instances like the first stirrings of net-consciousness at the end of DeLillo's *Underworld*. The significance of these almost living machines should not be underestimated, however; as one thinker in Pynchon's *V.* suggests, during a period of decadence, as people become "less human, we foist off the humanity we have lost on inanimate objects and abstract theories" (405). Once our objects and theories become more animate than we are, these novels seem to suggest, human beings will be at their mercy.

Such is the suggestion of the Whole Sick Crew's Slab, Catatonic Expressionist painter of innumerable cheese Danishes. In revolt against his own work, Slab creates in one of his paintings "the universal symbol I have decided will replace the Cross in western civilization," the partridge in the pear tree. "The beauty," claims Slab, "is that it works like a machine yet is animate. The partridge eats pears off the tree and his droppings in turn nourish the tree which grows higher and higher, every day lifting the Partridge up and at the same time assuring him of a continuous supply of good." This partridge-pear-shit-tree assemblage makes use of animate parts, but in the best Wienerian sense, deanimates them by transforming them into parts of a perpetual-motion machine. The bird, content to be caught in this arrangement and provided with an unending supply of pears, is in fact being carried to its doom by the growing tree; at the top of the painting, Slab points out, is "a gargoyle with sharp fangs," the largest fang of which "lay on an imaginary line projected parallel to the axis of the tree and drawn through the head of the bird" (*V.* 282). The ontology Slab envisions as a replacement for Christianity is thus self-destroying; life, become part of the machine, is destroyed by the machine.

In the case of *Mason & Dixon*, however, the bird in question—Vaucanson's duck—is not a living element of a machinic assemblage but a machine in its own right. Historically, Vaucanson's automaton-bird was designed as a shit-producing machine; the duck would take food offered to it and, swallowing, pass the food through a digestive system that culminated in excretion. Vaucanson expressly envisioned the duck as taking part in a contemporaneous debate about the nature of human digestion carried on between surgeons and anatomists who imagined digestion as a process of grinding and those who saw it as a more properly chemical process.[29] Such automatons, as Catherine Liu suggests in *Copying Machines*, thus serve not merely as mechanical curiosities but as representations of the presumed characteristics of the human. "The refusal to compare men and machine has recourse to absolute difference," Liu argues, "while the bringing together of man and machine takes place as a rhetorical gesture of comparison. Man can be *like* a machine and a machine can be *like* a man. In this kind of comparison, a relationship of analogical rather than absolute difference is established between what man (or human) is from what he is not" (79). Despite Vaucanson's sleight of hand—the material excreted by his duck was not, in fact, the remains of the food it "ate," but rather preprepared "droppings"—the duck-automaton thus draws inevitable comparisons to the human not only in its processes of digestion but in its entire ontology as well; the human is, in this rendering, *like* a machine to make shit with.

The "mechanickal Duck" represented in *Mason & Dixon*, however, is not this shit machine but a second, fictional duck imagined to replicate a different human bodily function:

> Vaucanson's vainglorious Intent had been to repeat for Sex and Reproduction, the Miracles he'd already achiev'd for Digestion and Excretion. Who knows? that final superaddition of erotick Machinery may somehow have nudg'd the Duck across some Threshold of self-Intricacy, setting off this Explosion of Change, from Inertia toward *Independence, and Power*. Isn't it like an old Tale? Has an Automatick Duck, like the Sleeping Beauty, been brought to life by the kiss of . . . *l'Amour*? (373)

Desire, in this second duck, allows the automaton to transcend its mechanical state, achieving independence, power—and, indeed, life. The duck's quest for the "erotick," which takes as its object France's foremost chef (who specializes, of course, in duck) thus reinscribes desire as central to humanness. The introduction of desire into the machine, in fact, effects such a profound metamorphosis that, following the chef first to the New World and then along Mason and Dixon's surveying expedition, the duck is finally able to control her motions such that she makes the leap from the "mechanickal" to the "Metaphysickal," transcending human existence altogether.

If the mechanical duck represents a conception of the human as shit-producing machine, and the metaphysical duck, a conception of the human as transcendent desiring machine, what then of *V.*'s humanoid automata? These two machines, SHROUD (synthetic human, radiation output determined) and SHOCK (synthetic human object, casualty kinematics), represent a specifically post-Hiroshima model of the human:

> In the eighteenth century it was often convenient to regard man as a clock-work automaton. In the nineteenth century, with Newtonian physics pretty well assimilated and a lot of work in thermodynamics going on, man was looked on more as a heat-engine, about 40 per cent efficient. Now in the twentieth century, with nuclear and subatomic physics a going thing, man had become something which absorbs X-rays, gamma rays, and neutrons. (*V.* 284)

In SHROUD and SHOCK, then, Pynchon devises a representation of the human as a machine for bombardment, an agencyless, purposeless object subjected to random bouts of radiation and car crashes. These synthetic human objects thus render visible the nature of V.'s and Benny's desires to achieve a "simple clockwork" of self; the two, along with many of the novel's other characters, long to return to an earlier, less chaotic model of the universe, with neither the uncertainties of Einsteinian physics nor the potential for heat death implied in Newtonian physics. Instead, the mechanical model of a clock is one that, even if agencyless, can be kept running eternally—provided there is a "Hand to Turn the Time."

Benny, who encounters SHROUD and SHOCK in the course of his night-watchman's job at Anthroresearch Associates (a subsidiary of Yoyodyne), bears in his own passivity an innate recognition of the position the two automata occupy, feeling "a certain kinship with SHOCK, which was the first inanimate schlemihl he'd ever encountered. But in there too was a certain wariness be-cause the manikin was still only a 'human object'; plus, a feeling of disdain as if SHOCK had decided to sell out to the humans; so that now what had been its inanimate own were taking revenge" (*V.* 285). But for SHOCK to have earned the animosity of its formerly "inanimate own," to have become the enemy of technology, the manikin must somehow have begun a metamorphosis similar to that of the "mechanickal Duck." On the one hand, it remains a "human object"; on the other, an "inanimate schlemihl." Neither description sounds terribly far from what the reader knows of Benny, and thus the question surfaces: what, exactly, is the difference?

While the humanist tradition, grounded in Cartesian dualism, rigorously maintains that difference, pointing alternately to language, reason, desire, or some other ostensibly unique aspect of human existence, Norbert Wiener, in *The Human Use of Human Beings*, dismisses the distinction altogether: "the problem as to whether the machine is alive or not is, for our purposes, semantic and we are at liberty to answer it one way or the other as best suits our convenience" (32). The difference between human and machine, and thus the significance of the label "human," has become negligible within the realm of cybernetics, a notion that provides little reassurance to anxious humanists, who find ominous cybernetics' equal application of its principles of control to both men and machines. The nature of contemporary cybernetic machines, however, makes categorization difficult. Even the television set, as Pynchon demonstrates in *Vineland*, has achieved such a level of animation that its inanimate, mechanical state no longer goes without saying. The machine is in fact an intimate player in family life, such that Debbi, Hector's ex-wife, names their set,

> a 19-inch French Provincial floor model, as corespondent [in their divorce], arguing that the Tube was a member of the household, enjoying its own space, fed out of the house budget with all the electricity it needed, addressed and indeed chatted with at length by other family members, certainly as able to steal affection as any cheap floozy Hector might have met on the job. (*Vineland* 348)

In a fit of jealousy, Debbi demolishes the television set with a frozen pot roast, which ends the liability of the television in their divorce.[30] However, Hector brings action of his own, having Debbi arrested under charges of "Tubal homicide." Both actions are immediately dismissed, but their presence before the court raises, as Hector notes, "deep philosophical issues. Is the Tube human? Semi-human? Well, uh, how human's that, so forth. Are TV sets brought alive by broadcast signals, like the clay bodies of men and women animated by the spirit of God's love?" (348). Hector's confusion reveals the real danger of the animate machine, whether television set, "mechanickal Duck," or synthetic human object—not that the machine in question actually might achieve life, but that human beings might think it has. The danger presented by the televisual machine is finally not ontological but epistemological, the confusing on a philosophical level of the categories of human and machine, categories upon whose distinction the novel has rested since the eighteenth century.

Benny, in considering these "deep philosophical issues," makes precisely this category mistake, one that Wiener might consider "semantic" but that for Pynchon strikes at the foundation of what it is to be human. Benny finds himself, on his rounds as night watchman, talking to SHROUD:

> "What's it like," he said.
> Better than you have it.
> "Wha."
> Wha yourself. Me and SHOCK are what you and everybody will be someday. . . .
> "What do you mean, we'll be like you and SHOCK someday? You mean dead?"
> Am I dead? If I am then that's what I mean.
> "If you aren't then what are you?"
> Nearly what you are. None of you have very far to go. (*V.* 286)

In trying to interpret SHROUD's enigmatic comparison, Benny attributes life to the machine, or at least the possibility of life, which death implies. The text of course suggests that SHROUD is hinting at technological inanimateness, that human life and machine being will merge in a kind of automaton. SHROUD's reversal of the comparison, however—first, you're almost what I am; second, I'm almost what you are—in fact suggests a mutual movement that finally undermines the coherence of the categories altogether.

And if a dividing line remains, it's become by novel's end a preciously fine one. Here, for instance, is the description of SHOCK, the humanlike machine:

> its flesh was molded of foam vinyl, its skin vinyl plastisol, its hair a wig, its eyes cosmetic-plastic, its teeth (for which, in fact, Eigenvalue had acted as subcontractor) the same kind of dentures worn today by 19 per cent of the American population, most of them respectable. Inside were a blood reservoir in the thorax, a blood pump in the midsection and a nickel-cadmium battery power supply in the abdomen. The control panel, at the side of the chest, had toggles and rheostat controls for venous and arterial bleeding, pulse rate, and even respiration rate, when a sucking chest wound was involved. In the latter case plastic lungs provided the necessary suction and bubbling. They were controlled by an air pump in the abdomen, with the motor's cooling vent located in the crotch. An injury of the sexual organs could still be simulated by an attachable moulage, but then this blocked the cooling vent. SHOCK could not therefore have a sucking chest wound and mutilated sexual organs simultaneously. A new retrofit, however, eliminated this difficulty, which was felt to be a basic design deficiency. (*V.* 285–86)

Compare this with Herbert Stencil's present-day projection of V., the machine-like human:

> skin radiant with the bloom of some new plastic; both eyes glass but now containing photoelectric cells, connected by silver electrodes to optic nerves of purest copper wire and leading to a brain exquisitely wrought as a diode matrix could ever be. Solenoid relays would be her ganglia, servo-actuators move her flawless nylon limbs, hydraulic fluid be sent by a platinum heart-pump through butyrate veins and arteries. Perhaps—Stencil on occasion could have as vile a mind as any of the Crew—even a complex system of pressure transducers located in a marvelous vagina of polyethylene; the variable arms of their Wheatstone bridges all leading to a single silver cable which fed pleasure-voltages direct to the correct register of the digital machine in her skull. And whenever she smiled or grinned in ecstasy there would gleam her crowning feature: Eigenvalue's precious dentures. (*V.* 411–12)

The differences are few: SHOCK is primarily mechanical while V. is electronic; V. is controlled by a "digital machine" in her head rather than SHOCK's control panel. The primary distinction, however, seems to boil down to wiring; otherwise, machines and humans, thanks to plastics, hydraulics, and the dentures of the inestimable Eigenvalue, seem to be moving toward the same, altogether alarming state of synthetic human object.

But one cannot help commenting on the abject misogyny contained in Herbert's imaginings of V. at seventy-six. While these imaginings are clearly those of a character, not necessarily of the author, they nonetheless demand consideration; as Stencil's historical project parallels Pynchon's, so his mediating consciousness reflects upon the author's own. Andreas Huyssen, writing about Fritz Lang's *Metropolis*, could just as well have been writing about *V.* when he claims that the machine vamp appeals to

> the male fantasy of the machine-woman who, in the film, embodies two age old patriarchal images of women which, again, are hooked up with two homologous views of technology. In the machine-woman, technology and woman appear as creations and/or cult objects of the male imagination. The myth of the dualistic nature of woman as either asexual virgin-mother or prostitute-vamp is projected onto technology which appears as either neutral and obedient or as inherently threatening and out-of-control. (73)

V. has all along been both virgin and vamp; by the novel's end, she has, in Stencil's rendering, become the ideal combination of computer, Barbie doll, and inflatable sex toy. She has been created, via Stencil's forcible dislocations, as the ideal nonhuman sexual object whose entire being is centered around pleasure, but who requires the insertion of that ever-missing phallus for the circuit to be complete. This is of course the future wished for by Benny Profane, who is chronically perplexed by the difficulties of dealing with real women: "Someday, please God, there would be an all-electronic woman. Maybe her name would be Violet." Benny's hope for a woman with no resistance—or at least none that can't be "measured in ohms" (*V.* 385)—is carried out in Stencil's imagination. And, of course, Stencil's imagination is carried out within Pynchon's imaginative prose.

And thus the reader is drawn back to the writerly consciousness that creates the terms in which the machine is represented, and the interests that are served by the continued "border war" between human and machine. Coupled with the femaleness of the "mechanickal Duck" and the ostensible femaleness of Hector and Debbi's television set (compared, as it is, to a "cheap floozy"), *V.*'s graphic sexuality indicates that the machine-human conflict serves as a kind of foil for anxieties about the dangers of the feminine. In the interface with the machine, it seems, is not merely a loss of some neutral "humanity" but a masculine loss of potency. Like Fergus wired to the television set, masculinity drains away into a passive stupor; in the television itself, the feminine principle gains sway. Thus Fergus, in his promotion of the television set to a form of synthetic human object, highlights the manner in which writerly anxieties about the passivity that the medium induces are heightened by the potential this abdication of human responsibility leaves for a new kind of machinic consciousness, a consciousness not under the sway of humanism's hierarchies.

This danger, in the view of the novelist of obsolescence, becomes all the greater when we remember the importance Descartes ascribes to language as the locus of the human. If, having renounced "humanity," humans foist it off on machines, and particularly televisual machines, these novels argue, then human beings leave themselves open to manipulation and control by those machines. And when those machines communicate not with words but with images, thus evading the linguistic center of the human, the possibilities presented by the humanist novel for resistance to the machine diminish all the more.

3
Spectacle

> Seeing comes before words.
>
> —John Berger

Let us begin with a brief return to the scene from DeLillo's *Americana* referenced in the last chapter, David Bell sitting before his television set:

> I looked at the TV screen for a moment and then found myself in a chair about a foot away from the set, watching intently. I could not tell what was happening on the screen and it didn't seem to matter. Sitting that close, all I could perceive was that meshed effect, those stormy motes, but it drew me in and held me as if I were an integral part of the act, my molecules mating with those millions of dots. (43)

David's television, which has drawn him in, and holds him fast, acts in a manner quite different from Pynchon's television, into which the couch potatoes of the past are physically wired. Here, the television's "meshed effect" produces a new kind of intertwining of human and television set, one that functions "as if" human perception were required to complete the broadcast. In this meshing, the "stormy motes" of the set's image pattern seem transformed into reproductive cells, "mating" with David and creating a new potential form of life. The interconnection David perceives is fundamentally imaginary, however, in both the common sense of unreality and in the Lacanian sense of a preverbal realm of the visual, because those reproductive cells themselves do not have a physical existence; they are merely the effect of the scatter pattern of an electron-scanning beam striking a phosphor-coated screen. These motes are pure evanescence, because they exist only as light, and only for a fraction of a second. They are, in other words, the purest form of image, pure visuality, communicating with the unconscious, fleeting and gone.

David's confusion of these image parts, these flashes of light, with a kind of materiality is not unique in DeLillo's fiction. One might remember Lyle's "discipline" of television watching in *Players*:

Sitting in near darkness about eighteen inches from the screen, he turned the channel selector every half minute or so, sometimes much more frequently. He wasn't looking for something that might sustain his interest. Hardly that. He simply enjoyed jerking the dial into fresh image-burns. He explored content to a point. The tactile-visual delight of switching channels took precedence, however, transforming ever random moments of content into pleasing territorial abstractions. (16)

The "image-burns," like David's stormy motes, communicate something beyond content that remains an abstraction and yet penetrates beyond consciousness. That this undiluted visuality is connected to a kind of tactility, however, suggests that these image-burns take on a sort of physical existence, at least in Lyle's conception of them.

Such a bleed between the visual and the tactile, between the ephemerality of the image and the solidity of the physical can be further seen in the transformation of Babette into a screen image in DeLillo's *White Noise*, and her family's response to that transformation. Having accidentally stumbled across a broadcast of her posture class on a local public-access cable station, the family races through a series of silent, terrified questions: "What did it mean? What was she doing there, in black and white, framed in formal borders? Was she dead, missing, disembodied? Was this her spirit, her secret self, some two-dimensional facsimile released by the power of technology, set free to glide through the wavebands, through energy levels, pausing to say good-bye to us from the fluorescent screen?" (104). This apparent disappearance is rapidly transmuted into a kind of reappearance, however, as the disembodied state of Babette's image mutates into a new form of embodiment:

With the sound down low we couldn't hear what she was saying. But no one bothered to adjust the volume. It was the picture that mattered, the face in black and white, animated but also flat, distanced, sealed off, timeless. It was but wasn't her. Once again I began to think Murray might be on to something. Waves and radiation. Something leaked through the mesh. She was shining a light on us, she was coming into being, endlessly being formed and reformed as the muscles in her face worked at smiling and speaking, as the electronic dots swarmed.

We were being shot through with Babette. Her image was projected on our bodies, swam in us and through us. Babette of electrons and photons, of whatever forces produced that gray light we took to be her face. (104–5)

In this "coming into being," Babette as image becomes more real than the physical Babette, producing a deeper communion with the members of her fragmented household, meshing with each of them. This image that is but isn't Babette, like the stormy motes on David Bell's television screen, creates an imaginary bond between viewer and viewed that in every case is associated with a decadent withdrawal from the real, and most particularly from the meaningful encounter with that real produced by symbolic forms of representation.[1] As Thomas Ferraro argues: "the rhetoric of light's physicality suggests that the screen's ultimate strategy is to destroy the distinction between flesh and image, re-presenting the image-in-all-its-fleshiness as the thing-in-itself. If the vehicle that generates perception is to replace the object perceived, then television can be said to seduce us with a major reconstruction of the nature of reality itself" (26). In this fashion, the "gray light" that her family takes to be Babette's face inspires not merely recognition—that image is an image of my wife, of our mother—but also mistaken identification: that image *is* my wife, *is* our mother.[2]

This obsession with pure nonsignifying visuality, this longing to mesh with the light from the electron-scanning beam, is only an extreme form of what Ferraro saliently calls the "image narcosis" (28) of contemporary U.S. culture repeatedly depicted in the novel of obsolescence. In this metaphor of image as narcotic are laden the supposed dangers the image presents: hallucination, incapacitation, addiction. Not all renderings of the role of the visual in the discourse of obsolescence are this extreme; however, that contemporary U.S. culture is image oriented has become nothing short of truistic in recent critical and popular cultural analyses. For instance, in an attempt to account for a surprising rise in museum going during the mid-1990s, the *New York Times* cites as a contributing factor the overwhelming visuality of the contemporary U.S. cultural scene. Again, the mere claim that the late twentieth-century United States is image driven says very little that is new; the surprise in the *Times's* assessment in this case lies in its sense that our connection to the visual could be responsible not just for MTV, but for something as socially uplifting as an appreciation of fine art. In making this claim, however, the *Times* recounts an abbreviated history of the image's rise to power:

> Image began to reign supreme over the written and spoken word once television started to dominate the national consciousness, beginning in the 1950's, a trend reinforced by the explosion of influence of movies and video. Americans, particularly young ones, learn their news on the tube and their history in the movie theater, and what interest they have in the high arts is best satisfied by the visual richness of museums. (Dobrzynski 1)

There is, first, something peculiar about the *Times*'s chronology, in which the image's reign "began" with television and was "reinforced" by film. "Television" has in this narrative become dislocated from history. Final cause has become first cause; television is here not the image's teleological endpoint but rather, by some logical shift, its origin. Television has, for the *Times*, as for numerous other participants in the cultural discourses of obsolescence, become less itself than a metonym for what has gone wrong.

But beyond this brief historical lapse, the *Times*'s replication of the conventional wisdom about the passionate relationship between U.S. culture and the image is revealing for what it says about the *Times* itself. It is no accident that the image is here described as "reign[ing] supreme over the written and spoken word"; the print form itself is endangered by all this visuality.[3] If Americans are indeed "learn[ing] their news on the tube," the newspaper reporting this fact is obsolete. Despite countervailing evidence that people persist in reading the *Times* even in the age of television, the newspaper apparently continues to operate with one eye checking nervously over its shoulder for the competitors that threaten to overwhelm it. Little wonder, then, that even that "old gray lady," the *Times*, had, by the date of this article, succumbed to the pressures of the image and begun printing in color.[4]

This lightly paranoid conviction, that one mode of communication is being forced out of existence by a newer, more technologically advanced medium, bears much in common with the novelist's anxiety of obsolescence. The discourse of obsolescence, as we have seen, flourishes across U.S. culture, surfacing in the journalistic realm as well as the novelistic, the popular as well as the academic. Participants in this discourse repeatedly depict older forms—here, the newspaper—as in danger of eradication by encroaching new technologies, a threat made possible by the birth of a postmodern, surface-oriented, sped-up subjectivity. The representation of this threat in the very forms presumably endangered—the newspaper's death announced in the newspaper itself—creates a protected space for these older forms, within which critics of contemporary U.S. culture can take refuge. The technological threats these critics uncover repeatedly differentiate, as I suggested in the first chapter, into three interconnected and yet distinct conceptual categories. Where older forms are assumed to be "human," new media are seen as mechanical; where older forms are individualist, new media are designed for an interconnected mass. And, as the *Times* here argues, where older forms are based upon the word, new media are founded upon the image. These new forms of mediation—machine, network, spectacle—are represented not simply as differences, however, but as active threats: a mechanical vision of the universe can only distort one's sense of the human; an affiliation with the mass undermines one's assumption of the individual's prerogative. In much the same way, concerns about the spectacle stress the ability of the image to weaken our cultural relationship with the word. These concerns assume a conflict inherent between visual epistemologies and typographic or linguistic ways of knowing; writing itself, these writers claim, is under siege.

This apparently threatening visuality, however, presents the novelist with another set of strategies for contending with the electronic media. In writing about the visual threat to writing, the novelist of obsolescence is able to create a cultural preserve, a protected distance from the contemporary that grants to writing important powers of political resistance. By delineating the epistemologies of text and image, and by repeatedly pointing to the dangers that the image ostensibly presents to a literate culture, the novelist of obsolescence is able to reclaim the primacy of text. In so doing, however, the writer must both represent and misrepresent the processes of the visual. As in the *Times* article, in which television is thought to precede film, the historical origin and development of the electronic media are manipulable narratives, free to be shifted and construed as the context of obsolescence demands. Similarly, the structure and functioning of the media are subject to appropriation and rewriting—including the very question of these forms' reliance upon the spectacle. Neil Postman argues, for instance, in *Amusing Ourselves to Death*, that television is primarily a visual medium, conducting a "conversation in images" (7). Many media theorists would insist, however, that this is an erroneous assumption, and that television, as an outgrowth of radio, is primarily an aural medium, pointing out the tendency of viewers to wander away from the set, only to be drawn back by the sounds that announce important images. Thus, according to John Fiske, "the look of the viewer is one of glances rather than the controlled gaze of the cinema spectator" (*Television* 57). The point here is not that Postman is wrong or that television is not reliant upon the image, but that the workings of the electronic media are not self-evident but subject to interpretation—and that these interpretations, as contained within the novel of obsolescence, reveal more about writerly perspective than they do about the media themselves.

Ekphrastic Fear

Near the beginning of *White Noise*, Jack Gladney takes his new colleague, the "visiting lecturer on living icons" (10) Murray Jay Siskind, out into the country to see a local tourist attraction: the Most Photographed Barn in America.

The much-hyped spot—Jack reports that they "counted five signs before we reached the site"—is designed for and replete with the technologies of image production. There is a "slightly elevated spot set aside for viewing and photographing," and Jack further observes that "all the people had cameras; some had tripods, telephoto lenses, filter kits. A man in a booth sold postcards and slides—pictures of the barn taken from the elevated spot." Despite all this concern for the visual aspect of the experience, however, Murray quite trenchantly suggests that "no one sees the barn," that, in fact, seeing the barn in such an environment has become quite impossible (12). In part because of this interest in the self-consuming nature of visual representations in contemporary U.S. culture, this episode has become the Most Written-About Scene in *White Noise*.[5] There is no small irony in this accomplishment. Critical and theoretical interest in the image—what W. J. T. Mitchell refers to as the "pictorial turn" (13)—has resulted in great attention to such representations of the relationship between the spectacular and postmodernity. And yet, to my knowledge, at least, few scholars have addressed a vital facet of this scene: the savage critique of the academic interest in the image that this pictorial turn evidences. Critical work on the scene has to this point largely focused in the same direction as those dozens of cameras, suggesting that critics, no less than visitors to the site, may be guilty of "taking pictures of taking pictures" (*WN* 13), as Murray smugly asserts.

None of this is to imply that the previous critics are "wrong" in their interest in this scene; such a focus on the production and reproduction of the image in the text is a result of DeLillo's own apparent concerns with visuality and its technologies throughout his work. *Americana* and *Running Dog* rely heavily on film both for their language and for their content; *White Noise* and *Mao II* examine both photography and television; *Great Jones Street* and *Libra* explore the more amorphous production of the celebrity "image"; *Underworld* sets in motion the range of twentieth-century media spectacles. In this rich vein of representations, particularly coupled with DeLillo's own critical treatment of the spectacle in articles such as "The Power of History," there is much that warrants consideration. Much of this chapter likewise explores these representations of images and their technologies, but I include an additional level of analysis by considering not only the images themselves and the modes of engagement demonstrated by those doing the looking within the text but also the mode of engagement of the text itself with those images: the critical content of the images as represented, as well as their critical function. From this angle, the Most Photographed Barn in America resolves not simply into an example of a peculiarly postmodern obsession with the visual but also into a demonstration of the means by which the novel can rescue culture from that obsession—and, not incidentally, of the means by which the novel can likewise rescue academia from its apparently unhealthy interest in images.

As Murray Jay Siskind's heavily satirized manner of "watching" the Most Photographed Barn in America suggests, critical and theoretical perspectives that foreground images are at times equated in the novel of obsolescence with the objects of their study, as the novel of obsolescence levels the same accusation at both: the abandonment of word in favor of image, resulting in textuality's loss of primacy among forms of mediation. This equation is of course suspect, but it reveals a contradiction inherent in the anxiety of obsolescence, which both proclaims the novel's death and provides for its continuance; which is simultaneously aimed at critical analysis of the postmodern phenomena it encounters and at an uncritical restoration of the primacy of the novel; and which is as such simultaneously elitist and populist in its renderings of those phenomena. Such is likewise the strategy of cultural critics such as Neil Postman, who see in the contemporary fascination with images an erosion in traditional literacy. Postman has repeatedly described, across his career, the dangers of the current prominence of the electronic media, most popularly in *Amusing Ourselves to Death* and *Technopoly*. The first is pointedly subtitled "Public Discourse in the Age of Show Business," pitting the seriousness of text against the empty flash of Hollywood spectacle. The second is subtitled "The Surrender of Culture to Technology," as though technology were culture's antithesis. In both texts, Postman insists that the rise of the image has revealed the decline of print-based U.S. culture. In fact, he argues, the "new imagery" that began to surface during the late nineteenth century, "with photography at its forefront, did not merely function as a supplement to language, but bid to replace it as our dominant means for construing, understanding, and testing reality. . . . The new focus on the image undermined traditional definitions of information, of news, and, to a large extent, of reality itself" (*Amusing* 74). For Postman, such technologies of communication as print and television cannot peacefully coexist. Instead, "new technologies compete with old ones—for time, for attention, for money, for prestige, but mostly for dominance of their world-view"; such competition leads to the present situation, in which U.S. culture faces "television attacking the printed word" (*Technopoly* 16).

The metaphors Postman chooses to describe the relationship between text and image are repeatedly those of conflict, as he sees in the frontier between these two modes of communication an all-out battle for supremacy between competing epistemologies: "television's way of knowing is uncompromisingly hostile to typography's way of knowing" (*Amusing* 80). The image-based media are represented as not contented with merely existing alongside text; instead, the image must destroy the word. Thus Postman, in referring to Daniel Boorstin's "graphic revolution," decries "the assault on language made by forms of mechanically reproduced imagery that spread unchecked throughout American culture" (*Amusing* 74). The image's spread, whether metaphorized as invading army or as raging virus, not only threatens to place visual ways of knowing alongside those of typography, according to Postman; the spectacle in fact actively works to undo typographic epistemology and thus threatens the very heart of print-based U.S. culture. And, as we shall see, contemporary scholarly interest in film as a form of art, or in television as a legitimate cultural artifact, hastens that decline, as the academy treacherously turns its back on the print-based epistemologies under which the university was founded.

Not everyone writing about the image is similarly convinced of its dangerous potential; for instance, in *The Rise of the Image, the Fall of the Word*, Mitchell Stephens works to avoid taking what he calls a "declinist" stance, while nonetheless carefully examining how the proliferation of images in twentieth-century communications has affected contemporary uses of language. In a slightly different fashion, a 1990 publication by a group of British communications scholars, with the neutral-sounding title *The Telling Image: The Changing Balance between Pictures and Words in a Technological Age*, champions the rise of the image as a means of communication, extolling its virtues for all manner of educational purposes. In this work, Duncan Davies, Diana Brathurst, and Robin Brathurst point out that "the pleasures of using pictures can sometimes be greater than those of writing or using words" (3) and boldly admit that "we want to try to add to the number of enthusiastic new potential picture-mongers" (4). While the crude sound of "picture-mongering" might only strengthen a declinist's resolve, Stephens convincingly argues that, rather than reducing the level of public discourse to silliness, as Postman claims, images present the possibility for conveying much more information with far greater speed than can text.[6] And, as the British scholars indicate, communication through images has existed far longer than has the written word:

> there were 250 centuries when we had pictures alone and could not learn how to use them generally and effectively. Next there were 20 centuries when we learnt how to use formalized pictures (pictograms and ideograms) as message carriers. There followed some 15 centuries or so during which clerks made the great leap forward of alphabetic reading and writing. During the next 5

centuries, reading and writing thrust picture-communication into the background. However, over the past one-third of a century, the picture has suddenly and explosively become the main means for "reading" and learning, but not yet the main means for the ordinary person's "writing." Not surprisingly, we are reeling from the shock. (Davies et al. 2)

The effect of this abbreviated history is, first, to resituate visual media at the center of contemporary communicative structures, indicating that print's dominance has been a brief diversion from the development of more effective modes of pictorial communication. Second, the extremely recent explosion of image-based communication accounts, in this history, for the dislocation experienced by print-based critics such as Postman; the shock comes from speed, not from decline. Third, this narrative indicates the importance of studying images, such that participants in an image-based culture find ways to use them not merely for "reading"—taking what is handed down—but also for "writing," thus becoming full contributors in an ongoing cultural conversation.

The rapid rise of image-based communication has nonetheless been the subject of much critique, as the image is variously implicated in Guy Debord's "society of the spectacle" and Jean Baudrillard's "precession of simulacra" and is generally read as evidence either of U.S. culture's use of the commodity form to quell potential revolution or that culture's more basic disconnection from reality. Such widespread concern with the image in academic and theoretical writing has resulted in Mitchell's philosophic "pictorial turn," as suggested earlier, in which "pictures form a point of peculiar friction and discomfort across a broad range of intellectual inquiry" (13). Mitchell intends this pictorial turn to play off and distinguish itself from what has been called the "linguistic turn" of structuralism and poststructuralism; I suggest, by contrast, the coimplication of the linguistic and pictorial turns. Neil Postman's narratives of decline indicate that it is precisely the rise of the image that has undermined the transparency of the linguistic sign; by this reasoning, the proliferation of image culture itself produced the linguistic turn in continental philosophy. Moreover, the same set of social and cultural factors that led Jean Baudrillard to explore the ideological determination of the linguistic sign in the early 1970s produced his consideration of the simulatory powers of the image ten years later. Both word and image are equally contained within the political economy of sign exchange and thus equally demand theorization and critique.

This equation of word and image under the rubric of "sign" is perhaps unnerving for the traditional literary intellectual; if these two modes of communication are in any sense equivalent, one could too easily be replaced by the other. This may be the reason for Mitchell's pictorial turn, the proliferation of writing, both novelistic and philosophical, about the distinctions between word and image. These texts often seek to control the image, arguing, for instance:

> Visual images don't provide the same kind of truth as words. What they say is not necessarily inferior but it is different. Meaning is much more on the surface, experienced immediately rather than discovered by extended in-depth analyses of the image. The meaning of the visual image is also far less complex, lacking the multiplicity of meanings characteristic of single words and the ironic ambivalence set up between words. (Kernan 149)

Or:

> visual imagery is more insidious than language, because it seems more "real." Individual words can be decoupled from the reality they represent (there need be no chair for the word to signify it) and can be combined and recombined endlessly into abstractions. Images are more limited in terms of the distance between the object and the picture of it; images are direct representations of things and cannot be entirely decoupled or divorced from them. For this reason, it is not true that a picture is worth a thousand words. Images carry less *meaningful* information than words because they cannot be combined to the same levels of complexity. (Slade, "Communication" 73)

The image is by these arguments inherently less meaningful than language—but "truth" or "meaning," in the sense that these writers intend, can be created only by interpreting symbolic signs; "meaning" can be produced only syntactically. Thus, by the definitional restrictions placed upon it, "meaning" can exist only in linguistic form, in ordered structures of symbolic signs; as Postman insists, the image "lacks a syntax, which deprives it of a capacity to argue with the world" (*Amusing* 72). However, this statement is true only if "argument" is conceived of in rationalist terms; if one can argue in terms other than those bounded by logic, the image is in fact quite capable of argument, as the history of propagandist photography demonstrates. The real danger, then, is less the loss of the "capacity to argue with the world" than the demotion of the linear to *one* form, rather than *the* form, of argument.

This demotion has produced the threat to typographic culture sensed in the rise of the image; as Postman goes on to argue:

> The new focus on the image undermined traditional definitions of information, or news, and to a large extent, of reality itself. First in billboards, posters, and advertisements, and later in such "news" magazines as *Life*, *Look*, the

New York *Daily Mirror* and *Daily News*, the picture forced exposition into the background, and in some instances obliterated it altogether. By the end of the nineteenth century, advertisers and newspapermen had discovered that a picture was not only worth a thousand words, but, where sales were concerned, was better. For countless Americans, seeing, not reading, became the basis for believing. (*Amusing* 74)

This concern about the substitution of images for text obtains only if, as the critics above suggest, the image's lack of depth, of ambivalence, of abstraction, indicates that its meaning lies on its surface, waiting to be experienced rather than analyzed. This too-closeness of meaning implies an uncomfortable relationship with objects, with the image's referent. In this, these authors echo Roland Barthes, who describes the photograph as a "transparent envelope" for the particular (*Camera Lucida* 5). This transparency is deceptive, however, hiding the image's status as sign behind an apparently unmediated presentation of the referent. In fact, while images may seem to be "direct representations of things" whose meanings are "experienced immediately," they are neither so direct and immediate as they seem, nor are they representations of *particular* things. To treat the photographic image, for instance, as no more than a "transparent envelope" reduces it to an indexical sign—like footprints, mere evidence that something once was there. On the contrary, images require reading just as do words. The chair signified by a photograph is no more "real" than the chair represented by the word; the photograph is a collection of iconic signs rather than a single indexical sign and communicates concepts through visual likenesses, not by directly presenting object traces.

However, while the image seems for these writers to be too "real," it is simultaneously not real enough; it is too tied to the world of objects to create "meaning," and yet too far from that object world to represent truth. The possibility that a viewer might assume that the photographic image depicts a once-existent reality is its greatest danger, for those concerned with the proliferation of the spectacle. Images are in a sense deceptive; they do not "represent" reality, but, as Baudrillard suggests, "simulate" it. Thus, by a demented sort of logic, for the traditional literary intellectual there is not only a dearth of interpretable meaning in the image but also too much meaning, telling the deepest sort of lie, fooling the viewer into forgetting that it is mere image and not a direct transmission of reality. By contrast, under this logic, the written word, which as symbolic sign always leaves its constructed nature visible, is a more "honest" means of representation and is thus a more appropriate vehicle for meaningful communication. The novel of obsolescence, by a self-reflexive consideration of its own uses of language and by its strategies for replicating the image in its content, thus confronts what Baudrillard has called "the murderous power of images, murderers of the real, murderers of their own model" (*Simulacra* 5), attempting to neutralize the image's power by capturing and transforming it in language.

Don DeLillo explores these conflicting concerns about the relative powers of the spectacle and the novel in his 1997 article "The Power of History." The article, which primarily purports to be an exposition of DeLillo's working method, reveals his combination of interest in and horror of the image in contemporary culture. In *Underworld*, as I argue later, DeLillo formulates a theory of mediation, and of the differences in effect of the various contemporary media, from radio to film to television to cyberspace. In "The Power of History," he lays this theory bare:

> Newsreel footage of Bobby Thomson's home run resembles something of World War I vintage. But the shakier and fuzzier the picture, the more it lays a claim to permanence. And the voice of the announcer, Russ Hodges, who did the rapturous radio account of the game's final moments, is beautifully isolated in time—not subject to the debasing process of frantic repetition that exhausts a contemporary event before it has rounded into coherence. (62)

The power of history—and, more importantly, the power that the media seem to be usurping from history—has long been at the center of DeLillo's novelistic concerns. What makes this article striking is his direct confrontation with the power of the image, and his determination to wrest that power away. Our sense of the power of the visual, DeLillo tells us, is no more than an illusion. The lower any image's quality, the more power it actually wields in the creation of a historical record. And, in fact, the most enduring, important media events are radio transmissions, which have no images attached whatsoever.

But that this sense of an inverse relationship between image quality and historical power is but a tentative, uncomfortable conviction for DeLillo becomes equally clear in "The Power of History":

> Maybe it is the evanescent spectacle of contemporary life that makes the novel so nervous. Things flash and die. A face appears, a movie actor's, say, and it seems to be everywhere, suddenly; or it is an entire movie that's everywhere, with enormous feature stories about special effects and global marketing and tie-in merchandise; or it is just an individual's name that haunts every informational nook, and you can't figure out who the person is inside the name or what the context is that gave such abrupt prominence to the name, but it never actually matters and this is the point. (62)

The problem with the image—and the thing that clearly "makes the novel so nervous"—is not merely a cultural evanescence, a lack of historical permanence, but that this evanescence is connected to spectacle. Images, often in the form of movies, are ubiquitous, are talked about, are successful in the marketplace, but the nature of moving images is to come and go quickly. By contrast, novels, while remaining still, are relatively ignored. Thus, for the novelist, the spectacle is to be deplored for creating an endless cycle in which there is always "another set of images for you to want and need and get sick of and need nonetheless, and it separates you from the reality that beats ever more softly in the diminishing world outside the tape" (63). The image is too concrete to be meaningful, and yet so ephemeral that it distracts from reality. It cannot create a sense of permanence, and yet it commands all desire. The problem with the image is that it is at once too real, not real enough, and, in fact, destructive of reality.

The answer to the problem posed by this "evanescent spectacle" is to be found, unsurprisingly, in the novel, and specifically in the novel's medium, language. The novel may attempt to rescue the power of history—and with reason, as Baudrillard suggests: "The age of history, if one can call it that, is also the age of the novel" (*Simulacra* 47)—from the images that have so weakened it. Baudrillard again: "Photography and cinema contributed in large part to the secularization of history, to fixing it in its visible, 'objective' form at the expense of the myths that once traversed it" (48). Like the radio broadcast, what gives the novel its vigor is that it is constructed in words only, not in pictures. In this, the novel resists the reifications worked by the image-based media; the novel's use of language instead resubjectivizes history, restoring its mythical qualities.

> Ultimately the writer will reconfigure things the way his own history demands. He has his themes and biases and limitations. He has the small crushed pearl of his anger. He has his teaching job, his middling reputation and the one radical idea he has been waiting for all his life. The other thing he has is a flat surface that he will decorate with words.
>
> Language can be a form of counterhistory. The writer wants to construct a language that will be the book's life-giving force. He wants to submit to it. Let language shape the world. Let it break the faith of conventional re-creation.
>
> Language lives in everything it touches and can be an agent of redemption, the thing that delivers us, paradoxically, from history's flat, thin, tight and relentless designs, its arrangement of stark pages, and that allows us to find an unconstraining otherness, a free veer from time and place and fate. (DeLillo, "Power" 63).

DeLillo borrows from the tools of visual representation—writing becomes "decorating" with words, thus obviating the need for the image—while he simultaneously valorizes language in its very differences from the visual media. History as it is conventionally known, it would seem from this passage, is built of images rather than words, given its "flat, thin, tight and relentless designs." Visuality is here central to history, while language resides on the margins as a form of "counterhistory." There is thus implied an otherness of medium that DeLillo seems to feel is experienced by the cultural practitioner who works in words rather than images. This is a problematic claim in two regards. First, as any good New Historicist would point out, history resides in its textual traces, and thus it is always already constructed in language.[7] Second, this desire to ascribe a historical otherness to language reveals the writer's claim to a kind of cultural marginalization, a claim that runs the risk of undermining attempts to redress social hierarchies based around human othernesses, such as those of race and gender.

The connection between these two types of otherness—human difference and difference of medium—reveals the cultural stakes in the novelist's battle to recenter language. Mitchell, in *Picture Theory*, suggests that the alterity of image and text presents the very terms in which alterity itself is expressed, including that experienced on a social (rather than cultural) level:

> The "otherness" of visual representation from the standpoint of textuality may be anything from a professional competition (the *paragone* of poet and painter) to a relation of political, disciplinary, or cultural domination in which the "self" is understood to be an active, speaking, seeing subject, while the other is projected as a passive, seen, and (usually) silent object. (157)

In this relationship between otherness of medium and the othernesses of subject position, then, one finds an important subtextual meaning of the anxiety of obsolescence: part of the concern about the visual in these novels revolves around the visual apprehension of the other—particularly the racially or ethnically marked other—and the inversions visual culture seems to threaten in the hierarchies of looking, in who gets to be the subject and who gets relegated to the object of the gaze. Given such complexities in all relations based on looking, the presumed binary of visual versus verbal is of course far too simple. As Mitchell points out, text itself is unavoidably visual, just as visual representations are often surrounded by text; "all media are mixed media," he acknowledges (5). But in exploring this inextricable relationship of words and pictures, Mitchell acknowledges the political import of the writer's colonizing gesture, particularly in the conventions of ekphrastic writing. Echoing more literal forms of geopolitical colonization, the assumption of ekphrasis, which Mitchell defines as "the verbal representation of visual representation" (152), seems to be that the colonized visual media cannot represent themselves and must rather be represented verbally to be "seen." Such colonization functions not simply as critique but as a resubordination of looking to language.

Mitchell delineates three stages in the fraught relationship between the verbal and the visual. The first he terms "ekphrastic indifference," in which the writer acknowledges the impossibility of fully capturing an image in words but is finally unconcerned about that impossibility. The second phase, "ekphrastic hope," develops out of a writer's sense that perhaps the visual can be captured in words on paper, and that some new, exciting relationship between the "sister arts" can grow out of such an attempt. Finally, however, there is "ekphrastic fear," which is the phase that may shed some light on the attempts of the novelist of obsolescence to confine the image within language. Ekphrastic fear is experienced by the writer as a threatening muteness, a terror not unrelated to the threat of castration; in ekphrastic fear, "the utopian figures of the image and its textual rendering as transparent windows onto reality are supplanted by the notion of the image as a deceitful illusion" (156). This fear of the image's powers of deception takes numerous forms; I here briefly sketch out three interrelated dangers often ascribed to the visual, to which I'll return in discussing the uses of ekphrasis in DeLillo's novels.

First, given its attempts to communicate solely through representations of concrete objects rather than abstract symbols, the image is thought to further a worldview in which things take precedence over ideas.[8] In this manner, culture itself becomes objectified. The threat of this focus on objects is twofold. The most apparent risk is commodification, the transformation of all cultural experience into marketplace exchange. Communication via images thus becomes a series of mail-order catalogs, advertisements for things one can own.[9] As Guy Debord argues in *The Society of the Spectacle*, because images have come to mediate all of social existence, the spectacle "corresponds to the historical moment at which the commodity completes its colonization of social life" (29). The purpose of the image for Debord is both to distract the subject from the processes of commodification and the inequities that the mode of production requires, and to further promote the commodity itself. Images thus work, for Debord, to heighten exchange value at the expense of use value: "The spectacle is a permanent opium war waged to make it impossible to distinguish goods from commodities" (30). What becomes important in such a commodified culture is not what one knows, but what one has.

There is a further threat in this focus on objects, however: in transforming all cultural experience into commodified, objectified form, the image presumably makes it impossible to think abstractly. Baudrillard's critique of the situationist commentary on the spectacle takes up this point; Debord reads the spectacle as "only an immense connotation of the commodity," Baudrillard contends in *The Mirror of Production* (120). Baudrillard moves beyond the connotative level to interrogate how the image has affected the semiotic code itself. He argues that Debord's society of the spectacle exists in "the third phase of political economy" (119), in which even the inalienable—language, for instance—falls under the sway of exchange value. In no small part, this assumption of previously uncommodified modes of exchange into the capitalist mode of consumption is due to an increasing traffic in images, which, in communicating through concrete representations of things, transform ideas themselves into objects. The first danger of the image resides, then, in this paradoxical transformation: in objectifying and commodifying culture, the spectacle insinuates itself between human perception and the "real," translating reality into images. In so doing, the spectacle eradicates the real by cutting off the subject's linguistic access to it, replacing the conceptual understanding of the real with the reifications of its image. In this manner, the abstract becomes exchangeable; what one knows *becomes part of* what one has.[10]

The second danger is an outgrowth of the first: the spectacle, in reducing the complexities of reality into images, unavoidably replicates the most dangerous aspects of ideology, setting the stage for explosive violence. As Debord points out, the spectacle is "a social relationship between people that is mediated by images" (12). Moreover, the spectacle's political implications exceed mere visuality: "It is far better viewed as a weltanschauung that has been actualized, translated into the material realm—a world view transformed into an objective force" (12–13). The problem is that the visual, given the reductions it works on abstract ideas, is incapable of dealing with such a reified worldview with any complexity. The result is that, on the one hand, the visual interest of the image comes to serve as a tool of state power, an ideological state apparatus, in Althusserian terms. The danger of this visual ISA rests in part in its ability to use the forces of visuality against the seeing subject, reclaiming the power of looking for the state; the images in question can thus be ideologically loaded displays that interpellate the subject into the dominant order, or, perhaps more frighteningly, they can *look back*. Mitchell distinguishes between these two directions of visuality by suggesting that "spectacle is the ideological form of pictorial power; surveillance is its bureaucratic, managerial, and disciplinary form" (327). These two specular forms nonetheless come together to create a terrifyingly inescapable visual feedback loop in which the individual is at the mercy of the unseen, all-seeing controllers of the image.[11] But in attempting to wrest control of the image away from such state apparatuses, revolutionary forces and lone individuals are led into desperate, violent acts that betray the impossibility of functioning in the zone between reality and images of reality. As Stacey Olster has argued about Pynchon's *Vineland*, there is a deep relationship between the image's reification of the human and violence inflicted against that human: "the media's representations of humans as characters, of *any* kind, on a screen, *any* screen, makes the act of extinction that much easier to effect" (126). In the image, then, is a kind of ideological violence that ultimately makes physical violence that much more possible.

The third danger the spectacle presents lies in its creation of a new reality that finally supplants the "real" to which its viewers have lost access. In this Baudrillardian hyperreal, a reality generated by its own models, the relationship between referents and their representations breaks down once and for all. This is the image's most profound deceit, that it may not simply create illusions, not simply provide distractions, not simply promote dangerous ideologies, but that it may be taken for the real, for that which it has already destroyed. Baudrillard, in "The Precession of Simulacra," describes the four "successive phases of the image," in which we can see the buildup of this threat created by the image's interference in the real:

> it is the reflection of a profound reality;
> it masks and denatures a profound reality;
> it masks the *absence* of a profound reality;
> it has no relation to any reality whatsoever:
>   it is its own pure simulacrum. (*Simulacra*, 6)

By the end, in becoming its own pure simulacrum, in abandoning any relationship to the "diminishing world outside the tape" that DeLillo laments in "The Power of History," the image also denies any relationship to representation, claiming instead transparency, authenticity, reality. This claim is, for the novelist, the most dangerous lie of all; if images become reality, can the novel any longer claim any access, privileged or otherwise, to the real? And if all the participants in contemporary culture can be convinced of the reality of the spectacle, will anyone any longer bother with, much less believe, the too apparently unreal symbolic representations of print?

The image is thus represented as corruptible and corrupting, in terms of both its deceptive proximity to "reality" and its Baudrillardian "murder" of that reality and its availability to representation. Horkheimer and Adorno sensed such a destruction of reality in film: because of its proliferation, they argue, "the whole world is made to pass through the filter of the culture industry. The old experience of the moviegoer, who sees the world outside as an extension of the film he has just left (*because the latter is intent upon reproducing the world of everyday perceptions*), is now the producer's guideline. . . . Real life is becoming indistinguishable from the movies" (126, emphasis mine). The blame for this confusion of reality and medium is here laid directly at the doorstep of the reproduction, in the form of the image, of visuality qua visuality. The equation of seeing images of the world with seeing the world—what Postman describes as the basis of the epistemological axiom "seeing is believing" (*Amusing* 24)—has not made the experience of film more real, for Horkheimer and Adorno, but rather made "real" life less. In undermining the importance of the real, the image has negated any possibility of substantive political resistance. Any, that is, except the novel: Baudrillard's disappearing profound reality is precisely the "diminishing world outside the tape" to which DeLillo refers, and which he claims the novelist has the ability to recuperate. Such recuperation of course requires the reassertion of the primacy of language and the cultural centrality of the novel, a reassertion that creates an elite capable of looking at images without being drawn in by them.

Ekphrastic fear, as manifested by the novelist of obsolescence, can thus revolve around the translation of the "real" into images, the reverse translation of those images into the "real," or the violence that simmers in the space between. In discussing the manifestations of each of these aspects of ekphrastic fear in DeLillo, I will in part associate commodification with photography, ideology with film, and simulation with television. This is of course not to suggest a one-to-one correspondence between fears and forms but to demonstrate a kind of progression: as the image becomes more technologically advanced, more pervasive, the nature of the novelist's anxiety heightens as well. In all cases, however, the novelist works to undermine the image's power through a form of colonization, capturing it in language. But implied within this ekphrastic fear is an even more wrenching terror: if language is, as DeLillo suggests, our last remaining agent of redemption, what happens when language itself has been so undermined through its co-option by the image-based media that it can no longer function? For Neil Postman, the writer's cultural death begins with the erosion of the epistemological foundation of typography; in this view, the problem resides in the public's lack of tools necessary to contend with print, in the inability to see the connections between language and the real. Alvin Kernan's narrative of decline places part of the blame for this linguistic decline at the feet of "theory"; poststructuralist thought, by revealing the lack of transparency in language, the slippery separation of signifier and signified, and the ideological motivation of the signifying process, has made any innocent use of language impossible (see Kernan, esp. 165). Baudrillard's political economy reveals the linguistic sign to be as rooted in exchange value as is the image; Foucault describes the ideological motivations of the discursive construction of language; Lacan's exploration of the symbolic order demonstrates the impossibility of ever accessing the Real, except through the impossible constraints of language. Thus we are reminded that before Mitchell's pictorial turn, there was the linguistic turn; each of the elements of ekphrastic fear could easily be turned back on language itself. The linguistic turn, as Mark Poster argues, put an end to the nineteenth century's sense of language's transparency, to the "stable, comfortable, knowable world where words clearly referred to things, where ideas represented reality. . . . There could simply not be articulated a 'revolution' in underarm deodorants" (Introduction 8).

That now there *can* be seems to indicate that the degradation of language into something unstable, uncomfortable, unknowable is directly connected to advertising and its attendant media. Horkheimer and Adorno, in considering advertising as part of the culture industry, point out that "the more completely language is lost in the [publicity] announcement, the more words are debased as substantial vehicles of meaning and become signs devoid of quality" (164), as though language had once been transparent and has been muddied—"words" devolved into "signs"—by its use in the electronic media. More recently, Sven Birkerts concurs: "If the print medium exalts the word, fixing it into permanence, the electronic counterpart reduces it to a signal, a means to an end" (123). In such an environment, the *only* revolution still possible is that in underarm deodorants; the very concept "revolution" no longer carries political potential but has, like all other words, been reduced to sign, to signal, to empty, slippery, nonreferential signifier.

This devolution of words into signs is made manifest in Pynchon's *V.* in the language of the Whole Sick Crew. As Rachel first notes about Paola, "the girl lived proper nouns." But her assessment of this situation just misses the mark: "Persons, places. No things. Had anyone told her about things?" (51). In fact, there is no need for Paola to have been "told about" things, as all the persons and places she wields as proper nouns have become, with their capitalization, fully thingified. It takes an onlooker from farther outside the Whole Sick Crew to better assess the Crew's uses of words as "signs devoid of quality": Dudley Eigenvalue. The Crew's language has, in his estimation, degenerated into

a kind of shorthand whereby they could set forth any visions that might come their way. Conversations at the Spoon had become little more than proper nouns, literary allusions, critical or philosophical terms linked in certain ways. Depending on how you arranged the building blocks at your disposal, you were smart or stupid. Depending on how others reacted they were In or Out. The number of blocks, however, was finite.

"Mathematically, boy," he told himself, "if nobody else comes along, they're bound to run out of arrangements someday. What then?" What indeed. This sort of arranging and rearranging was Decadence, but the exhaustion of all possible permutations and combinations was death. (297–98)

Words are for the Crew ponderously concrete, fully reified "building blocks" that can be moved and manipulated. But their very concreteness is the source of their inevitable destruction, for in their solidity they have become "finite." The physicality of the "sign" in this milieu, as opposed to the ephemeral abstraction of the "word," has sent language into what Tony Tanner calls in *The City of Words* "an inevitable decline"; worse, "the Whole Sick Crew seems to be hastening the entropic decline of language as a vehicle for the transmission of significant information, by playing with all its permutations regardless of what reference any of the permutations may or may not have to reality" (161). What has perhaps begun with advertising is being sped up by this decadent pseudo-intellectualization—and, one begins to suspect, in following Jack Gladney's progress through *White Noise*, by the same sorts of pseudointellectualization that run rampant through the university, posing as cultural studies and cultural theory.[12]

But Pynchon leaves a shred of hope in the face of this "inevitable decline": the possibility that "somebody else" might come along to introduce new possibilities, to reopen this closed, entropic system.[13] This "somebody else" is, of course, the serious writer who exists outside this realm of advertising, pseudointellectual chatter, and the university.[14] Perhaps, as DeLillo argues in "The Power of History," the novelist's use of "language" can rescue not simply the literary form but the culture itself from the degradation it is suffering at the hands of the image. But it can do so only if it can somehow rescue language first. For, as Fredric Jameson reads the postmodern novel—in his case, represented synecdochally by the *nouveau roman* of Alain Robbe-Grillet and Claude Simon—it is itself an enactment of "linguistic failure" in its very uses of language, in which the "breakdown" of the relationship between signs and referents "is experienced over and over again as a process, a temporary runoff between the habitual onset of linguistic belief and the inevitable degradation of the signified into its material signifier or the sign itself into a mere image" (139). Language in the novel threatens to degrade into images; this is perhaps the phenomenon that William Gass is referring to when he claims that the discovery "that novels should be made up of words, and merely words, is shocking, really. It's as though you had discovered that your wife were made of rubber" (27). Words as signs are, like the image, fakes, simulations of a reality that we cannot fully grasp. Gass's suggestion of this particular metaphor makes it clear, in fact, that the words that comprise the novel are, like the images they are devolving into, pornographic. The particular pornographies that the wife as latex doll represents—think back to Benny's Violet and Stencil's future V.—function, as does Gass's metaphor, to reassert and buttress traditional hierarchies: of subject and object, of watcher and watched, of verbal and visual.

But the flimsiness of these hierarchies remains, particularly that which attempts to differentiate the powers of linguistic signs from those of visual signs. Thus John Duvall raises the "problem" that "remains for DeLillo as a satirist: if he insists that the world is wholly mediated, what distinguishes the novel as a medium from the electronic media he criticizes?" (148n). The distinction is in fact minimal; the writer's fear for his own destruction includes his sense that there has been an apparent diversion of signifying power away from language, an awareness of language itself as a form of mediation—and worse, a creeping sense that the "media" are more practiced in manipulating these forms of mediation than are writers. In DeLillo's *White Noise*, for instance, we see repeatedly the withering of language during media-covered crises. After a plane nearly crashes, Gladney relates the story as told by one of the passengers: "Certain elements in the crew had decided to pretend that it was not a crash but a crash landing that was seconds away. After all, the difference between the two is only one word. Didn't this suggest that the two forms of flight termination were more or less interchangeable? How much could one word matter?" (91).[15] In fact, words cease to matter during such crises except as driven by the media itself; during the novel's central disaster, the nature of the crisis remains vague and undefined, not right, unnamed, until the radio announces the name it has been given, changing this name from the "feathery plume" to the "billowing black cloud," before finally settling upon the "airborne toxic event."[16] It is not that the words have no meaning; the point is that these meanings and the power to name them—the right of signification—seem to obtain only for the media, which has claimed (and been given) the powers of naming.[17] Moreover, it is possible to reread the "airborne toxic event" as the novelist's own description of television and radio themselves, which suggests that these powers of language *always* belong to the media and that the definition of a crisis is not, as Babette later suggests, "based on the fact that it's not an everyday occurrence" (174); a crisis is rather what the media says it is.[18] Any use of language in such a mediated culture remains undefined, unofficial, until verified by media sources: "Remarks existed in a state of permanent flotation. No one thing was either more or less plausible than any other thing" (129). The same holds for David Bell in DeLillo's *Americana*; in the corporate environment of the television network, "words and meanings were at odds. Words did not say what was being said nor even its reverse" (36). Words are not to be counted on at all within such an image-driven environment; what Marcuse has referred to as "the functionalization of language" (86) seems thus to stem directly from its co-optation by the forces of the electronic media. And if television has indeed succeeded in functionalizing language, the power of the novelist can only diminish.

The Most Photographed Barn in America

Given the degree of influence attributed to television in U.S. culture—remember the *Times*'s chronology, in which image culture was founded by television—it comes as a momentary surprise to reflect that the image need not move or employ sound to threaten the displacement of the novelist in his role as cultural producer. McLuhan, in claiming that "the step from the age of Typographic Man to the age of Graphic Man was taken with the invention of photography" (190), makes clear that the most basic technologies of image production were sufficient to create the circumstances of the novel's undoing.[19] This is true at least in part because the production of the image in particular is tied to commodity production in general. As Fredric Jameson argues, " '[t]he image,' said Debord in a famous theoretical move, 'is the final form of commodity reification'; but he should have added 'the *material* image,' the photographic reproduction" (125). The overt commercialism of network television, in other words, was not the necessary element in the absorption of signifying power within the corporate media machine; still photography itself already contains within it the mechanism for transforming the real into image, and thus into commodity.

We might best begin to approach this connection between commodity reification and photography in DeLillo through a return to *White Noise* and "the Most Photographed Barn in America," to which Jack Gladney takes Murray Jay Siskind. Murray is, as one might expect, a font of theories about the phenomenon of the barn. After an initial note-taking silence, during which he watches the orderly picture taking, the approved picture-taking locations, and the sale of official picture postcards and slides, he puts forth his first theory: "No one sees the barn. . . . Once you've seen the signs about the barn, it becomes impossible to see the barn." Murray here echoes Walker Percy on the impossibility of seeing the Grand Canyon; the real has been overcome by the process of signification surrounding it (see Percy). His second pronouncement invokes Benjamin's argument about the destruction of "aura" by the technologies of mass reproduction, claiming that by some twist, in the contemporary, "every photograph reinforces the aura" (12; see Benjamin 221). In contrast to the democratizing force Benjamin hoped for, the mechanical reproduction of the image has wound up having more in common with Horkheimer and Adorno's sense of the culture industry, in which the functionalization of cultural experience leads to a fascistic meaninglessness. As Murray finally concludes, "We've agreed to be part of a collective perception. . . . We can't get outside the aura. We're part of the aura" (12–13). The photograph solidifies a corporate ideology in such a fashion that the entire cultural experience becomes commodified; the picture takers, taking pictures of one another taking pictures, ultimately become part of the spectacle itself.

As does Murray, it appears, in finding himself "immensely pleased" (*WN* 13) with his own pronouncements: Murray's mobilizations of cultural theory appear at first to further the novel's desire to expose the fraudulence of the barn's claims to provide an enlightening visual experience, but that those mobilizations involve a number of crucial inversions in the theories he references seems finally to shift focus from the barn to Murray, from the spectacle proper to the academic approach to that spectacle. One of those inversions, that in the concept of "aura," has already been mentioned; that inversion undermines Benjamin's suggestion that the mechanically produced and reproduced image could democratize art by removing it from its ritual function and broadening access to its representations, allowing for a revolutionary displacement in intellectual hierarchies. Instead, in its postmodern inversion, this broadened access has deprived art of meaning, has reinforced its ritual value through its commodification and thus made it the tool by which the willing masses aid in their own oppression.[20] Is this shift from liberation to fascism, from the Benjaminian revolutionary proletariat to the Adornoan fascistic mass, meant to suggest that Murray, as a member of the intellectual elite, fancies himself immune to the forces by which the poor dupes taking and buying the pictures of the barn are so swayed? Or is it the novel, which controls the force of the image by recasting its representations into language, and which, as we'll explore further in the next chapter, ostensibly escapes the fascistic urges of the crowd by promoting the individualist experience of reading, that declares itself so immune?

This interpretation could probably be resolved in either direction—but for the inversion buried in Murray's first pronouncement: "Once you've seen the signs about the barn, it becomes impossible to see the barn" (*WN* 12). I suggested a moment ago that this was an echo of Walker Percy's analysis of the modern inability to truly see the Grand Canyon—except that for Percy it was the postcard snapshot of the Grand Canyon that made its material existence invisible. The proliferation of images of an object, such as we see surrounding this barn, renders the reality of the barn inaccessible; everyone looking at the barn is doing so through a mediating lens. For Murray, by contrast, it is the signs that render the barn unseeable, the five road signs that directed Murray and Jack to this place, textual signs announcing "THE MOST PHOTOGRAPHED BARN IN AMERICA." Thus, in Murray's revision, *reading* inhibits or disrupts the visual experience; rather than images destroying text, text undermines the image. In his implied nostalgia for a lost visual experience, Murray moves outside the novel's own perspective to become the object of its critique. Thus we might reencounter his final pronouncement on the barn:

> "What was the barn like before it was photographed?" he said. "What did it look like, how was it different from other barns, how was it similar to other barns? We can't answer these questions because we've read the signs, seen the people snapping the pictures. We can't get outside the aura. We're part of the aura. We're here, we're now."
> He seemed immensely pleased by this. (13)

Murray's pleasure ambiguously suggests a willingness to join the aura, to participate in the endless replication of the spectacle, or a satisfaction with his own analysis, an interpretation of the spectacle that ends with the meaninglessly tautological assertion of hereness and nowness. In either case, while Murray understands the act of sign reading to have undermined the production of meaning from the barn, shifting it from its previously (one assumes) functional existence to its new status as event, the novel suggests that the type of reading Murray performs equally obscures the meaning of the scene. Thus the novel gets to have its cake and eat it too, in a sense, both critiquing the barn as event and critiquing the critique, suggesting that in its transformation of the experience of text into an obstacle to seeing, cultural theory has done as much to undermine the act of reading as has the image. By this reading, the image may commodify objects, but cultural theory further commodifies the image, wrapping it in a new intellectual aura.

Another, younger, postmodern novelist, David Foster Wallace, connects this scene to the "metastasis of watching" he claims has been created by television, pointing out in it an infinite regress of spectators: "not only are people watching a barn whose only claim to fame is being an object of watching, but the pop-culture scholar Murray is watching people watch a barn, and his friend Jack is watching Murray watch the watching, and we readers are pretty obviously watching Jack the narrator watch Murray watching, etc." ("Pluram" 48). But one must note that, with this enumeration, Wallace eliminates the *novelist* from the regress of watching; DeLillo is somehow exempt from this chain of spectation. Moreover, Wallace, in linking Jack and Murray into the chain, conflates the critic with the audience, which amounts to an equation of watching and critical interpretation. Wallace reduces Murray's interpretation of and commentary on this popular event to "watching the watching," erasing the writing that Murray performs within the scene, both literal (as he is throughout "scrawling some notes" [*WN* 12]) and figurative (recasting the event in theoretical terms). Our own reading of this text is turned into watching as well, as though there were not experiential or interpretive differences between a novel and a film. Reading, interpreting, theorizing—all of which comprise the work of the critic—are by this argument reincorporated by and contained within the spectacle. In fact, Wallace derides Murray's academic attempts to remove himself from the role of spectator:

> most of the writing's parodic force is directed at Murray, the would-be transcender of spectation. Murray, by watching and analyzing, would try to figure out the how and whys of giving in to collective visions of mass images that have themselves become mass images only because they've been made the objects of collective vision. The narrator's "extended silence" in response to Murray's blather speaks volumes. ("Pluram" 49)

Murray's analysis, his attempts to understand this "collective vision," is thus transformed by Wallace into blather, while Jack's silent observation inverts into commentary; in fact, Wallace suggests that Jack is "DeLillo's alter ego" in the scene of the Most Photographed Barn in America, capable of "diagnos[ing] the very disease from which he, Murray, barn-watchers, and readers all suffer" (49). Here again, the compression of the various relationships to the object of sight of narrator, critic, participant, and reader into one uniform, diseased perspective speaks more about the conflict between the novelist and the culture of watching (and, not incidentally, about the conflict between the novelist and the academic) than about the critic, the scholar, or the reader at all. In reducing Murray's analysis to mere blather, Wallace recasts Jack as the novel's silent diagnostician, the novelist's stand-in. And in exempting the novelist from the regress of watching, in giving his writing "parodic force," Wallace suggests that DeLillo is the only player able to escape, and thus to transcend, the threatening culture of visuality.

Jack's silence in this scene, however, may be read more pointedly as commentary not on Murray's blather but on his own compromised state within the novel, a state that hardly lends itself to the kind of diagnostic prowess Wallace suggests. Jack is after all an academic himself, chair of the department of Hitler studies at the College-on-the-Hill. The one salient detail that the novel provides of Jack's academic life—that he "invented" Hitler studies in March 1968—is the key to *White Noise*'s reduction of the critic and scholar in the age of television, for what Jack studies is not Hitler's texts, not the political-historical significance of Hitler's reign of terror through Europe, but Hitler as image. The only class he still teaches at the College-on-the-Hill is described in cataloguelike terms as "Advanced Nazism, three hours a week, restricted to qualified seniors, a course of study designed to cultivate historical perspective, theoretical rigor and mature insight into the continuing mass appeal of fascist tyranny, with special emphasis on parades, rallies and uniforms, three credits, written reports" (*WN* 25). The irony of "written reports" in such a class aside, the course description betrays in its concern with "parades, rallies and uniforms" a focus on the visual aspects of Nazism, a focus that transforms National Socialism into a series of snapshots. This reduction of the historical realities of fascism into its images becomes even more disturbing when Jack reveals that "as the most prominent figure in Hitler studies in North America, I had long tried to conceal the fact that I did not know German. I could not speak or read it, could not understand the spoken word or begin to put the simplest sentence on paper" (31). Not only, then, does Jack fail to examine the substance of Nazism in his scholarly life, he is incapable of doing so; this mortifying inability to engage with the textual materials of his field reinforces the reader's suspicion that, for Jack, Hitler is about watching:

> Every semester I arranged for a screening of background footage. This consisted of propaganda films, scenes shot at party congresses, outtakes from mystical epics featuring parades of gymnasts and mountaineers—a collection I'd edited into an impressionistic eighty-minute documentary. Crowd scenes predominated. Close-up jostled shots of thousands of people outside a stadium after a Goebbels speech, people surging, massing, bursting through the traffic. Halls hung with swastika banners, with mortuary wreaths and death's-head insignia. Ranks of thousands of flagbearers arrayed before columns of frozen light, a hundred and thirty anti-aircraft lights aimed straight up—a scene that resembled a geometric longing, the formal notation of some powerful mass desire. There was no narrative voice. Only chants, songs, arias, speeches, cries, cheers, accusations, shrieks. (25–26)

These visual materials in their "geometric" quality suggest that "formal notation" in contemporary culture has come to be connected with a distinctly nonnarrative, nontextual form of inscription, inchoate collections of image and sound. Jack's role in producing this documentary pointedly fails to account for the political import of these images; he merely "edited" them together, resisting analysis and interpretation by refusing to include a "narrative voice." The inclusion of such narration, the novel seems to suggest, could appropriately contextualize these images in a way that would divorce them from their original purposes. Instead, in Jack's reification of these images, he reinforces that mass desire. In Jack Gladney, then, we can see the end result not only of a culture that made its history visual—Nazi Germany's—but also of a culture that learns its history, as the *Times* points out, not at the library but at the movie theater.

Worse, an academic culture that teaches history through the movie theater; sharing a building with the department of Hitler studies is Murray's department, that of "American environments," otherwise known as popular culture. According to Jack, these scholars "are here to decipher the natural language of the culture, to make a formal method of the shiny pleasures they'd known in their Europe-shadowed childhoods—an Aristotelianism of bubble-gum wrappers and detergent jingles" (*WN* 9). This "natural language" is clearly no longer textual, as these scholars have completely removed themselves from the study of typographic texts and instead now focus on the presumably empty images of packaging and advertising, utterly distracted from serious intellectual pursuits by the world's "shiny pleasures." Murray, in fact, first befriends Jack by suggesting his seriousness, his remove from the rest of the pop-culture crowd: "I understand the music," he says, "I understand the movies, I even see how comic books can tell us things. But there are full professors in this place who read nothing but cereal boxes" (10). Murray's presumed call for a return to text is of course disingenuous; as the multiple supermarket scenes throughout the novel reveal, Murray is an avid reader of food packaging.[21] Little wonder, then, that from DeLillo's point of view, nothing revolutionary emerges from the College-on-the-Hill. As Jack says of the college's home, Blacksmith:

> We don't feel threatened and aggrieved in quite the same way other towns do. We're not smack in the path of history and its contaminations. If our complaints have a focal point, it would have to be the TV set, where the outer torment lurks, causing fears and secret desires. Certainly little or no resentment attaches to the College-on-the-Hill as an emblem of ruinous significance. The school occupies an ever serene edge of the townscape, semidetached, more

or less scenic, suspended in political calm. Not a place designed to aggravate suspicions. (85)

It is entirely to the point that Jack here contrasts the college with television, as the novel throughout depicts a college besieged by the electronic media, an academia threatened with its own irrelevance. The College-on-the-Hill, in its serenity, in its abandonment of textuality as the object of study, in its denial of the politics that are inseparable from images of Nazism, has itself become "scenic," an object of watching.[22]

The moment of photography in the relationship of spectator to barn, then, has ramifications that ripple outward from the photograph itself, creating a "collective perception," an "aura," that absorbs both the takers of the pictures and the critic of the scene of photography in an incorporating, reifying gesture. As David Bell thinks in DeLillo's *Americana*, upon encountering a photographer in the lobby of his network's building: "Such is the prestige of the camera, its almost religious authority, its hypnotic power to command reverence from subject and bystander alike, that I stood absolutely motionless until the young man snapped the picture" (86). The picture-taking apparatus is of a piece with the corporate authority of the television network within which it functions. It is interesting to note, however, reading this moment against "the Most Photographed Barn in America," that the "subject" of the camera in this case is, in fact, another photograph, a huge enlargement of a prize-winning picture from the war. As Paul Virilio has noted, the codevelopment of the technologies of image production and of military domination has led each to be infused with the powers of the other; all photographs are, in some sense, photographs of the war (see Virilio, *War* and *Vision Machine*). Moreover, this image is displayed in the lobby of the television network that is growing famous for delivering real-time images of the war into U.S. living rooms; the prize-winning nature of this photograph, combined with the ratings success of the network, reveals the manner in which the photographic apparatus can commodify even the most extreme human suffering.

This is accomplished in part through the objectification of the photographed subject, who appears delivered directly unto the viewer. Roland Barthes, seeing the photograph as "literally an emanation of the referent," is led to muse about the enduring reality of this photographic subject:

> From a real body, which was there, proceed radiations which ultimately touch me, who am here; the duration of the transmission is insignificant; the photograph of the missing being, as Sontag says, will touch me like the delayed rays

of a star. A sort of umbilical cord links the body of the photographed thing to my gaze. (*Camera Lucida* 80–81)

This umbilical cord declares a gestational relationship between viewing self and viewed object, made possible by the interconnected relationship of the camera's gaze and the viewer's. Barthes would thus understand David's fear in *Americana* "that any small movement on my part might distract one of those bandaged children and possibly ruin the photograph" (86–87) as one of the results of the direct connection between viewer and "photographed thing"; shifting the connection might disturb the image. David, however, understands that these "radiations" begin and end with the photographic apparatus itself. The power of the connection between viewer and viewed is not an equivalence but a dominance, one structured by the machine that creates the image. It is the camera that has "prestige," that has an "almost religious authority"; it is the camera that commands him to be still. However, which photograph David's movement might ruin is uncertain. The primary camera has already produced the commodity reification of which Debord writes, transforming suffering into prize-winning photographs; nonetheless, the secondary camera is apparently powerful enough to reach back through this commodified object to the original subject and reify it all over again.

More than any other of DeLillo's novels, however, *Mao II* confronts this objectifying power of the camera head-on, particularly in its fraught relationship with the writer. While in *White Noise,* Jack Gladney claims that "[i]f our complaints have a focal point, it would have to be the TV set, where the outer torment lurks, causing fears and secret desires" (85), *Mao II* attempts to step back from the set, to seek the origins of this "torment" in the origins of the mechanically reproduced image, and thus discover how pervasive the "fears and secret desires" of the contemporary image-based culture are. The photograph is, in *Mao II*, the writer's death; the image's objectifying force dismantles the writer's necessary connection to the abstractions of language.

Brita Nilsson is the novel's photographer, the primary agent of the image's reifying power; she comes, at the request of Bill Gray (and expressly against the wishes of his assistant, Scott) to take Gray's picture. And "take" it she does; as the *New Yorker* wrote of the incident that inspired DeLillo's musings on the subject (the *New York Post*'s dispatching photographers to track down and shoot J. D. Salinger): "If the phrase 'take his picture' had any sense of violence or, at least, violation left in it at all, if it still retained the undertone of certain peoples who are convinced that a photographer threatens them with the theft of their souls, then it applies here" (Remnick 42). Though Gray has not been stalked or photographed against his will, this sense of violation appears to apply to his case as well; from the moment he is shoved, by the flick of a shutter, from writerly obscurity into the world of the image, he is unable to regain his balance. Brita, the producer of this ultimately disastrous transformation, has taken on as a life's project the photographing of writers, pulling them into the image's frame, as if preserving them against their own disappearance. There is something uncomfortably familiar about Brita's work, something redolent of a dying breed: "I'm simply doing a record," she says, but immediately follows it with the interpretation of one of her writer-subjects—"a species count" (*MII* 26). These photographs are an attempt on her part to save these disappearing writers from their own fated obscurity. As Gray comments during their photo session: "This is why you travel a million miles photographing writers. Because we're giving way to terror, to news of terror, to tape recorders and cameras, to radios, to bombs stashed in radios. News of disaster is the only narrative people need . . . you're smart to trap us in your camera before we disappear" (42). Gray immediately points out the tensions in Brita's project: novelists need saving because their work gives way before news of disaster, but the photographer "saves" through capture. Once caught within the camera, once transformed into an image-object, the novelist is trapped—and may not escape.

"[T]he logic of the photograph," claims McLuhan, "is neither verbal nor syntactical, a condition which renders literary culture quite helpless to cope with the photograph" (197). McLuhan's intent here was to depict the inept literary critic attempting to write about the photograph, but read against *Mao II,* this description seems to correlate with the writer's reaction to *being* photographed. For whether Bill Gray's initial desire to have his photograph taken— as he describes it, "to break down the monolith I've built" (*MII* 44)—is already a sign of a turning to exteriors, a desire to move into the "official memory" (*Libra* 279) of his culture, or whether the experience of being photographed itself, as in the fears of those "certain peoples" (the use of "peoples" signifying, of course, people of the "primitive" sort; writers are now classified as "primitive" in contrast to the electronic culture), has actually stolen Gray's soul, the result is the same. Gray relies upon the verbal and syntactical for his literary, not to mention his literal, life; as we saw in Chapter 1, his inability to cope with nontypographic visual cues leads to his being hit by an automobile. He is helpless in the face of the photograph; from the moment his picture is taken, the moment he becomes replaced by his own objectified image, his death becomes inevitable.

Scott recognizes this possibility right away as he ponders Gray's disappearance, a disappearance both necessitated and made possible by the photographs taken of him. "Bill had his picture taken," he thinks as he obsessively cleans Gray's manual typewriter, "not because he wanted to come out of hiding but because he wanted to hide more deeply, he wanted to revise the terms of his seclusion, he needed the crisis of exposure to give him a powerful reason to intensify his concealment" (*MII* 140). In a sense, Gray has disappeared *into* his photographs; he is now his own representation. Scott begins here to connect the photographs taken of Gray with those taken of Chairman Mao, who dropped out of sight with the effect of intensifying his power. But there is a crucial distinction: "Mao used photographs," Scott thinks, "to announce his return and demonstrate his vitality, to reinspire the revolution. Bill's picture was a death notice" (141). And in fact these photographs are Gray's obituary; to adopt Barthes's language, the fact of Gray's having emerged from his seclusion to allow his picture to be taken is mere *studium*. The *punctum*, the shock of these photographs is that

> he is going to die. I read at the same time: *This will be* and *this has been*; I observe with horror an anterior future of which death is the stake. By giving me the absolute past of the pose (aorist), the photograph tells me death in the future. What *pricks* me is the discovery of this equivalence. . . . Whether or not the subject is already dead, every photograph is this catastrophe. (Barthes, *Camera Lucida* 96)

In Bill Gray's case, the connection between the photograph and death is both more literal and more figurative. By the time Scott is able to see the proofs, Gray is dead. But his writerly death was effected long before his physical death; Gray's capture within Brita's camera forced him out of the abstractions of language and into the objectified world of the image, a world with which he was unable to cope. After Gray's death, Scott at last sees the pictures, the object-traces that remain:

> He took the magnifier to frame after frame and saw a photographer who was trying to deliver her subject from every mystery that hovered over his chosen life. She wanted to do pictures that erased his seclusion, made it never happen and made him over and gave him a face we've known all our lives.
> But maybe not. Scott didn't want to move too soon into a theory of how much meaning a photograph can bear. (221)

Whatever Brita's intent may have been, her pictures of Gray did erase his seclusion, did deliver him from the mysteries hovering over his life. Scott's earlier connection of the photographs with Gray's disappearance was valid; his only error lay in attributing motive and agency to the writer where in fact there was no such control. Gray's finally completed disappearance was not a matter of choice, but the final vanishing of the writer in an image-driven culture. Thus, that these images would have "erased" Gray's seclusion is the least of their violations. In delivering Gray from the mysteries of symbolic representation, in giving him a concrete presence, "a face we've known all our lives," Brita's photographs transform the writer into a trading card, something that can be owned rather than understood. And thus Scott's final uncertainty about the photograph's capacity to bear meaning is strangely valid; the photograph drains the world of meaning by erasing its connections to the real.

Yet the novel's epilogue seems to suggest that the only meaning remaining in the world is now contained by photographs. This final section of *Mao II* follows Brita to Beirut, where she has come to photograph Abu Rashid, the militia leader responsible for holding the writer whom Bill Gray was en route to rescue; having transformed writers into images of writers, she has now abandoned images of writers for images of bomb makers and gunmen. It hasn't been an announced shift but an anonymous one, like Gray's death, like the cultural abandonment of the writer felt throughout the novel: "She does not photograph writers anymore. It stopped making sense. She takes assignments now, does the interesting things, barely watched wars, children running in the dust. Writers stopped one day. She doesn't know how it happened but they came to a quiet end. They stopped being the project she would follow forever" (229–30). The writers were captured on film, and now even their images are destined to remain unseen. They, like Bill Gray, have disappeared.

The jacket copy of the novel's first edition claims that, "against this onslaught of images and cataclysmic events, DeLillo also tells an intimate story about faith, longing, and redemption." But one must ask, given this altogether dismal view of the writer's place in this world of terrorists, of bomb makers and gunmen—redemption for whom? The only possible answer appears to be for the photographer, ironically enough; if anyone can save the world from violence, it will be a person with a camera.[23] The very last moment of the novel reveals Brita standing on a balcony at 4 A.M., having watched a wedding party go past, now staring out at the darkness of the city. "There is a flash out there in the dark," we read, expecting it to be an explosion. It isn't:

> What could it be then if it's not the start of the day's first exchange of automatic-weapons fire? Only one thing of course. Someone is out there with a camera and a flash unit. Brita stays on the balcony for another minute, watching the magnesium pulse that brings an image to a strip of film. She crosses her arms over her body against the chill and counts off the bursts of relentless light. The dead city photographed one more time. (*MII* 241)

Perhaps the city can be brought back to life by the photographer recording the images of its death and destruction. Or perhaps the photographer, by impartially recording these images, by assisting in the reification that turns ideas into commodities, by silencing the voice of the writer within the great corporate, violent hum of mediated culture—perhaps the photographer is responsible for the death of the city and is now hard at work on the corpse left behind. In either case, in DeLillo's bleak vision of the world remaining, the creator of the visual image is the only cultural producer left standing.

A Camera Is a Gun

Throughout the last few examples of DeLillo's representations of the objectifying power of the photographic image, the transformation of the real into spectacle, has run an unmistakable thread of violence: the photograph of a photograph of the war, in *Americana*; Brita's "shooting" Bill Gray in *Mao II*, as the *Post* photographers "shot" Salinger; the photographs of bomb makers and gunmen; the photographer at work on the dead city. Barthes's suggestion of the equivalence between the photograph and the death of its subject and Virilio's exploration of the mutually reinforcing development of technologies of visuality and technologies of warfare both suggest the inevitability of such violence in a culture in which the image has replaced a significant portion of the real. This violence takes numerous forms—wars, both declared and undeclared, assassinations, and terrorism, as well as more subtle interpersonal violence—but each form in contemporary culture exists through a kind of collaboration with the image.

Given this dangerously collaborative interrelationship between violent conflict and the spectacle, the cold war stands out in recent history as peculiarly image based, even more so than the Gulf War, despite Baudrillard's insistence that the latter conflict did not take place except through its images (see *The Gulf War Did Not Take Place*). The peculiarity of the cold war, which was literally conducted in and through its images, is both that the images were the conflict's most significant events, and that the media that conveyed those images developed in tandem with the events themselves. The televised Army-McCarthy hearings; Kennedy on television, announcing the Cuban missile crisis; the aftermath of Kennedy's assassination; Nixon engaging Khruschev in the kitchen debate—the list of such cross-fertilizations of media and cold-war politics is plentiful. Even more, the technologies that made these events possible—television itself, most obviously, but also its conventions, including the live remote—are less mediators of, or even contributors to, than inventions of those events.[24]

In *Underworld*, Don DeLillo not only chronicles the cultural history of the cold war—a prodigious enough feat—but also along the way develops a theory of the twentieth-century forms of electronic media, particularly in their relationships to the cold war itself. His use of radio in the novel, in the form of Russ Hodges's broadcast of the Dodgers-Giants pennant game, has already been discussed. With regard to the Internet, I will here mention only that the novel may be read, as Adam Begley does in his review, as resembling "Mr. DeLillo's idea of the World Wide Web" (38), in which cyberspace represents both the potential for post-cold-war revolution—"The real miracle is the web, the net, where everybody is everywhere at once" (DeLillo, *U* 808)—and the ominous, containing corporate order that may in fact have brought the era to its conclusion: "It is all about the enfolding drama of the computers and fax machines. It is about the cell phones slotted in the desk chargers, the voice mail and e-mail—a sense of order and command reinforced by the office itself and the bronze tower that encases the office and by all the contact points that shimmer in the air somewhere" (806). What I would like to linger over momentarily is the novel's suggestion of the distinction between film and video in their relations to the period.

Part 2 of *Underworld*, entitled "Elegy for Left Hand Alone" and set during the period spanning the mid-1980s to the early 1990s, opens with a meditation on a videotape: "It shows a man driving a car. It is the simplest sort of family video" (155). Taken by a twelve-year-old girl on a vacation with her family, the video was intended to be a silly joke "recorded by a child who thought she was doing something simple and maybe halfway clever, shooting some tape of a man in a car" (156). Instead, the girl's videotape captures the man's murder at the hands of the Texas Highway Killer.[25] The images, like those of the Rodney King beating, immediately enter the public lexicon, played over and over on the national news. And as with the Rodney King incident, this murder becomes news, and thus only really "happens," because of the coincidence of the videotape, because there happened to be a camera trained on the events.

In fact, the connection of child and camera and murder seems inevitable, despite its equally apparent randomness. The incident becomes metaphorized as a fairy tale, on the one hand, a cautionary tale for children about the dangers of playing with images: "She wandered into it. The girl got lost and wandered clear-eyed into horror. This is a children's story about straying too far from home. But it isn't the family car that serves as the instrument of the child's curiosity, her inclination to explore. It is the camera that puts her in the tale" (*U* 157). On the other hand, the story is a grown-up one as well. That this murder could not have "happened" without the camera, that the camera puts the child in the tale, profoundly implicates the camera as weapon in the murder itself. In fact, as the narrative voice muses, the video camera may, in this murder, have found its true form:

> And there is something about videotape, isn't there, and this particular kind of serial crime? This is a crime designed for random taping and immediate playing. You sit there and wonder if this kind of crime became more possible when the means of taping an event and playing it immediately, without a neutral interval, a balancing space and time, became widely available. Taping-and-playing intensifies and compresses the event. It dangles a need to do it again. You sit there thinking that the serial murder has found its medium, or vice versa—an act of shadow technology, of compressed time and repeated images, stark and glary and unremarkable. (159)

Thus, the novel suggests, serial playing becomes serial killing; the repetition of images becomes, without metamorphosis, the repetition of murder. The easy exchange in this passage between murder and medium—"or vice versa"—suggests an interrelationship so profound as to be almost casual, and certainly wholly causal.

If the ultimate Aristotelian form of the videotape can thus be imagined to be the serial killing, *Underworld* posits the ideal form of film to be the assassination. Klara Sax, a conceptual artist, finds herself in 1974 at a secret exhibition, watching a film loop running in different sequences on a wall of television sets. The film loop is, of course, the finally leaked Zapruder home movie; this film, rather than calling attention to itself as a piece of history or as evidence of conspiracy, becomes for Klara a theory of itself:

> She knew she'd hear from Miles at dinner about the secret manipulation of history, or attempts at such, or how the experts could not seem to produce a clear print of the movie, or whatever. But the movie in fact was powerfully open, it was glary and artless and completely steeped in being what it was, in being film. It carried a kind of inner life, something unconnected to the things we call phenomena. The footage seemed to advance some argument about the nature of film itself. The progress of the car down Elm Street, the movement of the film through the camera body, some sharable darkness—this was a death that seemed to rise from the steamy debris of the deep mind, it came from some night of the mind, there was some trick of film emulsion that showed the ghost of consciousness. Or so she thought to wonder. She thought to wonder if this home movie was some crude living likeness of the mind's own technology, the sort of death plot that runs in the mind, because

it seemed so familiar, the footage did—it seemed a thing we might see, not see but know, a model of the nights when we are intimate with our own dying. (495–96)

The association of film with death—and particularly this most famous, most contested death of the cold-war era—again implicates the medium, the camera, in this shooting. The impossibility of clarifying the images on the one hand connects to the videotape viewer's impossible struggle to nudge the frame a little to the left to see the killer. On the other hand, given DeLillo's comments in "The Power of History," we are meant to sense that the poorer the image quality, the more "real" the event—though for Klara this very reality causes the film to leave the world of the phenomenal and become connected to "the ghost of consciousness." The film is "artless," and thus most completely itself in recounting this assassination. The "argument about the nature of film itself" advanced by this loop—or, rather, advanced by its representation in this novel—irrevocably connects the image with murder. Film is in *Underworld* murder made historical, conspiratorial; given its "openness," film is in fact, as the *Times* likewise suspects, the murder of history, that which renders impossible any unmediated understanding of the real. Videotape is by contrast murder robbed even of its facile historicity, become utterly random, sickeningly repeated. But in both instances, the camera, for DeLillo, is the gun. Baudrillard's conception of the "murderous power of images" is here literalized; the images are not *of* violence, but rather *are* violence itself.

This connection of camera and gun surfaces most literally in Pynchon's *Vineland*, as both the mission and the undoing of 24 fps. This group, formed from the remnants of the Death to the Pig Nihilist Film Kollective (described as a "doomed attempt to live out the metaphor of movie camera as weapon"), incorporates the concept into their manifesto: "A camera is a gun. An image taken is a death performed. Images put together are the substructure of an afterlife and a Judgement" (197). What the collective misunderstood, however—what doomed it to failure—was that these metaphysics of the image do not account for the image's material (or, rather, immaterial) properties; in any sense that an image can be "taken" and made revolutionary, it can also be taken back. Which is exactly what happens: the power of 24 fps's images is co-opted by precisely the hegemonic force they're trying to fight, as Brock Vond first appropriates copies of their footage and then gradually begins directing Frenesi on what to shoot. And then, finally, fatally, *whom* to shoot. Brock, in persuading Frenesi that her colleague Weed Atman must be killed, plays on her conviction of the interrelationship of camera and gun. When she protests, saying, "I can't bring a gun in the house," Brock counters: "But you can bring a camera. Can't you see, the two separate worlds—one always includes a camera somewhere, and the other always includes a gun, one is make-believe, the other real? What if this is some branch point in your life, where you'll have to choose between worlds?" (241). Brock thus counters Frenesi's fears of the gun with her comfort with a camera, finally convincing her that the two are mirror images of one another, and that the gun is real, while the camera is mere reflection.

In rendering the scene of the Kennedy assassination in *Libra*, DeLillo repeatedly cuts back and forth between these two vantage points, that of the man (men, that is) with the gun(s) and that of the onlookers, the picture takers, the people with cameras. In these images, as in the Zapruder film, the inevitable connection of the two kinds of shooting is made evident, mushrooming outward into not only a regress of watching, as in the scene of the Most Photographed Barn in America, but an infinite regress of violence:

> A woman with a camera turned and saw that she was being photographed. A woman in a dark coat was aiming a Polaroid right at her. It was only then she realized she'd just seen someone shot in her own viewfinder. There was bloodspray on her face and arms. She thought, how strange, that the woman in the coat was her and she was the person who was shot. She felt so dazed and strange, with pale spray all over her. She sat down carefully on the grass. Just let herself down and sat there. The woman with the Polaroid didn't move. The first woman sat on the grass, put her own camera down, looked at the colorless stuff on her arms. Pigeons spinning at the treetops. If she was shot, she thought, she ought to be sitting down. (401)

The woman's response does not simply enact a kind of dissociation in response to the unreality of the moment; it also betrays the glimmering awareness of the relationship of camera and gun.[26] Having taken a picture of someone who was in the process of the taking—"in her own viewfinder"—struck with a bullet, then on turning to find herself being photographed, the conclusion that she has been shot as well makes the kind of sense that the spectacle encourages: shooting is shooting, with whatever weapon. In this sense, the liminal space between Baudrillard's disappearing profound reality and the images that are overtaking it is the space in which the image and the bullet become one.

Throughout *Libra*, the reader is given the hazy sense that the bloody end of the novel's rendition of the Kennedy assassination comes about precisely because of the tenuousness of the distinction between image and reality in the cold war. The plot that spins out of control in the novel—the second time in

DeLillo's work that we are reminded of the "tendency of plots to move toward death" (221)[27]—is not a conspiracy to assassinate the president, but a conspiracy to commit the *image* of the president's assassination, a mere attempt on his life, a "spectacular miss" (51) that would have the effect of galvanizing the administration and its secret operatives into direct action against Cuba. "We want to set up an event that will make it *appear* they have struck at the heart of our government" (27, emphasis mine), Win Everett tells his supporters in setting the plot in motion. What goes wrong is not simply indicative of the secret life of plots in contemporary culture, but also the secret life of images; in their representations, both are uncontrollable, both are agents of death. In attempting to create an appearance, Everett unwittingly unleashes the image's violence on reality.

By the time of *Mao II*, the relationship described between the spectacle and violence has become more literal, as terror is conducted in no small part through its representations. As George Haddad, the political scientist spokesperson for the novel's terrorists suggests, the point of terror is the spectacle it creates and the attention that spectacle draws: "The more heartless, the more visible" (158). The point of kidnappings such as are enacted in the novel, the point of murders, is the images that can result from them; as Haddad tells Bill Gray, on suggesting that he might be used to take the place of the current hostage, such an exchange would enable the kidnappers to "[g]ain the maximum attention. Then probably kill you ten minutes later. Then photograph your corpse and keep the picture handy for the time when it can be used most effectively." Bill's print-oriented obsessions, however, lead him to miss the point: "Doesn't he think I'm worth more than my photograph?" (164), he asks, failing to understand that, for Abu Rashid (as, one might speculate, for Brita, who suggests early in the novel that "[t]he writer's face is the surface of the work" [26]), Bill's picture is worth all of the words he could possibly write. The picture is the act of terror, with a claim to visibility both literal and metaphoric that the writer, and his product, can never match.

Throughout *Mao II* these images of violence are replicated, most channeled through the television and its closest viewer, Karen. These images, as I discuss in the next chapter, are largely those of mass death, mass hysteria, mass destruction: the Sheffield soccer-stadium riot, the crushing of the revolt in Tiananmen Square, the Ayatollah Khomeini's funeral.[28] Karen watches these images in a most literal sense; she leaves the sound on her set off and relies wholly upon its visuals: "It was interesting how you could make up the news as you went along by sticking to picture only" (32), she thinks. But her interaction with these images is not really an invention of the news of the day; it is, rather, a merging with their violence on a visceral level. Such is her experience of photography, as well; she looks through books of photographs in Brita's loft, "amazed at the suffering she found. Famine, fire, riot, war. These were the never-ceasing subjects." The photographs, in fact, threaten to "overwhelm her" (174), a danger from which she is saved only by their contextualizing captions. The images themselves, in both photographs and television broadcasts, produce a horror that seems to absorb her:

> There were times she became lost in the dusty light, observing some survivor of a national news disaster, there's the lonely fuselage smoking in a field, and she was able to study the face and shade into it at the same time, even sneak a half second ahead, inferring the strange dazed grin or gesturing hand, which made her seem involved not just in the coverage but in the terror that came blowing through the fog. (117)

By novel's end, however, after being exposed to the unmediated spectacle of human suffering in Tompkins Square Park, Karen begins to speculate that, if she is so drawn in, so involved in the images of violence, maybe others are as well. Watching the funeral of the Ayatollah Khomeini, she wonders whether, "[i]f other people watched, if millions watched, if these millions matched the number on the Iranian plain, doesn't it mean we share something with the mourners, know an anguish, feel something pass between us, hear the sigh of some historic grief?" (*MII* 191). In this connection experienced between those watching and those watched, in the sympathies thus created, might perhaps lie an end to the violence.[29]

This vision of unity through watching is undermined by the novel, however, in two regards. First, this moment immediately precedes Karen's return to preaching the Moonie gospel and is thus posed as a sign not of a radical interconnectedness with the world but of a misguided evacuation of self. And second, the novel demonstrates repeatedly, through its orientalized images of otherness, the ways that such watching functions not to create intersubjective understanding but to heighten the divisions between individuals and their worldviews. As Karen's father notes during the mass wedding at Yankee Stadium, "I see a lot of faces that don't look American" (*MII* 5), thus suggesting that the unions these marriages will create cannot ultimately compete with the divisions of racial and national difference. That Karen later tells Brita that the marriages were arranged entirely via images—"The day before the ceremony Master had looked at photographs of members and he actually matched us by photograph. So I thought how great, I have an Instamatic husband" (183)—

only exacerbates the difficulty for the novel of imagining unity through spectacle: human difference is first apprehended visually, and the objectifying force of the photograph and other such visual technologies serve to reify those differences.

Such a link between visuality and the xenophobic sense of a dangerous otherness plays a key, if underconsidered, role in *White Noise*.[30] The novel's title concept is most commonly read as a representation of the static created in contemporary U.S. life by technology, primarily in terms of the electronic media that pervade the novel, endlessly intruding upon its action, a broadcast hum that serves as another "airborne toxic event" at the novel's center. This is the reading on the surface of the anxiety of obsolescence, which suggests that some essential element of our human nature is under constant assault by the images and technologies of late twentieth-century electronic life. But the repeated surfacing of a set of repressed anxieties about race and ethnicity in the novel suggest that this "white noise" may be fruitfully read as the noise, just out of the range of conscious hearing, made by the novel's white males as they are surrounded and displaced by members of other races.[31]

This noise largely comes from Jack Gladney, whose self-proclaimed "invention" of Hitler studies in March 1968 points directly to this sense of the dominant white male under siege: at a moment filled with the possibility of genuine social change, manifested in the United States in the civil rights movement, Jack retrenches himself in the most virulent forms of white supremacy.[32] This shocking representation of what would in the early 1990s have been labeled "white male anger" is of course a backlash against the changes produced by identity politics, and is thus wholly symptomatic of the time: March 1968 was the center of the Prague Spring; in five months, Soviet tanks would roll through the streets of Czechoslovakia. Just as Stalin moved in this historical moment to reign in a freedom that posed a threat to Soviet order and control, so Jack's specific turn to Hitler is an unavoidable echo of a specific type of European imperial domination, a reassertion of hegemony through military invasion and genocide. But perhaps more pointedly, given the too-apparent nature of the identity politics being asserted in presenting Hitler as an image of white male protest, in March 1968 the country was less than a month away from the assassination of Martin Luther King, Jr., one attempt at the reassertion of hegemonic control over the discourses of race in the United States. Jack, perhaps unconsciously, frames the very nature of his turn to Hitler during the "airborne toxic event," when he follows closely behind a pickup truck with extremist bumper stickers: "In situations like this," he helpfully advises, "you want to stick close to people in right-wing fringe groups. They've practiced staying alive" (*WN* 157). This desire to "stay alive" is an unspoken motive of Jack's turn to Hitler in 1968, and thus, unavoidably, questions of race, ethnicity, and domination become the subtext of the novel.

These questions of race and ethnicity in *White Noise* manifest themselves as a morbid curiosity on Jack's part about the ethnic backgrounds of those he sees around him. Many of the characters he meets throughout the novel appear "foreign" to him in some undefined sense, and thus become not only the object of speculation about their origins, but also the locus of some vaguely sensed threat. He feels this threat emanating, for instance, from the Sentra-driving "middle-aged Iranian" who delivers his newspaper, though he tries to discount his fears, claiming that it's the car that makes him nervous: "I tell myself I have reached an age, the age of unreliable menace" (184). The deliberate inscrutability of this comment points precisely to the gentility of Jack's racism: on the one hand, it sounds as though he is willing to admit that his sense of "menace" is "unreliable," that, given *his* age, it arises from an inanimate object, that any threat is his own paranoid construction. On the other hand, the newspaper-delivery man seems himself, in Jack's eyes, to represent an unreliable menace; given *this* age, an Iranian driving a Japanese car, delivering a U.S. newspaper, produces a threat that cannot be pinned down.

Pinning down the nature of the threat, and thus the nature of the other, is one of Jack's central preoccupations. The threat, for Jack, can potentially be read through the visual characteristics of the other. As he thinks to himself upon finally meeting Willie Mink, a.k.a. "Mr. Gray," whose indeterminate ethnicity makes his pseudonym appear all too appropriate: "His nose was flat, his skin the color of a Planter's peanut. What is the geography of a spoon-shaped face? Was he Melanesian, Polynesian, Indonesian, Nepalese, Surinamese, Dutch-Chinese? Was he a composite?" (*WN* 307). The shape of Mr. Gray's nose and the color of his skin combine for Jack into a full-fledged but undefined "geography" that foments in him a desperate need to locate, pin down, and contain. "Asian" more generally thus becomes a threat, one that must be controlled by being exoticized. The other option is the complete reification of "Asianness" itself as a quality that wholly defines the outlines of the individual in question, as seen in one of the novel's many grocery-store encounters:

> The woman waved at Babette and headed toward us. She lived on our street with a teenage daughter and an Asian baby, Chun Duc. Everyone referred to the baby by name, almost in a tone of proud proprietorship, but no one knew who Chun belonged to or where he or she had come from. (39)

Asianness is here nonthreatening, at least in part because the subject in question is literally an infant. But the baby's ethnicity, as represented by its name, is something to be owned, something toward which the adults of Jack's neighborhood can behave in a fashion that masks its orientalizing tone with broadmindedness. And that ethnicity is acceptable, on some level, because it is the baby's only aspect; no one knows where the baby "belongs" (clearly not here), where it came from (ditto), or even, apparently, whether it's a boy or a girl. Otherness is in this case something to be proud of, but only insofar as it has been purchased and displayed in a wholly white context.

That there remains a clear connection between these racialized concerns and the more apparent concerns about the media in the novel—and thus that the media provides an ideal location for burying the novel's fears about race and ethnicity—is suggested in a conversation between Jack and his stepdaughter Denise, who wants to know why he named his son Heinrich. Jack first claims that Heinrich was born just after he'd started the department of Hitler studies, and thus that "a gesture was called for." He then admits that he thought the name "forceful," that it might help make his son "unafraid":

> "There's something about German names, the German language, German *things*. I don't know what it is exactly. It's just there. In the middle of it all is Hitler, of course."
> "He was on again last night."
> "He's always on. We couldn't have television without him." (*WN* 63)

Hitler—and thus the most virulent form of ethnocentric violence—is at the heart of the electronic media and its participation in images of terror; television, as the primary purveyor of the dominant ideology, carries his message of whiteness and maleness twenty-four hours a day. But it is important to note that, for Jack, who ordinarily locates his "outer torment" in the television set, Hitler somehow justifies television's existence. Hitler makes it possible for the novel's characters to blame their "fears and secret desires" (*WN* 85) on television, rather than being forced to acknowledge their difficult, often inappropriate origins in human difference.

But the particular nature of the connection between the anxiety of obsolescence—in this case both the obsolescence of the white male in the face of this ethnic onslaught and the obsolescence of the writer in the age of the image—and Jack's obsession with race and ethnicity becomes especially clear when he meets his son's friend Orest:

> What kind of name is Orest? I studied his features. He might have been Hispanic, Middle Eastern, Central Asian, a dark-skinned Eastern-European, a light-skinned black. Did he have an accent? I wasn't sure. Was he a Samoan, a native North American, a Sephardic Jew? It was getting hard to know what you couldn't say to people. (*WN* 208)

This suggests another threat that lurks in visually perceived but uncontained otherness: not knowing what you can't say to someone of indeterminate ethnicity—the assumption being that what Jack would say might cause offense. This concern might not be based on the desire to make a racist remark, but instead might derive from the fear of "accidentally" saying something offensive. In either case, Jack feels the need to guard his words, a stifling of language that adds to the sense that visuality, and in this case, visually perceived human difference, is among the forces undermining the power of verbal representation.

The realm of the visual, then, is accused of doing violence both to cultural systems of representation and to the culture's sense of the human, making such desires to visually categorize and classify people inevitable. The supposed inevitability of this desire to classify serves, however, as a foil for an underlying desire to retain the privilege of whiteness. Of course, as Richard Dyer points out, the visual perception of difference works only through the suppression of whiteness's visuality: "We are seen, we do not (and could not possibly) actually inhabit the realm of the unseen, observing subject without properties—but because we are seen as white, we characteristically see ourselves and believe ourselves seen as unmarked, unspecific, universal" (45). This belief in the unmarked status of whiteness results in an appropriation of the powers of looking by the white subject; the unmarked universal functions to control the process of marking itself. Thus, in *Mao II*, some part of the image's violence arises from its attempts to mark the other as other, to reify difference as dangerous.[33] But there is also a countertendency glimpsed in *White Noise*, in which television's distribution of images makes whiteness itself visible. In Jack's confrontation with Willie Mink, for instance, Mink is able to call attention to what is otherwise suppressed:

> I took another step toward the middle of the room. As the TV picture jumped, wobbled, caught itself in snarls, Mink appeared to grow more vivid. The precise nature of events. Things in their actual state. Eventually he worked himself out of the deep fold, rising nicely, sharply outlined against the busy air. White noise everywhere.
> "Containing iron, niacin and riboflavin. I learned my English in air-

planes. It's the international language of aviation. Why are you here, white man?"

"To buy."

"You are very white, you know that?"

"It's because I'm dying." (310)

Mink, as I explore further in the next section, is too intimately connected with the television set, drawing a kind of life from its images, which (along with Jack's visual assessment of his face) deepens the sense of his otherness in this scene. Despite Jack's own assumption of a kind of otherness—in which it is suggested that he has only become "visible" because he is dying—Mink's ability to see his whiteness has deeper implications. From the vantage point of his marginalization, usually relegated to the watched and not permitted to be the watcher, and from his resulting understanding of the image's manipulations, Mink is able to comment on the novel's very suppressions.

The link, then, between the spectacle and violence may not be inevitable, because such a connection requires a particular viewing position for it to be complete. In this manner, in *Mao II*, while Karen's father can see only "faces that don't look American" (5), Karen is able to envision a bond of understanding between those watching and those watched. But these representations repeatedly suggest that the possibility of an intersubjective viewpoint, one that evades the hegemonic determination of the image, requires the subject's own partial erasure—by the processes of the media, in the case of Mink; by the mass consciousness of the cult, in Karen's case. Without that erasure, it seems, the viewer is always led to identify with the objectifying perspective of the camera—the camera that bears such a resemblance to the gun.[34]

At the end of *Mao II*, however, we return to Brita, agent of the image's spread. With her turn from reifying the writer into commodity form to thinking about bomb makers and gunmen, one wonders if her photographs will similarly defuse their cultural influence, removing them from the real and absorbing them into a specular realm. There is some evidence to suggest that it may; upon Brita's arrival in Beirut, her cab driver informs her that two rival militias have taken to "firing at portraits of each other's leader," a new form of warfare that has resulted in a "new exuberance" (227) among the fighters. Such a turn of events suggests that, if images are a kind of violence, they may also be able to channel violence by diverting *everyone's* attention from the real. On the one hand, there's a perverse sort of optimism in this suggestion, which hints that the photographer at work on the "dead city" may in fact contribute to its continued life by containing its destruction on film. On the other hand, there is simultaneously the sense of another threshold being crossed, of a much deeper destruction of the real, in which the image so effaces the real that, paradoxically, it becomes the real.

Cable Nature

This sense in which the image takes over the space of the real, giving rise to a Baudrillardian hyperreal, returns us at last to DeLillo's *Americana* and David Bell, sitting mere inches from his television set, meshing with the image's "stormy motes." David's merger with this image, while conveying a mistaken sense of the image's material existence, nonetheless exposes the core of its psychic existence; David's reality is comprised of images, images that do not represent but rather create the real. David's existence is early suggested to be wholly specular, as he relies upon images and reflections for his sense of self: "I had almost the same kind of relationship with my mirror that many of my contemporaries had with their analysts" (11). In understanding his core self, that which can ordinarily be accessed only through psychoanalysis, to exist instead on the surface of his reflection, David acknowledges that his reality is tenuous, at best. "There were times," he admits, "when I thought all of us at the network existed only on videotape. . . . And there was the feeling that somebody's deadly pinky might nudge a button and we would all be erased forever" (23). Such is the situation in a culture literally driven by television: reality, constructed by images, becomes infinitely mutable, even erasable. The desire for merger with the televisual image suggests at the same time the erasure of any phenomenal real that exists outside the videotape and a longing for a more permanent existence in the new real constructed by images.

David's desire for full entry into the hyperreal begins not with his job at the television network but with his youthful fascination with film, and particularly with the screen personas of those "American pyramids" (*A* 12), Kirk Douglas and Burt Lancaster. In watching them, David first comes to awareness of the greater "reality" to be found in an abandonment of the physical world and an entry into the spectacular: "I knew I must extend myself until the molecules parted and I was spliced into the image." The result of this desire is at once an existence as the reflection of a nonexistent celebrity—it is not an unusual event when David is approached on the street by a girl asking for his autograph, saying that "I don't know who you are . . . but I'm sure you must be somebody" (13)—and unanswerable doubts about the reality of the rest of the world. David thus achieves what the novel refers to as "the dream of entering the third person singular" (270), becoming, in his relationship with the image, "Bell looking at the poster of Belmondo looking at the poster of purposeful Bogart" (287).[35] His life is "an image made in the image and likeness of images" (130). But, on driving through the "country roads" of Connecticut—a suspect characterization of the area, already—he cannot help but "wonder how real the landscape truly was, and how much of a dream is a dream" (13). When images are more real than the real, when the real is paradoxically constructed of images, such questions become all but impossible to answer.

David's quest in the second half of *Americana* is to recover some sense of a real that exists outside the image, the "diminishing world outside the tape" that DeLillo claims the novel attempts to recapture ("Power" 63). The problem, however, is that David, so entrenched in the spectacle, attempts to encounter this real America by capturing it on film, thus creating yet another set of images that construct rather than represent reality. This problem first arises in the suggestion that David might not be able to tell the difference; he describes the town he grew up in, after all, as "American in our outlook, plain and meat-eating," before acknowledging that the town's inhabitants were "willing to die for our country, or for photographs of our country" (*A* 132). The implication is of course that the photographs *are* the country, or what sense of it the inhabitants have, which amounts to the same thing. Thus, when David emerges from the enclosure of New York into the openness of the West, it is first and foremost an image of the West that he finds, one created by its representations. Moreover, all the inhabitants of this America seem to acknowledge their image-oriented existence through their fascination with its apparatus. David merely "clutched the handgrip, rested the camera on my right shoulder, and walked through the quiet streets"; the presence of the camera galvanizes the town's inhabitants, and "[s]oon a small crowd was following [him]" (210). In fact, every time the camera is visible, all attention is directed toward it; local folk ask questions about it (211), ask for advice about their own camera purchases (212), ask how the apparatus works (215), and ask about David's relationship to it (213). Women in a supermarket parking lot wave to it, sensing perhaps that

> they were waving at themselves, waving in the hope that someday if evidence is demanded of their passage through time, demanded by their own doubts, a moment might be recalled when they stood in a dazzling plaza in the sun and were registered on the transparent plastic ribbon; and thirty years away, on that day when proof is needed, it could be hoped that their film is being projected on a screen somewhere, and there they stand, verified, in chemical

reincarnation, waving at their own old age, smiling their reassurance to the decades, a race of eternal pilgrims in a marketplace in the dusty sunlight, seven arms extended in a fabulous salute to the forgetfulness of being. (254)

Like David, then, these women seem to understand their lives to be verified only by images, which are somehow more real than they. Douglas Keesey points out in this moment that such an existence in relationship to the camera results in a deep disconnection from the self; "you are not yourself in space or time." However, it is important to note that Keesey reads this moment as describing "a group of young women outside a supermarket waving at TV cameras" and suggests that David in this moment comes to an awareness of his own disconnection from the space and time he occupies (17). I argue something slightly different, based on the evidence that the camera that the women are waving at is not from some unknown television station, but David's own Scoopic: his discovery is not of his own disconnection, but rather of his control as the image's creator, for he acknowledges at the end of the passage: "I could not help feeling that what I was discovering here was power of a sort" (*A* 255). Moreover, given that the Scoopic is not actually running, the suggestion is that the power of the image is such that even the *image* of the image is sufficient to construct the U.S. sense of self.

David's attempts to escape the image thus result only in its deeper entrenchment in his sense of the real. The violence of the latter part of his journey makes clear to him that all that exists of America is in fact composed of its "archetypes," that everything he confronts is built of "images that could not be certain which of two confusions held less terror, their own or what their own might become if it ever faced the truth." David fully reenters the hyperreal on board a flight back to New York, when he is once again assumed to be a celebrity: "Ten minutes after we were airborne," the novel's final line reads, "a woman asked for my autograph" (*A* 377). Moreover, while the novel ends on that flight, David's own chronology does not; he narrates the novel from a remote desert island—to which he has brought the film of his journey into America, which he watches obsessively. His representation for us, then, of the life lived within the novel, is constructed from the images he captured in his attempt to find the real that exists behind the screen's simulations.

That there may in fact no longer be such a real is a recurrent motif in DeLillo's fiction. Throughout, we find a trend toward simulation, in which representations, particularly images, take precedence over the objects they are ostensibly there to represent. Perhaps the most often noted evidence of such an interest in simulation is *White Noise*'s SIMUVAC, a group that ostensibly uses disaster simulations to prepare for real emergencies, but instead uses the airborne toxic event as preparation for future simulations.[36] When Jack asks a SIMUVAC representative how the actual evacuation as a "form of practice" is going, the answer is appropriately silly: "The insertion curve isn't as smooth as we would like. There's a probability excess. Plus which we don't have our victims laid out where we'd want them if this was an actual simulation. In other words we're forced to take our victims as we find them" (139). The ludicrousness of such a contortion of the relationship between representations and reality is apparent even to Jack, who is normally inured to such displays. The shock of discovering the event that may in fact kill him treated as a simulation of a simulation awakens him to the fundamental unreality of the world in which he lives. Upon encountering another SIMUVAC volunteer during an actual simulation, Jack turns snarky: "Are you people sure you're ready for a simulation? You may want to wait for one more massive spill. Get your timing down" (204). In a culture in which an actual event becomes less real than the simulation of that event, as Baudrillard suggests, images no longer bear a relationship to representation; instead, images become images of themselves.

Television is, in *White Noise*, particularly responsible for such simulation. As one of the novel's many media non sequiturs announces—one of the most prevalent forms of "white noise" in the text—television now channels to its viewers all the reality they could need: "CABLE HEALTH, CABLE WEATHER, CABLE NEWS, CABLE NATURE" (231). This "cable nature," whether images of a fast-receding undeveloped world or images of an equally fast-receding unmediated human essence, is more than anything the nature of cable: unlimited mediation, with round-the-clock access.[37] Just as cable opens the U.S. home to the onslaught of such representations, such that the images replace the reality they ostensibly represent, however, so another of the novel's mediating technologies opens the human psyche to the influence of such images: Dylar. Jack's fervent quest for the drug, produced by his painful encounter with the reality of his own potential death, comprises much of the last third of the novel. Dylar ostensibly interacts with the part of the brain responsible for the fear of death, easing this obsession. Beyond the drug, which is of course a feat of psychobiology, the tablet itself is "an interesting piece of technology" (187), according to Winnie Richards, the scientist Jack persuades to analyze it. The tablet is encased in a polymer membrane with one small laser-drilled hole, through which the drug seeps at a controlled rate; once the membrane has emptied, it "implodes minutely of its own massive gravitation" (188). Plastics, lasers, particle physics—Dylar is much more than a pharmaceutical breakthrough.

It is a constructed world in which the fear of death is relieved in controlled, even dosage. "Technology with a human face" (211), Jack claims, not terribly unlike cable nature.

Of course, like all technology, Dylar is not without its consequences, side effects that have caused it to be turned down for human trials. The part of the brain responsible for the fear of death is somehow also connected to the interpretation and understanding of language; as Babette says hypothetically, in recounting the drug's list of potential problems: "I could not distinguish words from things, so that if someone said 'speeding bullet,' I would fall to the floor and take cover" (*WN* 193). There is, in this linguistic disruption, an echo of the unnamed drug Bucky Wunderlick is first asked to hold and then dosed with by the Happy Valley Farm Commune in DeLillo's *Great Jones Street*. As it is described to Bucky just before he is injected, the drug, ostensibly developed by the U.S. government, "affects one or more areas of the left sector of the brain. Language sector. Still no market for this product. Street or otherwise. It damages the cells in one or more areas of the left sector of the human brain. Loss of speech in other words" (255). Critic Michael Valdez Moses compares the interactions of these two drugs, claiming that both promise "to return human beings to a blissful but subhuman state, free of either logos or the knowledge of personal finitude" (76); I suggest that Dylar has a very different function from Happy Valley's drug, and that this difference is what creates its "market." While the drug in *Great Jones Street* frees the subject from logos, eliminating the possibility of communication (see LeClair 100), Dylar in *White Noise* sets language itself adrift from meaning, eliminating not the signifying process but the distinctions between signs and referents. In this fashion the subject is not freed from logos but trapped within it, in an endless chain of signification that transforms the individual into the ideal television watcher. With this modification, a market is created for the drug at last.

The deep interconnection of language and the knowledge of death suggests that Dylar affects the nature of the human by changing its relationship to systems of representation. Such a conclusion can be read in the behavior of Willie Mink, *White Noise*'s most extreme representation of Dylar's side effects. Mink's dysphasia, the reader is quickly shown, is bound up in a too close relationship with television. Jack has, in the novel's penultimate sequence, at last discovered the identity and whereabouts of "Mr. Gray," the semi-anonymous man to whom Babette offered her body in exchange for Dylar. By the time Gladney finds Mink, carrying out a plot that is half revenge driven, the jealous husband out for justice, and half a quest for Dylar, the psychopharmaceutical grail, Mink has vastly overdosed on the drug. Throughout the scene, he randomly flings handsful of the tablets in the general direction of his mouth. Jack, out of curiosity, checks to see how the dysphasic effect is operating on Mink:

> I said, as a test, "Falling plane."
>
> He looked at me, gripping the arms of the chair, the first signs of panic building in his eyes.
>
> "Plunging aircraft," I said, pronouncing the words crisply, authoritatively.
>
> He kicked off his sandals, folded himself over into the recommended crash position, head well forward, hands clasped behind his knees. He performed the maneuver automatically, with a double-jointed collapsible dexterity, throwing himself into it, like a child or a mime. Interesting. The drug not only caused the user to confuse words with the things they referred to; it made him act in a somewhat stylized way. (309–10)

Dylar's technology has thus not only interfered with Mink's linguistic abilities, the power of differentiating between signs and referents, but also has made his actions "stylized," somehow inhuman. Jack's initial assessment, that Mink is acting "like a child or a mime," doesn't quite hit the mark, however; Mink is acting, rather, like he is *acting*. He may not be able to distinguish the words "falling plane" from the thing itself, but his response exists similarly on the level of simulation, an imitation of a *representation* of the human response to a plummeting aircraft, with none of the screaming, vomit, or blood of the novel's earlier near crash outside Iron City.[38] This response is thus doubly removed from reality—by the interference of televisual images of such crash positions, and by the destruction of the referentiality of language.

In erasing the fear of death, in fact, and in interfering with human linguistic abilities, Dylar seems to open the subject to "cable nature," making Mink, in this case, completely available to televisual suggestion and control. Mink's speech is peppered with bits of chatter from the television he is watching; for instance, as he explains Dylar's failure to Jack, he says, "The heat from your hand will actually make the gold-leafing stick to the wax paper" (*WN* 308), precisely the sort of non sequitur that has emanated from the television in Jack's house throughout the novel. Mink's speech has become infected by television's white noise; his actions are merely representations of human actions. The part of the brain responsible for the fear of death, which is also responsible for the linguistic separation of signs and referents, is apparently the locus as well of the ability to keep one's real ego separate from television's simulations.

The televisual spectacle, then, threatens disruption in the novel by erasing human access to the real through its objectifications, by replacing human knowledge of the real through its simulations, and by doing violence both to the nature of the human and to the processes of linguistic signification. The novel repeatedly proposes to rescue the reader (and, again, academic culture) from these threats by capturing and containing them in the novel's own language. In *White Noise*'s Willie Mink, as in *Mao II*'s Karen, however, we see a further kind of violence done by television: the decomposition of the ego into a radically fragmented, hivelike sense of self. In the multiplicity of television's voices, both its manifold interconnections and its teeming information, the novel imagines a further threat: the replacement of the individual with the mass-think of the network.

4

Network

> Everything is connected, but some
> things are more connected than
> others.
>
> —Howard Pattee

Fergus Mixolydian in Pynchon's *V.* and David Bell in DeLillo's *Americana*, in their peculiar relationships to the television set, reveal the anxieties about mechanicity and visuality explored in the novel of obsolescence; each allows the novelist room to explore the putative threat that television presents to the novel's future, while simultaneously valorizing the novel for its resistance to these dehumanizing and derealizing trends. Each allows the novelist to create for himself a protected space, and for the novel an elite status, that both belies the obsolescence he ostensibly fears and reveals a longing for a return of the form and its producer to both cultural and social centrality. But these two representations—Fergus with his sleep switch, and David with his stormy motes—each reveal a third area of concern in addition to those of the machine and the spectacle. Each is fundamentally concerned with interconnection—Fergus's literal, a physical wiring-in, and David's more figurative, an electronic mating of molecules. And in each of these moments comes an experience of unconsciousness, as Fergus operates the set by "drop[ping] below a certain level of awareness" (*V.* 56), and David's glance at the screen causes him to "find" himself in a chair in front of the set. The danger presented by this abandonment of the conscious self reveals writerly anxieties about such interconnection. What is on the other end of the television that Fergus and David connect themselves to? In which direction does television's networked control operate? And, having hooked into the network, are Fergus and David still themselves, or are they dissolving into something else, some identityless collective unconscious?

Such anxious questions throughout the writing of both Pynchon and

DeLillo about television's literal and figurative interconnections—between programmers and sets, among sets, and among individuals watching those sets—or what I am loosely calling the "network," shift the focus of this exploration from mechanicity and visuality to information, from the machines themselves and the images they convey to the wiring that connects them, and the impulses, both electronic and cultural, that those wires carry. This set of interconnections among individuals and across spaces by which electronic communication takes place—telegraph, telephone, radio, television networks, and the contemporary network of all networks, the Internet—has itself produced anxieties in the postmodern writing subject, visible, like the fears of the destruction of humanity by the machine and the destruction of language by the image, in the postmodern novel. Among these anxieties I include, and in this chapter explore, fears about the difficulties of communication within the increasing volume of information; fears about the entropic devolution of organization into chaos and the parallel emergence of a new, dangerous order from that chaos; and fears about the disappearance of the individual as he or she is wired into a potentially fascistic mass. In exploring these related fears, I draw upon recent work in the appropriately interconnected fields of information theory, systems theory, cybernetics, and theories of chaos and emergence; the efflorescence of such interest in the possibilities and the consequences of interconnection reveals that the network, like the machine and the spectacle, forms a peculiar point of pressure within contemporary academic, popular, and literary discourses, discourses that seem to point to the obsolescence of the novel. Kevin Kelly suggests, echoing Alan Kay, that

> the personally owned book was one of the chief shapers of the Renaissance notion of the individual, and that pervasively networked computers will be the main shaper of humans in the future. It's not just individual books we are leaving behind, either. Global opinion polling in realtime 24 hours a day, seven days a week, ubiquitous telephones, asynchronous e-mail, 500 TV channels, video on demand: all these add up to the matrix for a glorious network culture, a remarkable hivelike being. (28)

The shift from book to computer (via television) in this somewhat ecstatic rendering, as well as in the more anxious descriptions by less technophilic cultural critics, thus bodes more than simply a change of medium. Sven Birkerts, for instance, argues that our current networked culture may be "the first stages of a process of social collectivization that will over time all but vanquish the ideal of the isolated individual" (130). Left unspoken is for whom isolation, or individualism, is allowed to be an ideal, but it is nonetheless evident that such resistance to network culture is in part a resistance to the shifting of social hierarchies that have long upheld the meritocratic archetype of the post-Renaissance subject. In the wiring together of a "hivelike" electronic being, the novel (and critic) of obsolescence suggests, U.S. culture is abandoning not simply the individual experience of reading, but the very possibility of individuality itself.

That the network is itself a technology suggests that it could be considered an extension of the mechanizing forces of television explored in Chapter 2. The network's interconnections, however, and the electrical impulses that it carries, fundamentally transform the stand-alone machine and thus justify its separation and consideration as a distinct category of televisuality. For, as Friedrich Kittler argues: "before the electrification of the media . . . there were modest, *merely mechanical* apparatuses. These apparatuses could neither amplify nor transmit" (103, emphasis mine). Nor could they store information. But the electrical development of storage, amplification, and—most important for our purposes—transmission fundamentally changed the nature of communication, with profound implications for earlier mechanical technologies, including print. Where once these technologies maintained a power to surprise, to excite the imagination, "[e]lectricity itself has brought this to an end. If memories and dreams, the dead and the specters have become technically reproducible, then the hallucinatory power of reading and writing has become obsolete" (Kittler 110). Obsolescence—that terrifying concept for the contemporary writer—thus counts among its origins electricity itself, the wiring of the nation. McLuhan, of course, reads this wiring as an "outering" of the central nervous system, sending commands through the body public.[1] While Kittler concentrates in his essay on the development of the storage capabilities of the earlier mechanical apparatuses via their mating with electricity, his gramophone, film, and typewriter also have their "networked," transmitting equivalents in—and indeed, in McLuhan's sense, are the "content" of—radio, television, and the Internet.[2]

These broadcasting networks—in addition to the narrowcasting networks of telephone and telegraph—are the specific development of the integration of electricity and information. The network is not simply a machine but an interconnection of machines, its signals a language whereby transmitters speak to receivers. The interpretation and implementation of that language were explored in its early days by a number of related sciences: information theory, arising from mathematics; communications theory, derived from the social sciences; and, most notably, cybernetics, which brought the two fields together into a new discipline. Under the guidance of theorists such as Norbert Wiener and Gregory Bateson, cybernetics sought to translate the processes of communication into information, thereby creating a transparent mode of "communication and control" of machines.[3] As John Johnston argues, however, this early belief in transparency was rapidly undermined by the difficulty of defining "information" itself, producing "fruitful ambiguities and contradictions that later led theorists beyond these instrumentalist applications toward new visions of complexity, as in the study of self-organizing, or emergent, systems and chaos theory" (2). The shift from cybernetics to systems theory, and on to chaos theory, reveals a recognition of the complexity introduced by the network that makes its precise control impossible. In place of the technics of control, more contemporary researchers focus on interaction, organization, and change within dynamic, multiplicitous systems.[4]

What I am calling the "network" in this chapter bears something in common with what Tom LeClair refers to as the "system" in his study of systems theory as it pertains to contemporary fiction, and particularly the novels of Don DeLillo. According to LeClair's history, however, systems theory, and thus the systems it studies, originates in the natural, and particularly the biological, sciences. While systems theory may be *used* to study the network that is imagined in the novel of obsolescence, the network itself is not a system in this sense; it is rather an unnatural imposition on natural systems. The danger these novels intimate that the network presents is thus not inherent in systems themselves but in the artificially interconnected and controlled designs of "systems planning" (DeLillo, *A* 252) and cybernetics. The complexities and ambiguities of the network for writers such as Pynchon and DeLillo suggest less that the network is an emergent, potentially living form of organization than that the network may be prone to what LeClair refers to as "runaway," in which "positive feedback (which can be summed up as 'The more you have the more you get of the same') rules with no corrective, with no governor or negative feedback in the control loop. The result is eventual self-destruction of the system" (13). In a sense, then, the anxieties that I consider in this chapter—concerns about how and what the network communicates; concerns about how and what the network organizes; concerns about the network's mediation of the relationship between the individual and the mass—each has to do with the double-edged nature of "chaos" in contemporary culture, a concept suggesting alternately an entropic devolution of order into the random and meaningless and the spontaneous production of a finer and more pervasive form of order and meaning. Within the network's chaos, either nothing means or everything does; either one exists in a state of schizophrenia, surrounded, as Jameson would have it, by "a rubble of distinct and unrelated signifiers"

(26), or one is subsumed by paranoia, finding connections within and among everything.[5]

Anxieties about the network, then, reveal anxieties about the state of reading within a networked culture. In a world in which the relationship between signs and meanings has been disrupted by the irreconcilable, uncontrollable complexities of the network, the network appears not only to transmit messages but also to be a message itself, and in fact to have undermined the possibility of communication through an exponential increase in the number of messages. As a result, what the network communicates disappears within the process of that communication, and the medium truly becomes the message. Given the dominance and the pervasiveness of the network, paranoia becomes less a pathology than a reading strategy, a sense-making worldview, as the individual participant becomes a mere node on a system infinitely larger than himself that may allow for centralized, nefarious control of the individual, or may just as easily be radically decentralized and beyond any control.[6] Thus Lee Harvey Oswald, in DeLillo's *Libra*, watches two televised films about presidential assassinations and feels "connected to the events on the screen. It was like secret instructions entering the network of signals and broadcast bands, the whole busy air of transmission. . . . They were running a message through the night into his skin." Lee, paying attention to the connections rather than to the films themselves, knows with utter certainty that "[t]hey were running this thing just for him," that the network's controllers, whoever "they" may be, are capable of communicating directly with him through his connection to the network (370). What, exactly, "they" are trying to tell him is unclear; only the intent to communicate, the power of communication, and his absorption within it are certain.

Similarly, Hector Zuñiga in Pynchon's *Vineland* experiences a moment of extreme "Tubefreek" paranoia; while watching a late night television movie,

he saw the screen go blank, bright and prickly, and then heard voices hard, flat, echoing.

"But we don't actually have the orders yet," somebody said.

"It's only a detail," the other voice with a familiar weary edge, a service voice, "just like getting a search warrant." Onto the screen came some Anglo in fatigues, about Hector's age, sitting at a desk against a pale green wall under fluorescent light. He kept looking over to the side, off-camera.

"My name is—what should I say, just name and rank?"

"No names," the other advised.

The man was handed two pieces of paper clipped together, and he read it to the camera. "As commanding officer of state defense forces in this sector, pursuant to the President's NSDD #52 of 6 April 1984 as amended, I am authorized—what?" He started up, sat back down, went in some agitation for the desk drawer, which stuck, or had been locked. Which is when the movie came back on, and continued with no further military interruptions. (339–40)

This bit of anomalous intrusion into normal network programming may give Hector an accidental glimpse of the network's authority—or at least the network's potential for authoritative control—and thus may suggest an unseen order, a meaning in the network of which he was previously unaware. Or it may simply be a meaningless mistake bred out of the network's chaotic fragmentation, a random crossing of wires and no more. Hector, who is, as a Tubefreek, addicted to the "plug-in drug" and, as a DEA agent, aware of covert state maneuvering, opts for paranoia, associating this moment with "the classic chill" of secret operations, "the extra receptors up and humming, gathering in the signs, channels suddenly shutting down, traffic scrambled and jammed, phone trouble" and so on, all evidence that the network is the tool of state power, used not simply for transmitting information but also for gathering it (see Winn). This nervous sense of the multiple directions in which communication can run over the network gives this televisual moment its ultimate frisson: "As if the Tube were suddenly to stop showing pictures and instead announce, 'From now on, I'm watching you' " (*Vineland* 340).

In what follows, I investigate the connected ways in which Pynchon and DeLillo explore interconnection—Pynchon in extended fashion in *The Crying of Lot 49*; DeLillo more fragmentarily, in moments throughout *White Noise*, *Libra*, *Mao II*, and *Underworld*—thus unraveling the network of associations and representations by which the network is read as a threat to writing. First, the complexities and ambiguities of defining "information" within the network, and of determining how that information is transmitted and received, create a set of anxieties about communication and its potential for failure. If accurate and complete communication is impossible in network culture, might that impossibility have ramifications for print-based communication as well? Second, that these anxieties about communication arise from the inscrutable organization of the network itself, from the extreme multiplicity of its connections, highlights another area of concern: is the network's chaos a disintegration of order—entropy—or a complexity that masks a minute, even fractal, ubiquity of order that may spontaneously emerge into a new form of being? For that matter, is it possible to read the network sufficiently well to tell the difference? And third, in a fully networked culture in which chaos and emergence hold sway, is the individual threatened with extinction and replacement by an infinitely interconnected "hive mind"? If so, what will become of the "men in small rooms" to whom the novel is finally addressed?[7] Without these lone readers, can the novel as we know it, preeminent art form of the Enlightenment individual, survive?

Communication

For this study of the novel of obsolescence, the importance of information theory and the communications networks it conceptualizes begins with the fact that one of the early translations of cybernetics for the lay reader, Norbert Wiener's *The Human Use of Human Beings* (previously referenced with respect to the relationship of human and machine), informed Pynchon's exploration of these networks in *The Crying of Lot 49*.[8] The slight chill of Wiener's title— "use"?—echoes his functionalist treatment of communications networks and the individuals who connect to them: "In a certain sense," he claims, "all communications systems terminate in machines, but the ordinary language systems terminate in the special sort of machine known as a human being" (79). The interchangeable quality of human and machine in such networked situations indicates the significance of Wiener's importation of the principles of information theory to a broader conception of the network within cybernetics. This new field, as Wiener describes it, takes among its founding principles that the process of communication—between machines, between humans and machines, or between humans alone—is governed by general rules and involves generic messages, both discernable through careful study. Given the adequate control of those messages, and the sufficient understanding and implementation of those rules, the communication system in question could be used to control whatever "sort of machine" terminates the network, whether the mechanical type or the human type. Cybernetics from its earliest inception, then, imagined its sphere expanding beyond the realm of technology to influence social interaction.

The most basic requirement for such a discipline, which seeks to use control of the processes of communication to rationalize social interaction, is that it adequately define the concept of "information" itself.[9] In this seemingly small task, however, the early cybernetic theorists ran into an impasse. Claude Shannon in *The Mathematical Theory of Communication*, published in 1949 with his collaborator, Warren Weaver, created the field of information theory by suggesting that information is a mathematical quantity—not an index of meaning or signification, but "the probability of an encoded message in a communication channel" (Johnston 32).[10] Information, then, as Katherine Hayles

Figure 1: Schematic diagram of a general communication system

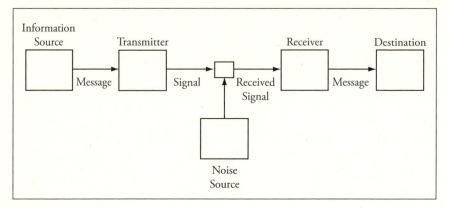

explores in *How We Became Posthuman*, was in this early moment equated with pattern rather than comprehensibility. Moreover, as John Johnston suggests, this definition of information, like Wiener's definition ("the content of what is exchanged with the outer world"), is wholly machinic, excluding from its purview the vagaries of human perception (see Johnston 32). In excluding both randomness and consciousness from these definitions, early information theorists and cyberneticists inadvertently drew attention to those categories, creating the ambiguities that would give rise to the next generation of systems and chaos theories: is there at times an invisible order in the apparently random? And can the observation of information ever take place outside the consciousness of the observer?

Such questions about the nature of what a communication system communicates, moreover, bled into similar questions about how such a system functions. Consider the model of the communications system developed by Shannon and Weaver, shown in Figure 1 (see Shannon and Weaver 34). In this model, an "information source" communicates with a "destination" via a transmitter and a receiver. The most significant aspect of this model for Shannon and Weaver's theory of communication is the distinction it draws between *signal* and *message*: the signal is the message's material, encoded form; only such a signal is communicable (see Hayles 18). The task of information theory is to determine, via a calculation of logarithmic probability, whether a message is contained within a received signal. The roadblock to such a determination in this model is noise, here represented by an external source of randomness that disrupts the signal's pattern. The questions that this model begs echo the questions raised by the mathematical definition of information. First, is noise genuinely external to the process of communication, separable from transmitter, receiver, and the signal that passes between them? Second, what are the roles of the information source and the destination in translating message into signal and back into message again? How might the roles of these observers alter the perception of the success of the communication system?

I pick up again the question of pattern, randomness, and noise later in this chapter in considering the network's organization. For the moment, I want to consider the effects of the human sources and interpreters of information, the consciousnesses left out of both this model of how the network communicates and what is communicated by it. Much of contemporary cultural studies, particularly as developed out of older sociological models of communication studies, focuses on this question of the human aspect of networked communication. Let us explore, for instance, the model of communication presented by Stuart Hall in his influential essay "Encoding/decoding" as reproduced in Figure 2 (see Hall 130). In this model, the sender, using both the cultural and symbolic knowledges to which he or she has access, "encodes" the message into the "meaning structure" traditional to the medium. The "message" thus encoded is then transmitted via the medium (in Hall's reference, primarily

Figure 2: Encoding/decoding

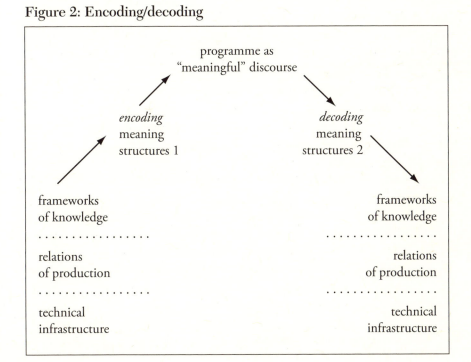

television, but Hall's model works generically) as a "programme" or other form of " 'meaningful' discourse." The receiver then takes the meaning structures gathered from the program and "decodes" them based on his or her own cultural and symbolic knowledges.

Where Shannon and Weaver erase human interaction from their communicative model, Hall erases the medium itself; but for the "technical infrastructure" implicated in the encoding and decoding processes, Hall's program flies mysteriously through space as an arrow. Despite their differences in emphasis, however, they agree on a fundamental point: both provide less for accurate communication than for distortion. The locus of that distortion in each model reflects its developer's particular concerns with communication; while Shannon and Weaver attribute this distortion to "noise" emptying from a third black box into the center of the network stream, Hall places the distortion in the origins and destinations of communicated messages, with the humans that encode and decode them. Hall takes great care to insist that the processes of encoding and decoding between the communicators "may not be perfectly symmetrical," that "[w]hat are called 'distortions' or 'misunderstandings' arise precisely from the *lack of equivalence* between the two sides in the communicative exchange" (131). In the context of Hall's argument about the functioning of the television network, this lack of equivalence is cause for optimism; given the different "frameworks of knowledge" produced by different subject positions, even the most culturally determined televisual texts become open to interpretation, and thus the "audience"—traditionally considered mute, passive, and stupid—can be understood to exert more control over the communicative process than earlier models of communication with the "culture industry" would suggest.[11]

Of course, the goal of cybernetics in studying and facilitating the communicative process is to do away with such ambiguities, to allow for more accurate ferreting-out of messages from signals, and more precise control of the messages' "destination," be that destination silicon- or carbon-based. Thus Mark Poster argues that, "[i]n principle, cybernetics is an elitist theory. It is a tool designed for technocrats to better manage what is seen as a chaotic society" (28). But, as John Johnston points out, such totalized control of communication exists just outside the realm of possibility: "while information has led to a new medium of control, it has also generated something that always exceeds control." For Johnston, this excess of information over control points to information's "viral power, its tendency to proliferate" (2). This out-of-control replication of information, however, does not wholly erase the potential for paranoia in confronting the network; as I further explore in the following section, the network in these two views presents itself as alternately a system of total control or total subversion, infinite order or infinite chaos. In either case true communication becomes impossible, for either all communication is reduced to the command, or the "lack of equivalence" between two communicating subjects so multiplies the quantity of information in any message that it renders exact comprehension of a sender's intent impossible.

Poststructuralist critical discourse, unsurprisingly, has tended toward the latter conclusion, suggesting through numerous texts, including Barthes's "The Death of the Author," Foucault's "What Is an Author?," and Derrida's "Signature Event Context" that there is no necessary correspondence, in what Wiener refers to as the "ordinary language system," between the message received by a reader and that sent by an author. The existence of the text, for each of these three theorists, becomes not the transmission of the author's will but rather the obliteration of that will. For each of these theorists, the very possibility of communication requires the sender's death. In the example of Barthes, of course, it is the death of the author that makes room for the birth of the reader. For Derrida, that death is inscribed in the technology of writing itself: "To write is to produce a mark that will constitute a sort of machine which is productive in turn, and which my future disappearance will not, in principle, hinder in its functioning" (8). Foucault, finally, insists upon death as the necessary condition of writing, and so performs the dead writer's postmortem:

> Writing is now linked to sacrifice and to the sacrifice of life itself; it is a voluntary obliteration of the self that does not require representation in books because it takes place in the everyday existence of the writer. . . . In addition, we find the link between writing and death manifested in the total effacement of the individual characteristics of the writer; the quibbling and confrontations that a writer generates between himself and his text cancel out the signs of his particular individuality. ("Author" 117)

For one strain of poststructuralist discourse, then, the model of communication enacted by written texts bears much in common with that proposed by Hall, in which the ultimate arbitration of meaning rests with the decoder, leaving the encoder finally mute, absent, dead.[12]

That one of Pynchon's sources in *The Crying of Lot 49* was early cybernetic theory, and particularly Wiener's *The Human Use of Human Beings*, then, highlights the difficulties posed to communication—and most particularly to reading—by the complexities of the networks represented in the novel. The central feature of the patterns of communications uncovered by Oedipa Maas in her California quest is their ultimate unreadability. In part, her difficulties are the result of the epistemological failures suggested in the previous chapters; in the age of the machine, in the age of the spectacle, but most importantly in the age of the network, the reasoned, linear reading strategies of the print era have become useless. Moreover, those printed documents that do filter through the novel—*The Courier's Tragedy*, of course, but most significantly the will of Pierce Inverarity—are themselves beset by unreadability, errata, omissions, inconsistencies. Print is in this rendering no longer imagined to be a reliable medium of communication; instead, it has become more akin to a spiritual medium, the mysterious—and perhaps nefarious—attempt to communicate from beyond the grave. This is a double-edged problem in the novel. On the one hand, Pierce's death is a literalization of Barthes's death of the author, a representation of the novelist's self-effacement in the presence of the reader. On the other hand, given that everything in the text, all of the order Oedipa attempts to read into the world around her, can be traced back to the will of Pierce Inverarity, in whose absence little can be known, the reader (like Oedipa) may begin to suspect that Inverarity, having, as Barthes suggested, gracefully died in order to make way for the reader, is having his revenge on his successor, purposefully creating unsolvable puzzles. The author may have died, and the reader may be nominally in charge, but perhaps Pierce took the possibility of meaning with him. The significance of the text, the author's *will*, is in this case vitally important and yet is left adrift in a sea of floating signifiers.

Don DeLillo's *Libra* presents similar difficulties for its character-reader, Nicholas Branch. Like Oedipa, Branch is overrun by signals that are indistinguishable from noise; like Oedipa, he faces the impossibility of adequately interpreting messages in the viral proliferation of information; like Oedipa, he finds himself increasingly distracted by links and connections, lost in a doomed attempt to read not the messages but the network itself. Branch, commissioned by the CIA to write the secret history of the Kennedy assassination, is surrounded by bits of evidence emanating from the long-dead—not simply the president, and not simply his assassin, but nearly everyone connected to the events—facing the impossibility of interpretation in the absence of these authors. Moreover, as the only author left standing, Branch feels the futility of his own attempts at communication, knowing that his history will never be read and will thus disappear into the network as well. For both these readers, then, in both these novels, the network generates not increased communication but impossibility: the impossibility of distinguishing information from noise; the impossibility of determining the source of any message, whether meaningful or not; the impossibility of interpretation, both of messages and of the networks themselves. "The irony for America," Peter Abernethy points out, "is that our human ability to communicate seems to decrease in proportion to the increase in our technical ability to communicate" (18). This continually expanding multiplicity, the viral force of both information and the systems that carry it, creates a point of anxiety for the novel of obsolescence, which explores through these networks its own failure to communicate.

In *The Crying of Lot 49* Pynchon seems to attribute this failure to communicate less to the cyberneticists' noise or Hall's differences among human subjects than to a generalized lack of agency on the part of those subjects, and an absorption of agency by the media themselves. This "agency panic" begins on the very first page.[13] Immediately Pynchon reveals how much more active are these methods of communication—presumed to be hollow shells without the messages devised and encoded by human subjects—than those who ostensibly use them: "Oedipa stood in the living room," he tells us, "stared at by the greenish dead eye of the TV tube" (9). Despite the fact that the TV's eye is "dead," the television is nonetheless the agent, the starer, while Oedipa is the passive object of its gaze.[14] Oedipa's fears for her own agency, in fact, are at the center of her crisis in the novel. The nature of the crisis is made clear at the end of the first chapter, as she remembers a trip she and Pierce made to Mexico City, and the Remedios Varos painting they saw there, "Bordando el Manto Terrestre" (Embroidering the Earth's Mantle), in which there were

> a number of frail girls with heart-shaped faces, huge eyes, spun-gold hair, prisoners in the top room of a circular tower, embroidering a kind of tapestry which spilled out the slit windows and into a void, seeking hopelessly to fill the void: for all the other buildings and creatures, all the waves, ships and forests of the earth were contained in this tapestry, and the tapestry was the world. (21)

The sadness that the painting inspires in Oedipa is based upon her identification with those imprisoned girls, who are in part trapped in the tower because there is nowhere else to go except the world created within that tower. "If the tower is everywhere and the knight of deliverance no proof against its magic," she asks herself, "what else?" (*CL49* 22). It's a good question—but the wrong question. The message sent her in this painting is not that the tower is all, that Oedipa is, despite what freedom she may feel, a maiden locked in a solipsistic experience of a world she is creating; the message is, conversely, that Oedipa is part of a tapestry woven by someone else. She is not trapped away from the social fabric but is rather part of that fabric, unable to separate herself from the network the communications complex has woven. In her confusion, however, Oedipa begins a desperate process of world creation, attempting to project, if not something outside the tower, then at least a tapestry of her own. By the novel's end, she is forced to acknowledge the paranoid possibility that the world she has imagined herself projecting may have in fact been built for her by the will of Pierce Inverarity, the novel's ultimate weaver, as well as the schizophrenic possibility that the connections she has discovered may be meaningless. The unresolvable nature of this tension between paranoia and schizophrenia is the logical extreme of the contemporary crisis of agency: either everything connects, or nothing does, and there is no particular way to tell the difference.

Oedipa's crisis of selfhood manifests as terror in the face of the world's communications networks. Given the eternal uncertainty, in Pynchon's paranoid representation, about what the networks are connecting one to, Oedipa's terror arises in part from the possibility that these networks are centrally controlled, devices of surveillance. Just as in *Vineland* Hector understands the mysterious military intervention in the television network as an announcement that the television is now doing the watching, *The Crying of Lot 49* begins with the suspicion that the "dead eye" of the television set may instead be a recording eye, transmitting information back through the communicative chain. But Oedipa's terror arises largely from the impossibility of knowing, the impossibility of reading the complexity of the network sufficiently well to understand whether it signifies ultimate order or ultimate randomness. The telephone—the last instrument through which Pierce speaks to Oedipa— inspires a particularly intense terror for precisely these reasons. When Pierce calls her—at 3:00 A.M., no less, a paranoia-inducing hour—Oedipa is aware, right through his repertoire of impersonations, that the long-distance line that carries their signals "could have pointed any direction, been any length" (*CL49* 12). But this phone call is the last bit of contact she has with Pierce until she is notified—by U.S. Mail, of course—that she has been named executrix of his will. That same night Oedipa receives another 3:00 A.M. call, this one from Dr. Hilarius, her shrink. The ringing of the phone produces, we are told, "clear cardiac terror, so out of nothing did it come, one second inert, the next screaming" (16). The immediate connections of this 3:00 A.M. call to the last, given the day's events, certainly account for some of its terror; is this Pierce, literally contacting her from beyond the grave? Although it isn't, and there is an earthly caller on the other end of the line, the "screaming" of the phone "out of nothing"—its lack of apparent connection to anything tangible, which suggests potential connection to the intangible—nonetheless produces not only Oedipa's terror, but later, Hilarius's own murderous insanity; it seems only natural that Hilarius's first act after his psychotic break is to "[take] a chair and [smash] the switchboard with it" (133). The network, possibly having developed agency of its own, or possibly serving as the tool of some other, malign agency, or possibly orderless and meaningless, in any case represents a threat to individual agency and thus the individual ability to communicate.

The indeterminate status of the network with regard to meaning—in which the network becomes not simply the mode of meaning's conveyance but potentially its source as well—troubles many of the novel's representations. Oedipa is repeatedly struck with the vague certainty that in the various networks of modern life exists not simply the form, but also the content of communication. As she sits in her car on a hilltop, for instance, the sprawl of houses and roads in the valley below makes her think "of the time she'd opened a transistor radio to replace a battery and saw her first printed circuit. . . . Though she knew even less about radios than about Southern Californians, there were to both outward patterns a hieroglyphic sense of concealed meaning, of an intent to communicate" (*CL49* 24). But the interpretive crisis Oedipa experiences has left her a desperate reader, overcome by a need to understand the patterns that surround her, to find the key to separating tapestry from world. She sees these patterns everywhere, from the layout of houses to the movement of an exploding spray can: "The can knew where it was going, she sensed, or something fast enough, God or a digital machine, might have computed in advance the complex web of its travel" (37). In her desperation to understand the networks by which she is caught, on the one hand, or to create intelligible new networks, on the other, Oedipa must insist that either the can has agency enough to determine the pattern by which it careens around the bathroom, or there is meaning in its pattern, a formula by which it can be known.

Her determination to interpret, if not create, these "complex webs" leads her to the mysterious Tristero, or at least leads her to see the Tristero everywhere, as "revelations . . . now seemed to come crowding in exponentially, as if the more she collected the more would come to her, until everything she saw, smelled, dreamed, remembered, would somehow come to be woven into the Tristero" (*CL49* 81). The Tristero becomes for her a kind of alternate reality, existing both within and outside the tapestry of network culture. In contemplating this alternative, however, Oedipa asks herself one crucial question, to which the answer is destined to remain ambiguous: "*Shall I project a world?*" (82). If she is in fact projecting the world of the Tristero, or if it has been projected for her, it exists within this world in the same fashion as the diegetic space literally projected by film. We see the simultaneous reality and unreality of this filmic space in the Metzger seduction scene: Metzger asks Oedipa if she wants to bet on the movie's outcome, but she says no, quite sensibly arguing that "the movie's made" (33). The end of the movie, already determined, exists in physical form in this world, projected onto a screen. Yet Metzger insists that betting would make sense, because Oedipa doesn't know the movie's ending; because she hasn't yet seen it projected, its meaning remains for her unfixed, yet to be discovered. And thus the film exists as a kind of alternate reality, both inside the "real" world and outside it, with a separate but internally coherent set of physical and metaphysical laws. Like the Tristero, the diegetic space of film and television represents both a world apart from Oedipa's and a world possibly projected from within. The complexity of interconnections between the "real" and its representations, between the world and the tapestry, augments the novel's sense that the networks of communications, ostensibly carriers of messages, may in fact themselves *be* the messages.

Such seems also the conclusion that Nicholas Branch in DeLillo's *Libra* circles in a somewhat Pynchonesque "approach and avoid" fashion.[15] Branch, having spent fifteen years in a small room surrounded by the proliferating information spun out by the Kennedy assassination, finds himself at moments taken aback by the "data-spew" (15) around him: "The stacks are everywhere. The legal pads and cassette tapes are everywhere. The books fill tall shelves along three walls and cover the desk, a table, and much of the floor. There is a massive file cabinet stuffed with documents so old and densely packed they may be ready to ignite spontaneously" (14). Beyond these textual materials—the previous attempts at narrativizing these events—however, there are the random bits of evidence, which may contain secrets or may be meaningless:

> Everything is here. Baptismal records, report cards, postcards, divorce petitions, canceled checks, daily timesheets, tax returns, property lists, postoperative x-rays, photos of knotted string . . . There is Jack Ruby's mother's dental chart, dated January 15, 1938. There is a microphotograph of three strands of Lee H. Oswald's pubic hair. (181)

On the surface, much of this data seems useless, and yet Branch cannot winnow it down: "He wants to believe the hair belongs in the record. It is vital to his sense of responsible obsession that everything in his room warrants careful study" (182). As in Oedipa's experience of the Tristero's clues, everything seems connected and thus demands interpretation. But this careful study of everything makes impossible the job that Branch, the "receiver" in this communicative chain, was assigned: not only can he not discern signal from noise and thus not interpret signal into meaning, but also he cannot relay the messages he uncovers through this study; he cannot write. Branch has "extensive and overlapping notes," we are told, but "of actual finished prose, there is precious little. It is impossible to stop assembling data. The stuff keeps coming" (59). This overflow of information, then, threatens the writing process with death by drowning in a sea of interpretation.

As the data piles up, Branch gradually and reluctantly turns his attention from what the "stuff" says to where it comes from. Despite his own assertion that his history is not intended to be "a study of the ways in which people succumb to paranoia" (*L* 57), the necessity of distinguishing the meaningful from the random induces precisely that response. This is in part the paranoia of the age; in an era of assassinations, investigations, and possible cover-ups, in an age partly driven by the covert operations of government, as conspirator Win Everett believes, "[s]ecrets build their own networks" (22). The nature of secret information is thus to call attention to its own pathways and interconnections, to induce paranoia by insisting upon an attendance to the evidence's chain of custody—who had it, whom they got it from, whether they are to be trusted. Oedipa, for her part, despite thinking at first that she is searching for the keys to escape the tower, finally shifts her quest by attempting to trace the tapestry in which she finds herself back to the tower itself, suggesting that one of the dark figures supervising the weaving in Varos's painting—figures significantly left out of the novel's description of the image—may be Pierce himself, that he may have left her the clues she has ostensibly discovered. Branch, literally trapped in his own small room, with data about the world being fed in to him but nothing beyond the room that can verify it, becomes increasingly nervous about the source of his information: the Curator. At first mention, the Curator is merely described as "quick to respond" (15) to Branch's requests for data; gradually, however, he comes to "send" without request information that bears an at times questionable relationship to the task at hand. "The Curator sends recent photos," we are told, "and Branch understands that he must study them, although they do not pertain to the case" (59). In this subtle change is the beginning of Branch's shift of attention from the meaning of the information to the meaning of the information *network*; the message Branch receives is not *in* the photographs but *about* them and their relationship to the Curator. By the novel's end, the messages Branch investigates are almost entirely those of the medium: "The Curator sends information on Bobby Dupard. Branch knows about Dupard only through the Curator. But how does the Curator know?" (441).

Branch's anxiety about the network through which he receives communications is heightened by the fact that a vast number of the original sources for this information, the "witnesses, informers, investigators" involved with the case from its outset, as well as those only tangentially connected, are "conveniently and suggestively dead" (*L* 57). In these many deaths, beginning of course with the president's own, is a kind of communication, a message that Branch cannot yet read. With each new death added to the roster, Branch sees not the meaning of that original death but rather the network it created: "the assassination sheds a powerful and lasting light, exposing patterns and links" (58). It is the network itself that draws him in, communicating to him not its origins but its conclusion, his own death. The network is, as DeLillo suggests in *White Noise*, composed of "waves and radiation, or how the dead speak to the living" (326), but in the alternately paranoid and schizophrenic contemporary environment, the language of the network communicates only itself.

Organization

In shifting the focus from what messages mean to who sends them and how, concerns about the network cease being communicational and become organizational. This transition, from reading messages sent by the network to reading the network itself, is due in part to what Friedrich Kittler describes as a leveling effect among thoroughly interconnected media; writing about the rise of optical fiber networks, he suggests that "[t]he general digitalization of information and channels erases the difference between individual media. . . . In computers everything becomes number: imageless, soundless, and wordless quantity" (102). The reason for the novel of obsolescence's apparent concern about this devolution of all communication into information is twofold. First, quantification implies a certain dehumanizing trend, a deindividualization in the flood of numbers. McLuhan suggests that "[i]n this electric age we see ourselves being translated more and more into the form of information" (57); it is not simply data that is thus quantified, but "we" ourselves. Some critics argue that this is an essential outgrowth of mechanization; for instance, Mark Seltzer points out that "two of the crucial control-technologies of machine-culture" are "statistics and surveillance" (100)—that is, the physical wiring that connects the individual to the system and the quantified information that passes along those wires.[16]

Second, however, statistics are arguably responsible not only for the translation of the human into information, but also for the vast overflow of data by which the individual is besieged, the endless stream of numbers that reduces all to sameness. Neil Postman, in writing about the "technology" of statistics, argues that contemporary U.S. culture's conception of the meaning

of statistical data is inherently flawed, its errors resident in problems of reification, ranking, and biased questioning patterns. But the function of statistics, he argues, is even worse than its flaws: "the elevation of information to
a metaphysical status: information as both the means and the end of human
creativity" (*Technopoly* 61). Ultimately, he claims—and the postmodern novel
concurs—the point of information is no longer any kind of human knowledge
but instead a self-referring justification: information for information's sake.
In historicizing this indictment of statistics in the explosion and devaluing of
information, however, Postman points to a very specific causal event, one at
the center of the networked culture under consideration in this chapter: "[t]he
presumed close connection among information, reason, and usefulness," he
claims, "began to lose its legitimacy toward the mid-nineteenth century with
the invention of the telegraph" (*Technopoly* 67).[17] The explosion of information
produced by statistics, along with information's dissociation from what Postman considers to be "reason and usefulness," created by the ability to transmit
this quantified information to areas far from its source, has contributed to
the cultural sameness Kittler sees in the movement of all media to a common
system of number and wiring: information in entropic decline. In statistics
and surveillance, then, we see the double-edged threat of the network's organizational principles: either connections and the information that flows across
them devolve toward the random and meaningless in their overproliferation,
or those connections in fact tie everyone in to a central source of authority.
This, again, is the dual sense of chaos in contemporary culture: a total lack of
order—entropy—or totalized order, an order so fine that it may spontaneously
emerge into a new, dangerous being of its own.

Considering entropy as a force in postmodern culture returns us to Pynchon's *The Crying of Lot 49*.[18] As Oedipa Maas's quest for some world outside
the tapestry woven by the networks of communications proceeds, as she seems
to find the solution to her desire for escape in the networks themselves, everything becomes for her a mechanism of communication capable of transmitting
some bit of information, from printed transistor circuits to the Southern California networks of highways to an old, filthy mattress absorbing the effluvia of
life "like the memory bank of a computer of the lost" (126). She even finds, in
John Nefastis and his Maxwell's Demon machine, both a physical representation of and a principle for this ubiquity of communication: entropy. As Nefastis
explains the principle to her, "there were two distinct kinds of this entropy.
One having to do with heat engines, the other to do with communication. . . .
'Communication is key,' cried Nefastis" (105). The first form of entropy Nefastis mentions is that described by the second law of thermodynamics; the

second form arises out of information theory. Norbert Wiener describes the former in *The Human Use of Human Beings*:

> As entropy increases, the universe, and all closed systems in the universe, tend naturally to deteriorate and lose their distinctiveness, to move from the least to the most probable state, from a state of organization and differentiation in which distinctions and forms exist, to a state of chaos and sameness. (12)

There are significant similarities between Wiener's definition of thermodynamic entropy and Callisto's description of a comparable cultural state in Pynchon's early short story "Entropy," in which Callisto claims that consumerism is moving the United States "from the least to the most probable, from differentiation to sameness, from ordered individuality to a kind of chaos" (*Slow Learner* 88). The overt parallels of language point to the basic texts of information theory or cybernetics as Pynchon's direct influences; the divergences—from thermodynamics to cultures in decline—point to his metaphoric treatment of entropy as a concept.

In examining this treatment, however, one must first contend with Pynchon's later dismissal of his use of the concept in both "Entropy" and *The Crying of Lot 49* as a mere "thermodynamical coinage" (*SL* 17), as well as with Oedipa's sense that John Nefastis is playing fast and loose with what amounts to a linguistic coincidence: " 'But what,' she felt like some kind of a heretic, 'if the Demon exists only because the two equations look alike? Because of the metaphor?' " (*CL49* 106). Oedipa's acknowledgment of entropy as a metaphor, rather than invalidating the connection, instead brings it inside the realm of interpretation, where, for the paranoid, all such "coincidences" are meaningful. In fact, the coincidence is not in this case merely linguistic, simply a matter of two concepts with the same name; the coincidence extends to mathematics, as the formulas for these two types of entropy, the thermodynamic and the informational, are identical. And, as Wiener himself points out, quantum theory has led to "a new association of energy and information" (38–39); one is no longer strictly separable from the other. The "coincidence" of these formulas thus appears more meaningful than coincidental; the connection suggests, first, that information, in parallel fashion to closed heat systems, is subject to entropic decline and has a tendency in its proliferation to devolve from organized messages into noise; and second, that the concept of entropy itself, in its connections between thermodynamics and information, is productive of meaning.

One finds in the connection of these two distinct entropies the notion that so terrifies the novel: networks of communication, rather than creating order through the distribution of information, may instead be hastening the entropic decline into meaninglessness. Communication, as Nefastis insists, is the key—but in an entropic universe, the proliferation of information is inextricably tied to heat death. The thermodynamic version of entropy is defined as the measure of the unavailable energy in a closed system, and thus the percentage of its proximity to chaos; in any heat engine entropy increases, tending toward greater dispersal of energy and thus the spread of disorder. This notion of the heat engine, and particularly its associated use as a metaphor for the universe, is connected to the nineteenth-century Newtonian model for man discussed in connection with *V.*; this is the vision of a premodern world, a universe set in motion by a God who has since disappeared. The replacement for this vanished God, and thus the source of hope for a means of ensuring the universe's survival, is Maxwell's Demon, proposed in 1871 by mathematician James Clerk Maxwell. The principle behind Maxwell's Demon, in the words of Stanley Koteks of Yoyodyne, is that of "a tiny intelligence" that could "sit in a box among air molecules that were moving at all different random speeds, and sort out the fast molecules from the slow ones" (*CL49* 86), thus concentrating energy, reducing entropy, and avoiding heat death.

However, to sort these molecules, the Demon must collect data on every molecule—both its speed and its position. Heisenberg's uncertainty principle declares such a task all but impossible, as certainty about one calls the other into question, and as the act of observing affects the result and therefore renders the knowledge useless.[19] The Demon must also enact this sorting without any use of energy, an impossibility that Oedipa calls attention to with an appropriate reference to the networks of communications: " 'Sorting isn't work?' Oedipa asked. 'Tell them that down at the post office, you'll find yourself in a mailbag headed for Fairbanks, Alaska, without even a FRAGILE sticker going for you' " (*CL49* 86). Scientific refutations of Maxwell's Demon have taken on many of these physical impossibilities, arguing, for instance, that the Demon would have to have some source of light in order to see the molecules, and that the light would more than use up the energy gained in the sorting. Pynchon, however, in his metaphoric deployment of entropy and the negentropic force of Maxwell's Demon, invents a solution: the Demon, in the Nefastis Machine, works in communication with a "sensitive," who gathers the necessary information through extrasensory means and then completes the network by communicating that information and setting the Demon in motion. The quite evident problem, of course, is that this vast proliferation of data is itself the other, informational form of entropy; the system may "lose entropy" as the molecules are sorted, but that loss is "offset by the information the Demon gained about what molecules were where" (105). Only by communicating this vast store of information can the Demon wholly rid the system of entropy by passing that chaos on to the sensitive.

In this sense, thermodynamic entropy and informational entropy, though determined by the same formula, are slightly contrary principles. Wiener argues that "the information carried by a set of messages is a measure of organization" (23); informational entropy is the opposite of information itself, and thus, in this mathematical sense, the more information in a system the more negentropic it becomes. However, as Orrin Klapp suggests in *Overload and Boredom*, contemporary network culture does not adhere to such ideal models; in entropic culture, information is a measure not of organization but of its opposite: "The larger the amounts of information processed or diffused, the more likely it is that information will degrade toward meaningless variety, like noise or information overload, or sterile uniformity" (2–3). Thus, through the notion of entropy, information and noise become indissolubly linked, and information becomes a measure less of organization than of noise. Moreover, quantum theory, in linking information to energy, reveals the cost of the information gathered by Maxwell's Demon; as Leo Szilard wrote: "any action resulting in a decrease in the entropy of a system must be preceded by an operation of acquiring information, which in turn is coupled with the production of an equal or greater amount of entropy" (qtd. in Mangel 199). Thus Maxwell's Demon merely trades one form of chaos for another, premodern for postmodern, heat death for information overload, which amounts to the same thing.[20]

Much of DeLillo's recent work posits this information overload as the baseline state of contemporary U.S. culture; as Johnston suggests, the trajectory of DeLillo's novels has functioned as a fictional assemblage "in which word and image, film and televisual effects are reconfigured as aspects of an englobing media assemblage, or multiplicity, within which the 'de-multiplication' of human identity and the collusion of agencies and institutions are the most striking consequences" (168). The "englobing" effect of the network and the sense in which information culture's multiplicity paradoxically results in "de-multiplication" of identity, the entropic chaos of sameness, is in part the focus of *White Noise*. The novel is, as many critics have pointed out, replete with lists, ranging in context from the brief non-sequitur triads of consumer products that appear as part of the novel's own "white noise"—"Dacron, Orlon, Lycra Spandex" (52); "MasterCard, Visa, American Express" (100); "Krylon, Rust-Oleum, Red Devil" (159); "Clorets, Velamints,

Freedent" (229); and so on, lists that communicate, as Nicholas Branch's evidence does in *Libra*, not meaning but the network itself—to more extended lists of lovingly crafted detail, such as that on the novel's first page, which catalogs the possessions brought to the College-on-the-Hill by students who are moving into the dorms:

> the stereo sets, radios, personal computers; small refrigerators and table ranges; the cartons of phonograph records and cassettes; the hairdryers and styling irons; the tennis rackets, soccer balls, hockey and lacrosse sticks, bows and arrows; the controlled substances, the birth control pills and devices; the junk food still in shopping bags—onion-and-garlic chips, nacho thins, peanut creme patties, Waffelos and Kabooms, fruit chews and toffee popcorn; the Dum-Dum pops, the Mystic mints. (3)

This enumeration of the means by which the multiplication of consumer goods has resulted in a kind of informational nonsense—the "Waffelos and Kabooms" through which these students and their parents discover their sense of self—finds its parallel, much later in the novel, in the accounting of the end results of those goods, in their final resting places. Searching through his kitchen trash for the Dylar he craves, Jack performs a kind of excavation of his family's compacted garbage, discovering the layers of waste resulting from consumerism's white noise:

> An oozing cube of semi-mangled cans, clothes hangers, animal bones and other refuse. The bottles were broken, the cartons flat. Product colors were undiminished in brightness and intensity. Fats, juices and heavy sludges seeped through layers of pressed vegetable matter. I felt like an archaeologist about to sift through a finding of tool fragments and assorted cave trash. . . . The compressed bulk sat there like an ironic modern sculpture, massive, squat, mocking. I jabbed at it with the butt end of a rake and then spread the material over the concrete floor. I picked through it item by item, mass by shapeless mass, wondering why I felt guilty, a violator of privacy, uncovering intimate and perhaps shameful secrets. . . . I found crayon drawings of a figure with full breasts and male genitals. There was a long piece of twine that contained a series of knots and loops. It seemed at first a random construction. Looking more closely I thought I detected a complex relationship between the size of the loops, the degree of the knots (single or double) and the intervals between knots with loops and freestanding knots. Some kind of occult geometry or symbolic festoon of obsessions. I found a banana skin with a tampon inside. Was this the dark underside of consumer consciousness? I came across a hor-

rible clotted mass of hair, soap, ear swabs, crushed roaches, flip-top rings, sterile pads smeared with pus and bacon fat, strands of frayed dental floss, fragments of ballpoint refills, toothpicks still displaying bits of impaled food. (*WN* 258–59)

The end of consumerism, and the continuous white noise of its advertising, is this entropic heap. In this repellent mass of contemporary civilization's detritus, however, which Jack studies so carefully as almost to negate its repellency, he senses—like Oedipa looking down at the highways of Southern California or at the pattern of filth on a discarded mattress—an intent to communicate so veiled as to appear wholly random, but with a randomness that seems to suggest pattern. The piece of twine, for instance, in which Jack detects an "occult geometry": finding meaning in the knots and loops requires sorting out the garbage heap's too-apparent entropy, a feat of organization and interpretation that can only add to the world's white noise another stream of pointless information, further decomposing all communication into chaos.[21]

Underworld centers much of its energy around such garbage heaps, produced on a much more vast cultural scale, as well as on the more dangerously noxious byproducts of the cold war. This encyclopedic narrative is, if anything, more relentless in its determination to read the networks of U.S. garbage, in part because the novel itself comprises such a network: "everything connects in the end," thinks one of its characters, "or only seems to, or seems to only because it does" (465).[22] The assumption of meaning in waste, and the production of waste through the cultural processes of signification, becomes important in the novel in part because the novel's own structure seems to rest on the relationship between meaning and waste. Jesse Detwiler, once a "garbage guerilla" (286) known for stealing and reading the trash of the famous and powerful, has become by the late 1970s a "waste theorist" (285) who suggests the role of such entropic decay in shaping U.S. culture: "Civilization did not rise and flourish as men hammered out hunting scenes on bronze gates and whispered philosophy under the stars, with garbage as a noisome offshoot, swept away and forgotten. No, garbage rose first, inciting people to build a civilization in response, in self-defense" (287). Or, more succinctly and more to the point: "Garbage comes first, then we build a system to deal with it" (288). Systems—whether of waste disposal or of meaning—in this rendering, are the necessary containment of the chaos that precedes them. This inversion of the expected ordering of things in a sense replicates the inversions implied by the novel's structure, which conducts a gradual archaeological excavation through the layers of history and into the past, finding, depressingly, only more chaos as the project ensues. The need to seek order—both in garbage's chaos and in the novel itself—is a result of the jangled significations produced by contemporary culture's entropy:

> Detwiler said that cities rose on garbage, inch by inch, gaining elevation through the decades as buried debris increased. Garbage always got layered over or pushed to the edges, in a room or in a landscape. But it had its own momentum. It pushed back. It pushed into every space available, dictating construction patterns and altering systems of ritual. And it produced rats and paranoia. People were compelled to develop an organized response. (287)

But this "organized response"—landfills, for instance—can only add to the problem; the systems meant to deal with waste produce only more insidious forms of waste. Thus, at novel's end, a company in Kazakhstan uses nuclear explosions to dispose of dangerous waste, ostensibly destroying it but in actuality—as J. Edgar Hoover thinks of the Soviet test blast in the novel's prologue—sending it "underground, to spawn and skein" (*U* 51).

If there is a way out of this entropic cycle in *Underworld*, a way to create meaning out of chaos, art provides it. As Mark Osteen notes in *American Magic and Dread*, the novel offers a significant number of representations of the reclamation of garbage within the aesthetic enterprise: Sabato Rodia's Watts Towers, Moonman 157's graffiti-painted tenement walls and subway cars, and, perhaps most significantly for the novel's own project of reclaiming the history of the cold war, Klara Sax's desert art project, *Long Tall Sally*, in which dozens work to create art from cast-off military aircraft. Describing her project to an interviewer, Klara is conscious of her interference in both the entropic systems of waste production and the destructive systems of social order and power:

> See, we're painting, hand-painting in some cases, putting our puny hands to great weapons systems, to systems that came out of the factories and assembly halls as near alike as possible, millions of components stamped out, repeated endlessly, and we're trying to unrepeat, to find an element of felt life, and maybe there's a sort of survival instinct here, a graffiti instinct—to trespass and declare ourselves, show who we are. (*U* 77)

In such acts of creation—or senseless acts of beauty, as the bumper sticker would have it—is a step outside the system that frees the world from the chaos in which it is mired, producing, at least momentarily, a negentropic clarity that allows for individual communication. Thus, as Osteen suggests, "DeLillo offers *Underworld* as a similar act of resistance and redemption, submerging us in the culture of weapons and waste so that we may re-emerge transformed"

(216). In fact, DeLillo's hope, expressed more than a decade earlier in an interview with Anthony DeCurtis, is that fiction can "rescue history from its confusions," creating a multiplicitous new order by pointing out the chaos within patterns, and the patterns within chaos (DeCurtis 56). The complexity of this fictional assemblage, as Johnston suggests, claims to counter the "de-multiplying" effects of the media assemblage through its access to the aesthetic, the imaginary. As DeLillo's "Author's Note" at the end of *Libra* suggests, the novel is fundamentally a "work of imagination," and while it may aspire to "fill some of the blank spaces in the known record" (458), those spaces are not primarily factual in nature; rather, the novel's work is "providing the balance and rhythm we don't experience in our daily lives . . . correcting, clearing up and, perhaps most important of all, finding rhythms and symmetries that we simply don't encounter elsewhere" (DeCurtis 56). The novel's work is to build a multiplicity that can take the reader out of the alternately entropic chaos and strangling uniformity of the network. The novel, given its presumed powers of resistance, can escape the entropic winding down of contemporary culture and, like Maxwell's Demon, concentrate energy anew.

Art is thus, for DeLillo, comparable in a sense to the "non-equilibrium thermodynamics" pioneered by Ilya Prigogine, which explores "environments where the laws of entropy are temporarily overcome, and higher-level order may spontaneously emerge out of underlying chaos" (Johnson 52). The artists throughout *Underworld*—as well, of course, as the novelist himself—thus become a kind of humanist "singularity," a point at which matter shifts into something completely unlike its prior state. Of course, the singularity, in its popular-science and science-fiction conceptions, has no such traditional, benign, or aesthetic results; Vernor Vinge, for instance, argued in 1993 that once the singularity—which he defines as "the technological means to create superhuman intelligence"—is reached, "the human era will be ended" (Vinge). Bruce Sterling, moreover, explores posthuman evolution in *Schismatrix*, creating a fully posthuman culture in which, at such points of singularity, being proceeds by "Prigoginic leaps" as the chaotic elements of systems both technological and living spontaneously reorganize into new, higher levels of complexity. Thus, while art allows DeLillo, through both his characters and his texts, to escape the entropic trend of contemporary culture via the singular transformation of the chaos of waste into the order of art, such points of singularity in networked culture can prove dangerous to the humanist ideal, in that they demonstrate, in Kevin Kelly's phrase, just how "out of control" complex networks are.

Thus, in *The Crying of Lot 49*, Nefastis's (and Maxwell's and Oedipa's) desire for the existence of the "tiny intelligence" that can possibly forestall the universe's demise is doomed to failure, not simply because of the Demon's impossibility—a nonthermodynamic creature that functions in a thermo-dynamically closed system—but also because of the danger presented by the interposition of a mechanistic control within an out-of-control system. The longing for such a control parallels V.'s desire for a mechanized self overseen by an all-powerful, if slightly outré deity; it is less a longing for a world rescued from the brink of chaos by an aesthetic order than one controlled by a ruling principle. The problem is, first, that such control is inevitably oppressive and, second, that it always calls attention to other, uncontrolled possibilities; wit-ness, for instance, the ill-fated Scurvhamite heresy, a Puritan sect that operated under the strictest possible assumptions about predestination:

> Nothing for a Scurvhamite ever happened by accident. Creation was a vast, intricate machine. But one part of it, the Scurvhamite part, ran off the will of God its prime mover. The rest ran off some opposite Principle, something blind, soulless; a brute automatism that led to eternal death. The idea was to woo converts into the Godly and purposeful sodality of the Scurvhamite. But somehow those few saved Scurvhamites found themselves looking out into the gaudy clockwork of the doomed with a certain sick and fascinated horror, and this was to prove fatal. (*CL49* 155)

While for the Scurvhamites, the opposition between the controlled and the chaotic finds its expression in a universe either organized and maintained by an omnipotent God or one, like clockwork, fated to run down, this same divi-sion is echoed in the contemporary, post-Nietzschean scene of *The Crying of Lot 49* in the contrasting beliefs in the possibility of Maxwell's Demon and the inevitability of the gradual winding down into entropy. While the existence of the Demon would allow for an escape from the rigors of the second law of thermodynamics, the out-of-control presence of such a Prigoginic Demon—and the potential for its malignity—suggests that order is not entropy's true opposite but its flip side, potentially just as dangerous.

Thus we return to the double-edged sense of "chaos" in contemporary culture: chaos is popularly defined as a state completely lacking order, but as the late twentieth-century developments in multiple branches of science ex-plored in James Gleick's *Chaos* make clear, the apparent randomness of chaos may in fact conceal an order that is both pervasive and dynamic. Thus, sys-tems that appear entropic or chaotic in the first sense might instead contain a deep, fractal order that suggests the potential for the system's control. As Kelly suggests: "there are two kinds of complexity: inherent and apparent. Inherent complexity is the 'true' complexity of chaotic systems. It leads to dark unpredictability. The other kind of complexity is the flip side of chaos—apparent complexity obscuring exploitable order" (427). This exploitability is precisely the danger of such order, and particularly the danger of unseen levels of order; can a complex network that wires together the citizens of a nation, for instance, be used against those citizens? Perhaps worse, can the network itself become sufficiently complex that it develops a kind of intelligence in its connections, evading by exceeding centralized control? In either case, the novel of obsolescence seems to argue, while chaos is dangerous, the order it masks may be even more so.

The first of these possible threats posed by order within the network operates in the top-down fashion of ideological or governmental control of the networks of communications. Such networks betray ideological biases in their very wiring; as Erik Barnouw argues in his history of the rise of television, *Tube of Plenty*, the contemporary structures of broadcasting are rooted in the military purposes for which the technologies were originally developed—surveillance and reconnaissance—and the corporate purposes to which they were later turned over.[23] The ideological nature of such development and use of the network reveals another key aspect of McLuhan's formulation "the medium is the message," particularly as reinterpreted by novels and critics of obsolescence; the structure of any network of communication will determine what can be said over its connections.[24] This deterministic view of the media of communications perhaps lessens the irony that Peter Abernethy sees at work in *The Crying of Lot 49*, as pointed out earlier: "our human ability to communicate," he claims, "seems to decrease in proportion to the increase in our technical ability to communicate" (18); all channels of information, all conduits, are imagined to limit the shape of what flows through them.

John Stark has claimed that Pynchon's novels are an effort to "organize satisfactorily the enormous amount of information available to contemporary people." Despite Stark's admission that such a task is "probably hopeless" (4), this argument is nonetheless a bit curious, given that the last feeling any reader would claim to have at the end of a Pynchon novel is that of having had an "organized" experience. Rather, that Pynchon's magnum opus, *Gravity's Rainbow*, ends on a maddening note of fragmentation and disintegration seems precisely the point. Nor does DeLillo's own claim of the ability of fiction to "rescue history from its confusions" seem to bear out, as even his speculative interpretation in *Libra* of the Kennedy assassination leaves us with more questions than it answers. What the reader, like Nicholas Branch, is finally left with at the end of such apparently chaotic novels are mounds of information and the vaguely paranoid sense that it should all connect. This is the paranoia of the network: that the novel of obsolescence is, as Stark rightly points out, obsessed with the *process* of the organization of information, of plot making, is distinctly related to the paranoid late twentieth-century sense that networks of communications may serve as covert means of individual control, whether they are used for state surveillance and reconnaissance or corporate commodity production and distribution. The effort to organize information in the novel suggests the attempt to divine the network's order; the failure of such organization reflects at the same time the network's overwhelming complexity and the novel's drive to free itself from its sticky grasp.

An early suggestion of the potentially controlling nature of the networks of communications surfaces in the work of Norbert Wiener. In *The Human Use of Human Beings,* he responds to concerns about his grouping, in the earlier technical text *Cybernetics* (1948), of "communication" and "control" within the same classification:

> Why did I do this? When I communicate with another person, I impart a message to him, and when he communicates back with me he returns a related message which contains information primarily accessible to him and not to me. When I control the actions of another person, I communicate a message to him, and although this message is in the imperative mood, the technique of communication does not differ from that of a message of fact. (16)

What began in cybernetics, at least in theory, as the study of the communication of commands necessary to control a machine already betrays hints that it is moving, at this early moment, into the altogether similar study of the communication of commands necessary to control a human being. The medium is, indeed, the message; to study communication is to study control. Thus Neil Postman's claim that "[t]he milieu in which Technopoly flourishes is one in which the tie between information and human purpose has been severed" (*Technopoly* 70) seems quite wide of the mark. The link between information and meaning—between information and individual purpose—may have been dramatically weakened, if not severed entirely, but the pattern of the circulation of information, even in Technopoly, has ideology at its heart, and what does ideology serve if not some human purpose? Postman himself quite rightly reads educational institutions—which Althusser declared in 1970 to be the dominant ideological state apparatus—as "a mechanism for information control" (71; see Althusser 152). However, he either does not notice or is unconcerned by the ideological ends which the control of information is inevitably made to serve.

Wiener's chapter entitled "Law and Communication" makes even more explicit the connection between the dominant ideology and the control of communication, claiming that "[l]aw may be defined as the ethical control applied to communication" (105), and that "the problems of law may be considered communicative and cybernetic" (110). This intimate connection between communication and the pressures of legal structures heavily inflects *The Crying of Lot 49*. In fact, subterranean ties between lawyers in this novel, or government officials in *Vineland*, and the period's most evident and pervasive network, the Tube, strongly suggest the medium's complicity with centralized forces of control. Remember, for instance, Hector's late-night vision of the military cooption of the network in *Vineland*; it is no accident that the officers on-screen claim to be operating under the auspices of a presidential directive or, for that matter, that the viewer on the other side of the screen is himself a government agent. Television, the conduit of "official" messages and representations, bears a covert relationship to these representatives of the dominant ideology, one that may ultimately be exploited for purposes of control. And yet, as Hector's addiction attests, it's frequently a love-hate relationship; in *The Crying of Lot 49*, for instance, Oedipa discovers her family lawyer, Roseman, "brooding over the Perry Mason television program" (18), having gone so far in his contemplations of the lawyerly representations of this show as to draw up a "rough draft of *The Profession v. Perry Mason; a Not-so-hypothetical Indictment* . . . in progress for as long as the TV show had been on the air" (19). One assumes that Roseman's fury is over the show's departures from the standards he holds for lawyering; nonetheless, despite his concern over these breaches of "reality," he is unable to distinguish the show itself as unreal, drawing not the program but the character into a still-potential but not so hypothetical legal battle.

This is a common failure in *The Crying of Lot 49*, this inability to distinguish between the *representations* of the law and the *representatives* of the law; Oedipa has the same momentary difficulty at Metzger's entrance. Having never met the lawyer, she finds herself put off when "[h]e turned out to be so good-looking that Oedipa thought at first They, somebody up there, were putting her on. It had to be an actor . . . she looked around him for reflectors, microphones, camera cabling" (28). Meeting Metzger, Oedipa finds herself transported into an episode of *Candid Camera*. And as it turns out, Metzger, with his history as a child actor, and with his apparent lawyer's fluency with the tube, is much more adept at manipulating the medium than Oedipa is. While Oedipa uses the television as a weapon, wielding its rabbit ears to fend off Miles's advances, Metzger uses it as an instrument of seduction, "accidentally" finding *Cashiered*, a movie he'd starred in as a child, on the air: "Either he'd made up the whole thing, Oedipa thought suddenly, or he bribed the engineer over at the local station to run this, it's all part of a plot, an elaborate, seduction, *plot*. O Metzger" (31). Metzger is much closer to the truth of the medium here in his uses of it than is Oedipa; as demonstrated in *Vineland*, television will come to be used more as an instrument of seduction than as a tool of overt domination.[25]

In Oedipa's ability to create a "plot" out of Metzger's seduction, though, are the incipient traces of Pynchonian paranoia. Paranoia in Pynchon, as Joseph Tabbi argues, is "not a clinical condition or even a psychological state so much as it is a conceptual commitment to systems of connection" (*Postmodern* 53). Paranoia, in its emphasis on "connection," thus becomes the opposite end of the information spectrum from the schizophrenia of entropy; rather than disorganization and chaos, a complete separation of information from meaning, paranoia is the state in which *everything* means.[26] This state of paranoia seems inevitable given any visible means of organizing information—particularly in patterns and connections like the networks of communications themselves. As Leo Bersani suggests:

> paranoia is a necessary product of all information systems. . . . Information control is the contemporary version of God's eternal knowledge of each individual's ultimate damnation or salvation, and both theology and computer technology naturally produce paranoid fears about how we are hooked into the System, about the connections it has in store for us. (103)

Between theology and computer technology, however, there is television, the system of communication that appears to bring the world into the home. Paranoia about television, like that exhibited by Roseman with regard to Perry Mason, frequently has to do with the vagueness of the diegetic boundary between "television" and "life," the difficulty in determining which direction the information is flowing across that border, and the sense in which that border may be crossable.[27]

Metzger's fluency with the medium, his seemingly instinctive awareness of its uses for seduction rather than physical domination, goes so far as to make him capable of moving with some ease back and forth across its diegetic boundary; when Oedipa questions him on some point of his knowledge of German U-boat maneuvering during the war, he responds offhandedly,

"Wasn't I there?" (*CL49* 32), taking his filmic experiences as equivalent to reality.[28] Oedipa, by asking in the first place and then by attempting to object to this response, reveals her inability to make this same kind of cross in and out of the network. Metzger tries to explain this facility to her, and what it has to do with the law, but to very little avail:

> "But our beauty lies," explained Metzger, "in this extended capacity for convolution. A lawyer in a courtroom, in front of any jury, becomes an actor, right? Raymond Burr is an actor, impersonating a lawyer, who in front of a jury becomes an actor. Me, I'm a former actor who became a lawyer. They've done the pilot film of a TV series, in fact, based loosely on my career, starring my friend Manny Di Presso, a one-time lawyer who quit his firm to become an actor. Who in this film plays me, an actor become a lawyer reverting periodically to being an actor. The film is in an air-conditioned vault at one of the Hollywood studios, light can't fatigue it, it can be repeated endlessly." (33)

Metzger's explanation of the reason for the connection between lawyers and the Tube—that lawyers are actors in some fundamental sense—feels highly unsatisfactory, or perhaps only partial; that lawyers are actors seems to imply something more about the relationship of both to the system of "preferred meanings" that makes up the dominant ideology. John Fiske, in *Television Culture*, claims that the "ideological" codes of television "work to organize" television's other codes—those inscribed in and by a program's use of lighting, camerawork, makeup, music, and so forth—into "a congruent and coherent set of meanings that constitute the *common sense* of a society" (6). Actors and lawyers thus are both entrained in the project of this "organization," the transformation of codes into common sense. Metzger's ability to move back and forth across the boundary between these two worlds reveals only the identity of the codes involved.

However, when Manny Di Presso, Metzger's actor-double, shows up, chased by the mob, even Metzger loses his bearings. "Are we on camera," Metzger asks "dryly" (without benefit of question mark). "This is real," Di Presso responds, clarifying which side of the screen we're on (*CL49* 57). Like Jesús Arrabal's anarchist miracle, this is the intrusion of the filmic universe into the real one—and for a moment, even Metzger can't tell them apart. In fact, the lines between the electronic media and reality begin to blur uncontrollably. As Oedipa discovers later in the novel, speaking with Mr. Thoth in the Vesperhaven retirement home (a part, of course, of the estate of Pierce Inverarity), the television is bleeding out into the "real" world just as easily as the lawyers are moving in the other direction. Mr. Thoth attempts to relate a dream he has just had to her but then says that " '[i]t was all mixed in with a Porky Pig cartoon.' He waved at the tube. 'It comes in your dreams, you know. Filthy machine. . . .' " (91). That the content of this Porky Pig cartoon is "the one about Porky Pig and the anarchist" (91) brings us right back to Jesús Arrabal, defining his anarchist miracle as "another world's intrusion into this one. Most of the time we coexist peacefully, but when we do touch there's cataclysm" (120). The blurring, through the network, of the boundary distinguishing "media" from "life," then, appears not to be innocent or inconsequential; while Arrabal seems to suggest that such cataclysm might be revolutionary, the exploitation of television by the state's ideological apparatuses indicates that the coming explosion is one of reaction instead.

The dangerous nature of such top-down control of the network is not alleviated through a shift in controllers, however, as Oedipa discovers in her encounters with the Tristero. Whether a real or imagined entity, the Tristero seeks its escape from the web of governmental power by attempting to wrest control of the networks of communication away from "official" sources. It is within this framework that Bortz describes the history of the Tristero to Oedipa, or rather pitches it to her as though it were a script for a movie:

> "He looks like Kirk Douglas," cried Bortz, "he's wearing this sword, his name is something gutsy like Konrad. They're meeting in the back room of a tavern, all these broads in peasant blouses carrying steins around, everybody juiced and yelling, suddenly Konrad jumps up on a table. The crowd hushes, 'The salvation of Europe,' Konrad says, 'depends on communication, right? We face this anarchy of jealous German princes, hundreds of them scheming, counter-scheming, infighting, dissipating all of the Empire's strength in their useless bickering. But whoever could control the lines of communication, among all these princes, would control them. . . .' Prolonged cheering." (*CL49* 164)

The Tristero's response to the entropic decline into which the German Empire is falling is thus to eliminate the official couriers, Thurn and Taxis, and to institute a new system under which communication would be controlled by the underground couriers; this is not anarchy but a new reign of terror. The Tristero may be imagined to correspond to the "tiny intelligence" of Maxwell's Demon, which would handle the gathering and sorting of information, but it also reflects in its awful brutality the "soulless" Principle of the anti-Scurvhamite universe, an equally entropic world of information overload. Control of the network in any form—by God or by Principle; by government or by corporations; by Thurn and Taxis or by the Tristero—produces the same bloody results for those who attempt to communicate through it. That this scene is pitched to Oedipa, as would be such a scene from a film, clearly places this scenario on the other side of the diegetic border, with Metzger's movie in the realm of the law. And it's impossible for Oedipa to tell what of it may be real and what of it is sheer coincidence, as "[e]very access route to the Tristero could be traced also back to the Inverarity estate" (170). Perhaps this is all the will of Pierce Inverarity, and thus those elements that appear to exist outside the network's tapestry are merely that tapestry's underside.

During Oedipa's overnight adventure in the Bay Area, she discovers that "[t]he repetition of symbols was to be enough" (*CL49* 118), that in her paranoia she doesn't after all need connections to be drawn for her through a specific sequence of signifiers in order to discover the world she is seeking, for she has made, as Tabbi suggests, the "conceptual commitment to systems of connection" (*Postmodern* 53). In fact, she need not "discover" this world at all but can project it for herself. As Joseph Slade points out with regard to *Gravity's Rainbow*: "Most of Pynchon's characters believe that the information [they receive] comes from 'outside,' that their senses are like movie cameras recording what is there, but an occasional character worries that he is instead a projector, that something 'inside' is responsible for the film he sees and hears" ("Humanist" 59). This anxiety about which side of the diegetic boundary she falls on follows Oedipa through her wanderings in the Bay Area. By the signs she reads around her, she is able to project a world in which "here were God knew how many citizens, deliberately choosing not to communicate by U.S. Mail. It was not an act of treason, nor possibly even of defiance. But it was a calculated withdrawal, from the life of the Republic, from its machinery" (*CL49* 124). This withdrawal from the legally controlled lines of communication is precisely what Oedipa is seeking, some other world outside the tapestry, something not created and ordered for her. The conflict, however, is painfully evident, just as it is with movies: there is certainly an alternate world here, but is it, like a film, merely a diegetic world? Does it really exist, or has it been projected—by Oedipa, by Pierce—from within this world, a mirage, an image? And if there is a mode of control other than the machinery of the republic, is it in fact any less dangerous?

This confusion remains unresolved at the end of *The Crying of Lot 49*. Oedipa finds herself circling a dim awareness that, if the Tristero is just her projection, she must embrace it as such, seeing that there is either

> [a]nother mode of meaning behind the obvious, or none. Either Oedipa in the orbiting ecstasy of a true paranoia, or a real Tristero. For there was either some Tristero beyond the appearance of the legacy America, or there was just

America and if there was just America then it seemed the only way she could continue, and manage to be at all relevant to it, was as an alien, unfurrowed, assumed full circle into some paranoia. (182)[29]

The only way to be relevant to contemporary culture is to assume the truth of the Tristero, to find meaning in the patterns she reads around her, to accept this bit of communication as meant for her. For such appears to be the only possibility for true communication which exists in this fully networked world; Oedipa reads the Tristero as "a network by which X number of Americans are truly communicating whilst reserving their lies, recitations of routine, arid betrayals of spiritual poverty, for the official government delivery system" (170). If there is to be communication, it seems, it must happen outside the tapestry; something rests at the center of the "official" that prevents real communication, transforming everything into "lies," "routine," "spiritual poverty."

And yet: the first piece of correspondence Oedipa sees delivered via this alternative system is a meaningless letter to Mike Fallopian, delivered solely because of the organization's regulations: "To keep it up to some kind of a reasonable volume," he confesses to Oedipa, "each member has to send at least one letter a week through the Yoyodyne system. If you don't, you get fined" (*CL49* 53). And thus, again, alternative forms of centralized control allow for no more freedom, no greater communication, than do the governmentally controlled networks; they merely shift the locus of the order's oppressions. And thus, whether Oedipa has in fact found "[a]nother mode of meaning behind the obvious, or none. Either Oedipa in the orbiting ecstasy of a true paranoia, or a real Tristero" (182), comes to matter precious little. The choices she is left with—Tristero or no Tristero; a way out of the tapestry or just more tapestry; heat death or information chaos; paranoia, in which everything is connected, or entropy, in which nothing is—are not true opposites but mirror images. She is left, in the end, waiting for a middle ground, "waiting for a symmetry of choices to break down, to go skew. She had heard all about excluded middles; they were bad shit, to be avoided; and how had it ever happened here, with the chances once so good for diversity? For it was now like walking among the matrices of a great digital computer, the zeros and ones twinned above" (181). That these twinned choices resolve into the inner workings of the next dominant instrument of communication, the computer, is no accident. The officially controlled lines of communication have rationalized the world's flow of information, creating a quite reasonable paranoia, making it impossible to discern on which side of the diegetic border one stands. Neither choice of any pair means anything, as all choices lead to the same end, one and zero contained by the same computer. Right and Left, anarchy and fascism, are equally meaningless, as the exclusion of the middle through the network's centralized control has eliminated all possibility of diversity, of individual freedom.

The true alternative to such top-down, centralized, exploitable order obscured by the complexities of the network is of course a more diffuse, bottom-up control, in which the elements of the network, not ruled by any imposed order, self-organize into a spontaneous, emergent form of order. That this second kind of hidden order is not imposed by a central source of authority but draws its authority from the network itself, from the complexity of its interconnections, does little to alleviate the contemporary paranoia about organization and control, as this kind of unlocatable, diffuse, interconnected power is the power of conspiracy. Theories of conspiracy, as Timothy Melley argues, are the result of a postwar state of "agency panic," in which individuals, feeling "a nervousness or uncertainty about the causes of individual action" (12), attribute the motive force for such action to outside sources, imagining that such "controlling organizations are themselves agents—rational, motivated entities with the will and the means to carry out complex plans" (12–13). The more complex the action, and the more complex the organization, in fact, the more individual agency is threatened, and the more power the network itself absorbs. Thus, while Win Everett claims in *Libra* that "[s]ecrets build their own networks" (22), it is equally true, and far more threatening, that networks form their own secrets, that the power of connections among individuals quickly outstrips the ability of those individuals to control it.

DeLillo explores throughout *Libra* the "tendency of plots to move toward death," a quality Win believes inherent in "[a] narrative plot no less than in a conspiracy of armed men" (221). Conspiracies are thus self-organizing, dynamic systems whose structures take on the emergent qualities explored in contemporary systems theory, chaos theory, and theories of complexity. Despite Win's clear attempts at communicating his plan for a staged—and, most importantly, failed—assassination attempt, the multiplication of interconnections among the men involved in the conspiracy causes the network to take on a life of its own. David Ferrie, one of the key figures of this plot, suggests the dynamic nature of such interconnections to Lee Oswald years before the central conspiracy begins to take shape: "I've studied patterns of coincidence," he tells Lee. "Coincidence is a science waiting to be discovered. How patterns emerge outside the bounds of cause and effect" (44). Such spontaneous organization is currently studied in an appropriately interdisciplinary fashion under the rubric of emergence—as author Steven Johnson defines it, "a higher-level pattern arising out of the parallel complex interactions between local agents"

(19). Ferrie's sense of coincidence as more meaningful than random—as he tells Carmine Latta, later in the novel, "We don't know what to call it, so we say coincidence. It goes deeper. . . . There's a hidden principle" (*L* 172)—is evidenced, in fact, by the strange multiplicity of his relationship with Lee: having first met when Lee was a teenager in the Civil Air Patrol, they cross paths again, seemingly randomly, in the office of Guy Banister just as the conspiracy gets underway.

Lee in fact becomes, in *Libra*, the ideal focal point for such a conspiracy, precisely because he is constructed as a network of identity fragments, complexly interconnected and yet without apparent direction or purpose. Win Everett, in setting the conspiracy into motion, assumes that such a figure will have to be crafted; he plans to "script a person or persons out of ordinary pocket litter" (28), creating evidence of alternate identities, false records, fake identifications, all intended to "show the secret symmetries in a nondescript life" (48), to "[a]stonish them. Create coincidence so bizarre they have to believe it" (147). And yet the coincidences he doesn't create are all the more bizarre. He is profoundly unsettled to discover that Oswald, creature of the network, "existed independently of the plot" (178), that he has already constructed for himself all the documents Win is busily forging for him, that "the fiction he'd been devising" is "living prematurely in the world" (179). Thus Lee, who is more network than individual, simultaneously evades the control of individual members of the conspiracy and becomes of a piece with the larger plot's operations, as if spontaneously created by the plot itself.

Late in the novel, Lee comes to understand, if only partially, his emergent existence; having spoken with Ferrie about the Kennedy administration's perhaps imagined plots against Castro one day, he reads an article about those same plots in the newspaper the next:

> Of course it was only coincidence that Ferrie mentioned the thing one day and it appeared in the paper the next. But maybe that was even stranger than total control.
>
> Coincidence. He learned in the bayous, from Raymo, that Castro's guerilla name was Alex, derived from his middle name Alejandro. Lee used to be known as Alek.
>
> Coincidence. Banister was trying to find him, not knowing what city or state or country he was in, and he walked in the door at 544 and asked for an undercover job.
>
> Coincidence. He ordered the revolver and the carbine six weeks apart. They arrived the same day.
>
> Coincidence. Lee was always reading two or three books, like Kennedy.

Did military service in the Pacific, like Kennedy. Poor handwriting, terrible speller, like Kennedy. Wives pregnant at the same time. Brothers named Robert. (*L* 336)

The desperation in some of these "coincidences"—the painful, conflicted desire to identify with both Castro and Kennedy, the random vagaries of postal delivery—suggests that Lee's dyslexia, evident throughout the text in the difficulties he has with both reading and writing, carries over to his understanding of his own interconnections. The "coincidence" of his appearance at Banister's office, however, hints at the deep order of the networks of conspiracy, an order that is "stranger than total control" in its diffuseness. The very impossibility of predicting such a connection, combined with the vastness of its effect, suggests that what Lee thinks of as coincidence is instead, as Ferrie insists, determined by the network itself. Ferrie attempts to explain his undiscovered science to Lee, using, appropriately enough, imagery that draws the network in a series of connections:

> Think of two parallel lines. . . . One is the life of Lee H. Oswald. One is the conspiracy to kill the President. What bridges the space between them? What makes a connection inevitable? There is a third line. It comes out of dreams, visions, intuitions, prayers, out of the deepest levels of the self. It's not generated by cause and effect like the other two lines. It's a line that cuts across causality, cuts across time. It has no history that we can recognize or understand. But it forces a connection. It puts a man on the path of his destiny. (339)

Coincidence, conspiracy, the network—all are emergent structures that self-organize seemingly random parts into deeper levels of order. However unsatisfactory may be Ferrie's analysis of the origins of such spontaneous organization, the tissue of "dreams, visions, intuitions" and the desire to be "on the path of his destiny" are all that comprise Lee's character; if there were no connection between those parallel lines prior to this moment, Ferrie's speech creates one, completing the network that gives the conspiracy life. In this fashion, by coming to sense the inevitability of coincidence and the emergent connectedness of his own life, Lee is prepared to understand how the television networks, running films about presidential assassinations, could be speaking directly to him, "running a message through the night into his skin" (370), even without the controlling presence of any empowered "them."

The risk, however, of interpreting coincidence through the concept of emergence, of understanding interconnection as fate, is the violence that such a vision does to the concept of individual agency. As Melley suggests in *Empire of Conspiracy*, conspiracy theory, or the ostensibly paranoid psychic commitment to divining deep levels of interconnection in the supposedly random, is largely driven by agency panic, and thus serves both to explain away individual powerlessness and to displace that lost sense of power onto the networks that seem vaguely to have absorbed it. Like the anxiety of obsolescence, which announces the death of the novel in order, paradoxically, to augment its cultural influence, conspiracy theory functions to "sustain a form of individualism that seems increasingly challenged by postwar economic and social structures. Conspiracy theory, paranoia, and anxiety about human agency, in other words, are all part of the paradox in which a supposedly individualist culture conserves its individualism by continually imagining itself to be in immediate peril" (6). The danger of the network as represented in the novel of obsolescence is not simply the threat it poses to reading, but that which it poses to readers; not simply the difficulties it creates for coherent communication, but the effect it has of undermining the modern conception of the individual. While top-down control of networked systems directly oppresses by subjecting the individual to governmental, corporate, or other ideological domination, the more diffuse structure of bottom-up control may in fact be riskier, in that the spontaneous development of order out of nothing that occurs at a given level of complexity serves to transform the individual elements of a network into something entirely different: a mass.

Massification

In a sense, then, just as the novel of obsolescence's anxieties about television's machinic existence reveal less about the television itself than about the novel's attachment to at times conservative definitions of the human, and as such anxieties about television's spectacular qualities reveal the novel's desire to valorize its own uses of language, so the novel's apparent anxieties about television's networked status function to support the novel's own appeal to the Enlightenment individual as the foundation of freedom. Such an appeal requires a vilification of its opposite, the mass, that figure of equal anticommunist and antifascist fervor. As Lynn Spigel suggests in *Make Room for TV*, anxieties about the relationship of the individual to the communications network are implicated in the earliest popular discourses that surround the introduction of television into the U.S. home, discourses fractured by a profound ambivalence about the new medium. This ambivalence, Spigel argues, "is part of a long history of hopes and fears about technology; . . . communications technologies such as the telegraph, telephone, and radio were all met with a mixture of utopian and dystopian expectations—both in intellectual circles and in popular culture" (3). On the one hand, television could bring the world into the U.S. home; on the other, "television posed the intimidating possibility that private citizens in their own homes might be rendered powerless in the face of a new and curious machine." These fears, however, though apparently focused on "powerlessness" before the "machine," are in fact connected to the use of television's technology in "surveillance and reconnaissance" during World War II (47). That the locus of this anxiety turns on the notion of surveillance reveals that the issue is perhaps less with the machine itself than with the unknown quantity to which the machine is wiring private citizens. If this concern begins to sound a bit familiarly paranoid, as Spigel describes the suburbia that the television network webbed across, the connection becomes increasingly clear:

> There was an odd sense of connection and disconnection in this new suburbia, an infinite series of separate but identical homes, strung together like Christmas tree lights on a tract with one central switch. And that central switch was the growing communications complex, through which people could keep their distance from the world but at the same time imagine that their domestic spheres were connected to a wider social fabric. (101)

Like Oedipa's connection of such suburban networks to printed transistor circuits in *The Crying of Lot 49*, Spigel's sense that these homes are "separate but identical," strung together and controlled by the networks of communications, imagining connectedness but longing for distance from the whole, reveals a profoundly cold war–influenced U.S. anxiety about collectivity, or what happens to individuality when the citizenry is wired not just to a central authority but to one another as well.

The connection between collectivity, or "massness," and television originates in Marshall McLuhan's thinking, particularly his suggestion that the "mass" in "mass-production" is not indicative "of size, but of an instant inclusive embrace. Such is also the character of 'mass media.' They are an indication, not of the size of their audiences, but of the fact that everybody becomes involved in them at the same time" (349). The mass, according to Lewis Lapham in his introduction to the 1994 edition of McLuhan's *Understanding Media,* is what results when "[t]he individual voice and singular point of view disappears into the chorus of a *corporate and collective* consciousness" (xxi, emphasis mine). Lapham here echoes McLuhan's own reckoning of the "outering" of the central nervous system produced by the wiring of the United States: "Rapidly, we approach the final phase of the extensions of man—the technological simulation of consciousness, when the creative process of knowing will be *collectively and corporately* extended to the whole of human society"

(3–4, emphasis mine). The repeated conjunction of "corporate" and "collective" in the network is, for Marxist critics of the postmodern such as Fredric Jameson, inseparable from its capitalist inflection; as Jameson suggests: "our faulty representations of some immense communicational and computer network"—and thus, ostensibly, our representations of the masses who participate in these networks—"are themselves but a distorted figuration of something even deeper, namely, the whole world system of a present-day multinational capitalism" (36). By contrast, for McLuhan, the conjunction of "corporate" and "collective" in considerations of network culture is focused not on the structures of capital built upon the mass but rather on the mass as a kind of superorganism, the unification of multiple parts into one body.[30] "If there is any sense in deploring the growth of corporate and collective art forms such as the film and the press," McLuhan goes on to argue, "it is surely in relation to the previous individualist technologies that these new forms corrode" (189). Among those individualist technologies, of course, is the novel in its putative obsolescence.

For contemporary theorists of emergence and complexity, such a process of unification appears radically different than it does for critics of obsolescence. While Jameson imagines McLuhan's wired-together "global village" as the dehumanized product of the totalization of capital (this despite understanding postmodernism as the late age of capital, wherein no such totalized structures survive), Kelly, for instance, understands the mass less in its "global" than in its "village" implications. Arguing that emergent, adaptive network technologies cannot survive on a mass scale without local adaptability, Kelly insists that "[t]he logic of the network induces regionalism and localism" (173) rather than planetary conformity and domination. The view from the standpoint of obsolescence is of course nowhere near so benign; television, from this perspective, has led to the disappearance of the individual within a mindless, uniform, crushing whole that functions primarily by leading the viewer to misunderstand his or her individuality through the structures of that multinational conglomerate. Thus, as Melley suggests, Lee's assumption that the network is speaking directly to him through its broadcast of the assassination movies is one of the confusions inherent in the public experience of the media: "a misrecognition of generic, social . . . messages for private communications and sources of individual identity" (152). In this manner, for the novel of obsolescence, the massness of media address continually contradicts and is contradicted by its apparent enunciation of individuality. When the network addresses the individual—as in commercials that exhort the viewer to "be yourself" by purchasing corporate products—the viewer is assumed to overlook naïvely the massness of that address, instead equating individuality with mass consumption. Among the functions of the anxiety of obsolescence is thus to restore awareness of the "mass" in mass media, encouraging readers to return to an ostensibly pure source of individual experience: the novel.

The terror of such "corporate and collective" experiences of the media for the novel of obsolescence, then, encompasses both anxieties about the controlling web of international corporations and anxieties about a more bodily merger of individuals into a superorganism. In David Riesman's *Lonely Crowd*, for instance, the media induces a corporate-driven group-think: "The mass media play the chief role in . . . reducing to impersonality and distributing over a wide area the personal styles developed by individuals and groups" (84). By contrast, in Kelly's *Out of Control*, the interconnection of individuals via the network will produce rather than group-think a more literal merger, a hive mind: "what is contained in a human that will not emerge until we are all interconnected by wires and politics? The most unexpected things will brew in this bionic hivelike supermind" (13). In many popular representations of the hive mind—the most infamous being *Star Trek*'s Borg collective—members of such a network can no longer function as individuals but instead become drones capable only of laboring toward collective goals. This anxiety about the hive mind emerges in part from a confused equation of human experiences of collectivity with the collectivities of beehives and ant colonies, in which "the intelligence of the colony actually relies on the stupidity of its component parts" (Johnson 97). In the equation of human massness with the hive or the colony, critics of obsolescence assume that individual intelligence will of necessity be lost. As Cyrus Patell argues, however, in reading the novels of Rudy Rucker, such loss of individual intelligence is not a given but an ideological assumption: "The utopian and post-individualistic idea that Rucker's novels imagine is a hive populated not by drones but by individuals. The hive intelligence that would then emerge is beyond our current conception of intelligence as singular. What would it mean, Rucker's novels ask, if intelligence were plural?" (296). To equate human collectivity with that of an ant colony is to assume that intelligence can be only singular, that it can be resident only within individuals, and that if intelligence begins to develop within a network, it must of necessity evacuate the component parts of the network. Such is one of the founding assumptions of post-Cartesian liberal individualism, which equates the discrete, rational, humanist (and, not incidentally, white, Western, male) individual with the very possibility of intelligence itself.[31]

What such anxieties about massness and corporate intelligence miss is that, as individuals, we are all already hive minds; human consciousness exists in no unitary location but is rather an emergent phenomenon developed out of the complex interactions of millions of local agents. That the human body, and the brain in particular, may thus be understood as a giant parallel processor is deeply buried, however, under centuries of assumptions about the nature of individuality. As Kelly points out, one "great irony puzzling cognitive scientists is why human consciousness is so unable to think in parallel, despite the fact that the brain runs as a parallel machine" (339). A potential explanation may be found in the ideological assumption that "I" refers to a singular agent, and therefore the "I" of which I am conscious can think only serially. Even postmodernist theories that attempt to disrupt the primacy of the individual in contemporary culture posit a fragmentation of self, which suggests the breaking apart into pieces of a formerly or potentially unitary and coherent self, rather than arguing for that self's inherent multiplicity. In this manner, just as the individual is imagined to be fractured but nonetheless singular, the participation of that individual in a networked mass is imagined in the novel of obsolescence to create not a plurality of intelligence but rather, as Johnston has suggested, "the 'de-multiplication' of human identity" (168). As in the Borg, networked intelligence, and thus networked identity, can never be more than one.

This odd connection between fragmentation and demultiplication of identity in network culture can be seen in Pynchon's *The Crying of Lot 49* in the appropriately named Mucho Maas. Mucho, Oedipa's husband, is introduced in the novel as "a disk jockey who worked further along the Peninsula and suffered regular crises of conscience about his profession" (12). Mucho's relationship to his chosen medium is reminiscent of Raoul's connection to television in *V.*, an uncomfortable combination of dependence and loathing. Like Raoul, Mucho is an extension of the communications network, an encoder of its messages, working in its service—yet, unlike Raoul, as we shall see, it is not his industry's "sponsor fetishes" he distrusts but the communicated product itself. He is perhaps well to be wary, as radio, part of Horkheimer and Adorno's "culture industry"—a conjunction of collectivity and the corporate closer in its implications to Jameson's rendering of multinational capital than to McLuhan—is deeply implicated in the novel's exploration of the disappearance of the individual. "What is individual," Horkheimer and Adorno posit, "is no more than the generality's power to stamp the accidental detail so firmly that it is accepted as such. . . . In this way mass culture discloses the fictitious character of the 'individual' in the bourgeois era" (154–55). The demultiplication of identity performed by the radio network (in an era that might more accurately be described as postbourgeois) creates a faceless mass in which "accidental details" come to replace genuine differences between individuals. The wiring of suburbia thus comes to produce what Lynn Spigel describes as an "antiseptic electrical space" (109), in which radio and television broadcasting serve as "a cultural filter that purifies the essence of an 'American' experience, relegating social and ideological differences . . . to a kind of programming ghetto" (112). Through this erasure of difference—a literal demultiplication of human identities—radio and television eliminate the need for uncomfortable contact with others. This process of "purification" is thus in part responsible for the "excluded middles" that Oedipa understands to have eliminated the "chances . . . for diversity" (*CL49* 181) in the United States; the network has exiled difference to the farthest reaches of the broadcasting spectrum.[32]

Mucho's crises of conscience about radio seem to have only in part to do with his role in that purification as a sort of huckster for the system. His guilt is intended to be an indictment of radio as a medium of cultural exchange, particularly given his thoughts about his former life as a used-car salesman; he is aware of all of the negative stereotypes of that position, and yet, he claims, "at least he had believed in the cars" (*CL49* 13), the inference being a complete lack of belief in the products of the radio. His sense of complicity in radio's exploitation of the least common denominator to construct a hive mind is, however, augmented by his simultaneous need for the medium itself, for the stratifications of the broadcasting spectrum, regardless of its products. Something has driven him into radio despite his clear lack of belief in its ends; Oedipa begins to touch on that something when she reveals her suspicion that "the disk jockey spot . . . was a way of letting the Top 200, and even the news copy that came jabbering out of the machine—all the fraudulent dream of teenage appetites—be a buffer between him and that lot" (15). In fact, Oedipa is not far from the truth, but it is significant to note that it is less the content of the radio—the Top 200, the news copy, the "fraudulent dream"—that serves this purpose for Mucho than the medium itself, the network.

Oedipa begins to understand the distinction by the end of the novel, as she comes to think of the wiring itself as part of "the secular miracle of communication" (*CL49* 180), a miracle that exists apart from the messages it carries. The networks of communication come to serve an iconic—or even oracular—role for Oedipa, in her quest; however, the object of Oedipa's quest, unlike that of her (possible) namesake, is not to be discovered in a proper interpretation of the relationships between people, but rather in the relationships among things in their networked interconnections, as though the answer were not provided in the content of the message from the oracle at Delphi but in the mechanism of the oracle itself, the fact that the oracle spoke at all. Radio serves such an oracular function for Mucho, giving him not the answers to the meaning of his dreams but a vehicle by which he can avoid their threat. Mucho is besieged, five years after the fact, with nightmares about the used-car lot; once he is finally able to relate the dream to Oedipa, he reveals the locus of its horror in a sign (of course) hanging in front of the lot: "We were a member of the National Automobile Dealers' Association. N.A.D.A. Just this creaking metal sign that said nada, nada, against the blue sky" (144). The radio, the "net" of communications, is all that can protect him from the abyss of his used-car-lot nightmares, all that stands between Mucho and nada. Much or nothing: the massness of communications is apparently all that separates Mucho from the void.

However, this sense that safety from chaos can be found in any technology is, as I have pointed out, always a fundamental error in Pynchon; as Marcuse suggests, mass transportation and communication, mass production and consumption, and mass entertainment all "carry with them prescribed attitudes and habits, certain intellectual and emotional reactions which bind the consumers more or less pleasantly to the producers and, through the latter, to the whole" (4), a connection that produces an ultimate one-dimensionality of society, a sameness. This sameness, as we have seen, is depicted in Pynchon's early short story "Entropy" as a product of U.S. consumerism, which results in a devolution "from ordered individuality to a kind of chaos" (*SL* 88). Given the apparently entropic force of such massness, Mucho's attempt to escape the void by using the networks of mass communication as a shield is doomed to failure.

Mucho's ultimate merger with the radio network, however, is not metaphoric but frighteningly literal. On his reappearance late in the novel, he evidences an LSD-produced insight into the structures of communication, a bizarre understanding not of the human differences that distort the encoding and decoding process, but of the mysterious noise factor in the mechanical model of communication. In taping a live remote with Oedipa, after Hilarius's capture, he refers to her as "Mrs. Edna Mosh." When Oedipa asks, he tells her that "[i]t'll come out the right way . . . I was allowing for the distortion on these rigs, and then when they put it on tape" (*CL49* 139). He's developed a strange synesthesia with the radio, a chemical sense of oneness with the media. But while it's true that the effects of LSD do seem, for Mucho, to produce the benefits of this understanding and control of communication, among the other effects of this deep interconnection with the media is a total loss of individual identity.[33] Like *Gravity's Rainbow*'s Slothrop, whose oneness with the rocket in the persona of Raketemensch produces a simultaneous fragmentation and massification of self—"Some believe," the narrator tells us, nearing the end of the tale, "that fragments of Slothrop have grown into consistent personae of their own" (*GR* 742)—Mucho's union with the radio triggers both a fracturing of his identity and a merger with some collective technological unconscious, an entry into the hive mind. As Funch, the station manager, tells Oedipa, "they're calling him the Brothers *N*. He's losing his identity, Edna, how else can I put it? Day by day, Wendell is less himself and more generic. He enters a staff meeting and the room is suddenly full of people, you know? He's a walking assembly of man" (*CL49* 140). In this assembly of man, however, is not a true multiplicity of self, for the selves Mucho has fragmented into are generic; despite there seeming a crowd present wherever he appears, Mucho is not more in his massness, but less. Mucho, becoming part of the communications network, discovering that he can now do "spectrum analysis" in his head (142), is afflicted by a kind of human entropy, a devolution from individuality into sameness. He explains to Oedipa that he uses LSD not because he's addicted, but because of the communications he receives: "Because you hear and see things, even smell them, taste like you never could. Because the world is so abundant. No end to it baby. You're an antenna, sending out your pattern across a million lives a night" (143–44). Mucho has in fact become an antenna, and a receiver, and in the process has lost his individuality in the "million lives" of the hive; as he attempts to demonstrate, any two people who say the same words—especially media-generated words like "rich, chocolaty goodness" (142)—are indistinguishable, inseparable. For the novel of obsolescence, the media collapses all into one.[34]

These anxieties about the disappearance of the individual into the massness produced by the world's communications networks find their apotheosis in DeLillo's *Mao II*. Bill Gray, a Pynchon-like reclusive novelist and the "arch-individualist" of the text, manages in the course of the novel to escape the watchful protection of his assistant, Scott, to emerge from his seclusion—and to enter the world of terrorist violence.[35] Ironically, this reemergence leads to Gray's ultimate disappearance; *hiding* from mass culture is perhaps the only safe place for a writer, as "the disappearance of the author would seem in every case to be a disappearance *into* the materials of contemporary culture" (Tabbi, *Postmodern* 181).[36] In *Mao II,* terrorism is connected not simply to the spectacle, as argued in the last chapter, but to the threat of massness as well. The spread of terrorism via both literal explosions and the coverage and transmission of those explosions by television represents the end state of networked communications, the final proliferation of the materials of contemporary culture, and the triumph of the communications complex over the lone voice of the novelist. The fraught relationship between the pervasive violence of televisual communication and a waning print culture is a crisis, however, that has developed over the course of DeLillo's career; traces of it may be seen as early as *Americana*. In the last meeting David Bell attends before beginning his nightmarish quest into the heart of America, the executives of David's television network discuss the potential introduction of the "live satellite pickup" into their coverage of Vietnam. The problem they feel must be solved is, quite simply, that "[r]atings on the warcasts are way down" (62); the immediacy and danger of live transmission would beef things up, bringing the war via the network directly into the U.S. home. Ted Warburton insists, however, that such a connection is "ghoulish beyond belief" (62). Warburton's concerns, almost throwaway and ignored within the context of the meeting, are clearly intended to be taken more seriously by the reader. Warburton is, as David's narration informs us, the "tribal consciousness" (62) of the network, but the "tribe" of a long-gone era must be clearly distinguished from the "mass" of the televisual era. Warburton's tribal values are displayed in a series of mysterious, anonymous memos distributed to the network at large:

> messages from Zwingli, Lévi-Strauss, Rilke, Chekov, Tillich, William Blake, Charles Olsen and a Kiowa chief named Satanta. Naturally the person responsible for these messages became known throughout the company as the Mad Memo-Writer. I never referred to him that way because it was much too obvious a name. I called him Trotsky. (21)

Trotsky's memos espouse the values of an older, individualist, print-based culture that theorizes, contemplates, strikes moral stances, a culture Neil Postman has referred to as "Typographic America" (*Amusing* 30). Warburton's conscience is that of the writer; his opinion of these live broadcasts from the war zone is closest, perhaps, to the novelist's own sense of the "ghoulish" power of such intimate connection to images of destruction.

White Noise reexamines the issue of the mass embrace produced by television's coverage of violence and disaster from a vantage point of nearly fifteen years later, and it is clear that the live telecasts from Vietnam have directed the development of television over those years. Jack Gladney's family members, as a rule, enforce their unity by watching television together on Friday nights; one particular Friday night, early in the novel, the entire family is mesmerized by the images of destruction they find there, the "floods, earthquakes, mud slides, erupting volcanoes." Worse, Gladney's family gets caught up in the hysteria of these images: "Every disaster made us wish for more, for something bigger, grander, more sweeping" (64). Gladney, on the one hand a scholar (and thus writer), but on the other a self-designated scholar of Hitler studies, of the twentieth-century cult of celebrity, lives in a rather more attenuated relationship to the culture of the mass media than does *Americana*'s Ted Warburton, having clearly forsaken the tribe for the mass. Nonetheless, in his discomfort with his reaction to these piped-in pictures of disaster, Gladney seeks out Alfonse Stompanato, the chair of the department of "American environments," asking him, "Why is it . . . that decent, well-meaning and responsible people find themselves intrigued by catastrophe when they see it on television?" Alfonse responds: "Because we're suffering from brain fade. We need an occasional catastrophe to break up the incessant bombardment of information" (64–65). Jack, still unsettled, tries to clarify: "You're saying it's more or less universal, to be fascinated by TV disasters." Alphonse responds: "For most people there are only two places in the world. Where they live and their TV set. If a thing happens on television, we have every right to find it fascinating, whatever it is" (65). Jack is all too willing to accept this line of reasoning; as a scholar, he thinks of himself as apart from "most people," and yet the novel progressively makes clear that he, like the rest of his family, is part of a wholly mediated, networked environment. He is wired into the mass consciousness—which wiring makes acceptable his "celebration" of Hitler, given that "[w]e couldn't have television without him" (63)—but with just enough remaining individual self-consciousness to need to seek absolution for his "universal" fascinations.

DeLillo's *Mao II* is replete with similar communications of mass disaster and hysteria—transmitted within the content of the novel itself, but also reproduced within the still images on the flyleaves separating the novel's sections—beginning with the mass wedding conducted at Yankee Stadium by the Reverend Sun Myung Moon, through post–soccer game riots, to the desperate grief of the mourners at the funeral of the Ayatollah Khomeini. Interestingly, all these images of massness, as broadcast on television and described in the novel's content, are given to the reader from the point of view of Karen, Scott's (and Gray's) lover. As suggested earlier, Karen is affected by these images almost to the point of delirium; unlike Gladney's family in *White Noise*, however, rather than craving greater and greater disasters, she imagines that this absorption into the spectacle can create a common bond of humanity among those who watch it, resulting in an intersubjective experience of human understanding. *Mao II* repeatedly undermines this reading, however, by treating Karen as its best example of the death of the individual, the wholly vacated subjectivity created by the massness of the electronic media: the drone in the Moonie hive who has no identity of her own but takes on the personae of those around her. Gray and Scott, caught up in their own individualist battles, do not read Karen's overempathic responses as evidence of any void. Karen, says Gray, is "smart about people. Looks right through us. Watches TV and knows what people are going to say next. Not only gets it right but does their voices" (65). But what Gray misses is that Karen in fact bears a striking resemblance to the television; she does not *understand* people but *channels* them. She is the multiplicitous and yet demultiplied subject of the future, a future that, as the narrator tells us, "belongs" not to people, but to crowds (16).

This anxious acknowledgment of the "mass" created by the media networks that carry daily images of crowd hysteria is symptomatic of the impossibility, for Gray, of maintaining his solipsistic, isolated, writer's life; as he tells Brita during their photo session: "Years ago I used to think it was possible for a novelist to alter the inner life of the culture. Now bomb-makers and gunmen have taken that territory. They make raids on human consciousness. What writers used to do before we were all incorporated" (*MII* 41). This link in Gray's thought between terrorism and the fall of the novelist, between this fall and an encroaching corporate culture, is a central part of the critique of information society; remember Jameson's reading of such novelistic renderings of communications networks as "distorted figurations" of multinational capitalism (36). Gray makes this connection literal: the reason writers can no longer affect human consciousness is the fact of their "incorporation"—both bodily assumption and re-creation as commodity—within the consciousness industry. As Joseph Tabbi points out: "*Mao II* is about all the ways in which the mainstream writer in America can become absorbed and incorporated not only as a 'consumer event' but as yet another cultural narrative" (*Postmodern* 197). The mass absorbs the writer—even the writer who resists—and reincorporates his dissident position as part of the dominant ideology.[37]

In this fashion the massification produced by television's network reveals its deep political implications; the loss of individuality experienced as a demultiplication of identity and an absorption into a hive mind is equated in the novel of obsolescence with the disintegration of the modern political achievements of democracy. Robert Golden describes Pynchon's concern with the political ramifications of massness, reading in *V.* his apparent conviction that "the increasing role of the masses in political life means the end of individual choice and responsibility" (5). John Duvall likewise explores, through DeLillo's representations of television as a mediating force in *White Noise*, the novelist's treatment of "the ways in which contemporary America is implicated in proto-fascist urges" (127). Fascism, however, while the most obvious target of such critique, is not the only potential outcome of the hive mind. In fact, fascism, constructed through the top-down control of an identityless mass of drones, violates the principles of emergence on which the hive mind is founded, producing not a spontaneous self-organization but an imposed structure. A true beehive or ant colony—as already discussed, significantly flawed models for human collectivity—is a bottom-up structure, with no supervising ruler. (As Steven Johnson points out in *Emergence*, the adoption of human monarchical metaphors to describe bee and ant "queens" misses the fact that in such collectives, the queen's sole purpose is reproduction; she has no authority whatsoever over the other members of the swarm or over the swarm's holistic direction.) Such a colony, rather than fascist in its political structure, would be more accurately thought of as communist in nature, the bottom-up self-organization of identityless drones working toward a dimly perceived common good.

These connections between the hive mind and communism, however, are redolent of the stream of popular films and novels produced during the cold war that depicted the devastation wreaked upon a society of free individuals by an identityless mass of invaders: the pod people in *The Invasion of the Body Snatchers*; the nematodelike multiplication-when-divided of *The Thing*; *Them!*'s ravenous ants; *The Blob*'s amorphous mass of strawberry jam. As Patell points out, however, such anxious cultural representations of the devouring of the individual by teeming masses of identical drones have an earlier precedent in "nineteenth-century yellow peril fictions . . . which depicted all Asians as insect-like automata who, if allowed to immigrate and participate in U.S. democracy, would inevitably overrun the United States and assimilate its culture" (291). That such ethnocentricity and xenophobia may in part still underwrite anxieties about the emergence of hive mind in network culture, even if unconsciously, can be inferred from a number of discomforting representations in the novels of obsolescence previously discussed—*Mao II*'s endless images of Middle Eastern terror and hysteria; *White Noise*'s disturbing obsession with the races and ethnicities of its tangential characters, as well its central character's invention of "Hitler studies"—as well as other representations not previously touched upon: *Gravity's Rainbow*'s nervousness about the vivid nature of blackness in contrast to the whiteness of death, as well as the novel's inclusion of "Takeshi and Ichizo, the Komical Kamikazes" (690) among the characters of Slothrop's final disintegration; *Vineland*'s suggested connection between the undead Thanatoids and Eastern mysticism. None of this is to suggest conscious racism on the part of either DeLillo or Pynchon, as each has clearly taken, both in his fiction and in his nonfiction, a series of oppositional stances with respect to the dominant culture; Pynchon, for instance, in his article "A Journey into the Mind of Watts," expressly confronts the violence inherent in U.S. race relations in the mid-1960s. This is, however, intended to point to the deep alignment between the contemporary U.S. investment in individualism and the hierarchical social structures that have long supported white supremacy and Western domination.[38] It is not accidental that, in a nation in which individualism is represented as the political ideal, otherness is often equated with the loss of individuality; the television network, in binding a disparate citizenry together, thus threatens the loss of the individual's primacy and the equation of the privileged form of the individual—white, male, Western—with those others he has for so long dominated. Equating such a wired-together populace, a hive mind (not unrelated to that singular "mind" of Watts), with fascism serves as a simultaneous diversionary tactic and a means of protecting individualism's sanctity.

As Patell points out, however, in suggesting that intelligence is not necessarily but only ideologically singular, other possibilities for networked emergence nonetheless remain. Remembering that the examples of the ant colony and the beehive are insufficient models for human collectivity, we must ask: if, in the popular imaginary, the top-down organization of mindless drones replicates the political structures of fascism, and the bottom-up organization of mindless drones replicates the structures of communism, what revolutionary possibilities might be contained in the bottom-up organization of complex, plural intelligences? What if *more* resulted not in the destruction of individual subjectivities and identities in the superorganistic mass, but in a spontaneous self-organization of still-extant individuals? What if more can really be more, rather than less? Johnson points out in exploring the politics of emergence that such structures of bottom-up organization, particularly in their association with technology, are today most frequently aligned with the libertarian Right's drive to escape governmental interference, but similar weblike emergent political structures are also being explored and used by activists working toward progressive causes, most notably in the organization and coverage of the numerous anti–World Trade Organization protests by small, independent, but cooperative groups. However one may feel about the anarchists and their tactics, this leaderless group of movements has been, with cause, frequently credited for using both the technologies and the structures of the network in a manner that breathes new life into democracy by reempowering the individuals it was meant to serve.

More *is* different, as Kevin Kelly repeatedly points out in *Out of Control*; moreover, true difference requires more—more individuals who are more interconnected. As Kelly argues: "a plurality of truly divergent components can only remain coherent in a network. No other arrangement—chain, pyramid, tree, circle, hub—can contain true diversity working as a whole" (27).[39] Kelly does indicate that there exists a level of connectivity beyond which networks themselves cease functioning, a point at which more interconnection becomes too much; the possibilities to be gained from networked, distributed intelligences nonetheless outweigh the disadvantages for him: "When the sum of the parts can add up to more than the parts, then that extra being (that something from nothing) is distributed among the parts" (469). For the novelist of obsolescence, the network seems inescapably prone to runaway, to the continual piling up of positive feedback until the system self-destructs. In these novels, the free flow of information across the network results in information's too-muchness, and in that too-muchness is the end of information's freedom; by the same token, in the free flow of individuals through the networks' masses is the too-muchness of humanity, and in that too-muchness is the end of individual freedom. Despite obvious questions that stand to be asked about the nature of the individual—particularly who gets to be one—in such an environment, it seems to the novelist of obsolescence, in a world of information overload and the entropic devolution into sameness, that the individual act of reading an individual text cannot survive.

5

Obsolescence, the Marginal, and the Popular

> Pynchon and DeLillo were
> ahead of their time.
> —David Foster Wallace

> Thomas Pynchon. Now there was someone
> you never saw on "Oprah Winfrey."
> —Henry Louis Gates, Jr.

The Anxiety of Obsolescence, Reconsidered

Throughout this book, my intent has been to explore a particular group of postmodern novels by arguing not merely for a specific way of reading these texts but for a particular kind of hermeneutic in the textual encounter. This interpretive method looks to cultural studies in its exploration less of specific artifacts than of the circulation of discourses and ideas about those artifacts. By structuring my argument about the anxiety of obsolescence as a fruitful mode of reading around three conceptual categories—the machine, the spectacle, and the network—I have sought to examine the ways in which the novelists I consider mobilize popular and theoretical discourses about contemporary culture in formulating their own responses to television and the other forms of electronic media. My analysis has been aimed at another triad of connected (if potentially paradoxical) conclusions that focus less on what the anxiety of obsolescence *means* than on what it *does*: first, that the novelists reveal through their representations of the media a cluster of anxieties about being displaced from some possibly imagined position of centrality in contemporary cultural life; second, that these anxieties are in certain ways a pose, an assumed stance that provides access to a number of useful writing strategies that assist the novelist in trying to regain his ostensibly faltering importance as a cultural critic; and third, that this focus on the shifts in contemporary cultural life produced by new media developments is at times employed to obscure other, unspeakable anxieties about shifts in contemporary *social* life that pose a lesser threat to the dominance of the novel than to the hegemony of whiteness and maleness long served by the structures of traditional humanism.

Given this final implication of the anxiety of obsolescence, it may seem that I have unfairly set up Pynchon and DeLillo, overlooking the obviously critical positions that each has struck toward the contemporary status quo, asking these two novelists to take the fall for a failing endemic to the whole of Western culture. The question thus remains: is the anxiety of obsolescence, the novelist's represented fears of an encroaching electronic media (and submerged fears of a similarly encroaching otherness), unique to the writers I have addressed in these pages? Or is it a formation common to the entirety of literary culture, all of which is apparently under threat by television and responding in similarly defensive fashion? In attempting to answer these questions, my work turns its gaze in this chapter from Pynchon and DeLillo to look both forward and outward: forward to David Foster Wallace, a writer often thought of as their descendant, and outward to Toni Morrison, a writer who, though very different from them, has often been considered their peer. In the work of these two exemplary novelists, I hope to unpack two related concerns. The first is the relationship between the representations produced by Pynchon and DeLillo, taken as metonyms for what might be thought of as a group of "first-wave" postmodernists (including Gaddis, Gass, Coover, Barth, et al.), and those more recently produced by a younger group of authors whom many critics have begun to think of as the "second wave" of postmodernism. Do these younger authors, born after television had made its incursions into the U.S. unconscious, carry the same anxieties about the medium that nursed them through their childhoods? The second is the correlation between the rise of new media and the waning social influence of humanism—an influence that has for centuries supported (or been misused to support) the putatively universal ideals that function to reinforce the hierarchies of racism, sexism, heteronormativity, ethnocentricity, nationalism, and individualism. Are those new media experienced and interpreted with the same anxiety by novelists who write from the social margins of contemporary U.S. culture, those who, in other words, write from and about a subject position that is not aligned with whiteness, maleness, Westernness, straightness, and so on? Is the novelist's anxiety about television a historically specific phenomenon? Or is it socially specific?

These two concerns come together in the incident with which I began this book, the Jonathan Franzen/Oprah Winfrey entente. This literary brouhaha was for more than a year discussed in terms both irate and offended, invoking notions of conflict, of malfeasance, of blame. Witness the following off-hand remark in an April 2002 *New York Observer* article that explored the phenomenon of the "media coach," referring to one such consultant as "the same woman summoned by Farrar, Straus and Giroux to help Jonathan Franzen express himself on the idiot box after he made the mistake of dissing Oprah Winfrey" (Jacobs). As the rest of the article's tone meanders between amusement at the level of the contemporary literati's cluelessness about the media and stifled horror at publishers' too-apparently profit-induced attempts to polish up their writers for the camera, it's hard to tell how to take this suggestion of Franzen's "mistake." The author could be suggesting that the locus of this conflict resides in Franzen's stupidity or, just as easily, in Oprah's ego; the reader could infer from this description that Franzen holds an unduly high opinion of his own cultural superiority (given the "idiot box") or that Oprah's sense of her own power as an arbiter of contemporary culture was too easily bruised by Franzen's mouthing off (given the "dissing"). In either case, however, the story begins as one of personalities—Franzen v. Oprah; snooty writer v. purveyor of daytime fluff—and winds up as another battle in the contemporary (media) culture wars, with few of its myriad analysts thoroughly considering the full range of issues that such a conflict might contain.

Nonetheless, the conflict between these two figures raises the hackles of so many in the literary community precisely because of the multiplicity of issues with which it intersects, and the passionate desire of so many to narrow this multiplicity down to a concrete sense of what the "real" issue is. The real issue, for instance, is the way that Oprah's powerful branding/merchandising mechanisms have transformed book publishing and selling into an offshoot of her media empire, terrorizing authors, editors, and retailers alike with the power of her *Good Housekeeping*–style seal of approval, and threatening withdrawal of literary stardom if one fails to pay the proper obeisance. Thus, Franzen's questioning this power, and most particularly the power that Oprah's name would hold over the reading of his novel, demonstrates his integrity in deciding to withdraw from the corporate scheme, or at least his discomfort with profiting from it, to his eternal credit.

Or the real issue is the elitism so endemic to the contemporary literary scene, particularly among writers who self-consciously consider themselves "serious" novelists, and who wish to hold themselves above popular culture, suggesting that their work contains meanings of a more delicate and nuanced character than do contemporary movies and television programs or even popular novels, and further suggesting that their books cannot be properly read or understood by the viewing audiences of such popular daytime treacle as talk shows. Thus, Oprah's decision to disinvite Franzen's participation in the book club and appearance on the show was the only reasonable one, because the viewers watching this show are not cultural dupes and have no desire to be condescended to by literary snobs who have no sense of the nuanced ways that viewers in fact participate in such shows, and that the pleasures of such shows are thus not passively experienced but actively created.

While each of these narratives is satisfying, though of course in very different senses, I would argue that Franzen v. Oprah should not be read simply as a cautionary tale about high-brow against low-brow, or about the purity of art against the corruption of corporate culture, or even about the damage that individual personalities can do when they take themselves too seriously. Rather, this kerfuffle is these things and more, at its root a complex enactment of all the perceived conflicts between the novel and television that emerge in the anxiety of obsolescence. Franzen resists Oprah because of the threat that her viewership poses to the seriousness of his position as cultural producer. In so resisting, and in the rebuff that his resistance produced, Franzen creates a loyal following among those "marginalized" folks who take fiction seriously in the contemporary United States, thus assuring himself a steady audience (and a *New York Times* bestseller, and a National Book Award, and a follow-up contract). But in that invocation of the "marginalization" of serious fiction and its readers, Franzen/Oprah inadvertently reveals the uglier issues that all the talk about the inappropriateness of the "Oprah" logo on the book jacket serves to conceal: insofar as the conflict is about the relationship between literary products, their readers, and the mass marketplace, it is also in large part about the subject positions of the novel's readership and, not incidentally, the subject positions of Franzen and Oprah themselves.

The modernist moment in Western culture, as Andreas Huyssen documents in *After the Great Divide*, was characterized in part by a perceived need on the part of its "high" artists to separate themselves and their work from the products of mass culture, work produced by and for the popular. Modernist artists experienced, he argues, an "anxiety of contamination," a need to fend off "an increasingly consuming and engulfing mass culture" (vii); the locus of this anxiety was not, then, that mass culture threatened modernism with marginalization but that it threatened art with popularization, with an audience composed no longer of the elite few but of the heterogeneous many. While Huyssen argues that the postmodern has successfully located itself "after" the great divide between high and mass culture, I suggest that Franzen/Oprah reveals the extent to which this threat of contamination still obtains for some contemporary artists. The novelist's concerns about being culturally marginalized by television seem, in the age of Oprah, radically inapropos; the danger for Franzen was less in remaining unread than in being read by the wrong audience.

And thus the component of this conflict that the dozens of commentators haven't mentioned, perhaps because in an age in which we like to think such concerns are behind us, it didn't seem important, or perhaps because it just seemed impolite to say: this battle between the literary and the televisual pits a white male literary humanist against a black female producer of mass media, each vying for control of the cultural arena. Moreover, Oprah's audience is overwhelmingly female, and certainly more diverse in terms of race, class, and educational background than is Franzen's previous readership. These facts are not mere demographic coincidences but part of U.S. literary culture's self-definition—being by, of, and for the unmarked "universal" (that is, white, male, middle-class, educated) individual. It remains true, as it was in Huyssen's modernist moment, that "mass culture is somehow associated with woman while real, authentic culture remains the prerogative of men" (47); only those granted such cultural prerogative have the wherewithal to scorn the popular. For this reason, the threat television poses to the novel, and thus the threat Oprah poses to Franzen, is not (or at least not merely) a dehumanizing mechanicity, or a depthless spectacularization, or a corrupting commercialism, but a dangerous democratization. Television's democratizing reach is dangerous to the novelist in part because of the power it wields to level disparities in access to cultural products, exposing the writer to the scrutiny—and, indeed, the judgment—of others who may not be like-minded, who might exist in the terrifying spaces beyond the writer's personal knowledge, and who might for that reason understand his universalizing view of the human condition to be an ideological construct conditioned on privilege. Moreover, as the specific case of Oprah Winfrey should make clear, the danger in democratized access is worsened for the novelist because of the authority new media often grant to those outside the traditional humanist structures of power: the power not simply to listen, but to speak back.

In Franzen v. Oprah, then, is enacted the full range of conflicts that exist between the postmodern novel and television as the two vie for what appears to each to be a kind of cultural market share. While television as a medium is clearly beset by its own anxieties, worries about being taken seriously perhaps foremost among them, I have focused throughout this book on the writer's anxieties about television: anxieties about being incorporated, being consumed, being driven into obsolescence. And while I have attempted throughout to deconstruct those anxieties with an eye toward exploring the multiplicity of beliefs, desires, and motives that underlie them, this one scene of conflict, and the vast number of column feet it inspired, should suggest the seriousness with which players on both sides take the divide between the literary and the televisual. Pynchon and DeLillo are of course far from alone in their perceptions of this divide; as I hope the myriad of sources I have consulted throughout this study suggests, the anxiety of obsolescence is merely a local manifestation of a culturewide concern about literacy, about novelty, and about cultural hierarchy. The selection of these two novelists as the objects of my inquiry has in this sense been in part a matter of taste, in part a matter of convenience—and in part a matter that bears some unpacking: generational and social change.

New White Guys

The desire to characterize or, better still, to name generational clusters of literary authors is inevitably in part a canon-forming bent, a desire to label both the major trajectory of contemporary literature and the major players within that trajectory. Such naming can be seen in the second-order postmodernist debates, the continuing wrangle about what it means to be a postmodern novelist—is a postmodern novelist necessarily pro-postmodernism, or rather a critical chronicler of the postmodern condition?—about the distinction between high modernism and postmodernism (and, indeed, whether such a distinction can be supported), and about who falls in which category, when viewed from what angle. As I suggested in the first chapter, the canon-forming lists of postmodern novelists developed and debated by Barth, Hassan, and numerous other critics set the stage for the debate to follow, in no small part because of these lists' stellar uniformity. With the rare exception of a Kathy Acker or an Ishmael Reed, these lists of the postmodern canon are a roll call of white male novelists: Barth, Burroughs, Coover, DeLillo, Gaddis, Gass, McElroy, Pynchon, et cetera. This insularity, as Molly Hite suggests in introducing her revised list in the *Columbia History of the American Novel*, has made a lasting mark on perceptions of the genre: "the American novel is widely perceived—and criticized—as a white male genre" (698). Hite works, in her entry, to debunk this notion with regard to the postmodern novel, exploring the work of a number of nonwhite and/or nonmale authors whose work is aesthetically in keeping with the interests of postmodernism, and who should thus be included in an opened, revised canon. That such an argument has to be made, however, suggests both the power of early adopters to define generational terms and the political realities that underlie all such ostensibly disinterested descriptions of cultural phenomena.

For this reason, recent characterizations of the second wave of postmodernist writers are revealing, particularly as they have spread memelike through popular considerations of the contemporary literary scene. Consider, for instance, the following lines from the *Orange County Weekly*'s review of Rick Moody's collection of short stories, *Demonology*: "Moody's not alone here [in the difficulties he's faced locating his literary ambitions as more properly Updikean or Pynchonesque]: the other New White Guys—as [David Foster] Wallace has dubbed the group that includes him, Moody, Jeffrey Eugenides, Jonathan Franzen, Donald Antrim, and for good measure, let's throw in that upstart Dave Eggers—have almost had the same trouble" (Bonca). The multiple suggestions in this quote—that there is a group, that it has been named, that it has been named by one of its own members—are readily adopted in this review as evidence of these writers' importance: Antrim, Eugenides, Franzen, Moody, and Wallace (and one might add others who've been suggested for membership, such as Eggers, Jonathan Lethem, and William T. Vollmann) are the new canon because everybody says so.

This reading of the "New White Guys" misses two key points, however: first, that the term itself, as attributed to Wallace, is a reduction of a more complex (and more complexly expressed) thought both about the group and about its existence as a group; and second, that this thought is doubly conscious, that it both is and is not meant to be taken seriously, that it is at its root aware of the contested nature of the terms it invokes.

The first point first: after exhaustive searches among the myriad databases of the new information economy, after reading dozens of author interviews and profiles and transcripts of nonprint interviews and profiles, after querying the fantastically obsessive readers of the Wallace-L listserv and the caretakers of the Howling Fantods Web site, and, finally, after asking the author himself, I can find no evidence anywhere that Wallace ever uttered the now oft-cited words "New White Guys," least of all with canon-forming intent. He has commented in several places on the newness and whiteness and guyness of these particular writers, but less as a means of declaring them a group than of pointing out the superficiality of the criteria by which they might be considered a group. Consider, for instance, the following comment published in a *Time Magazine* article that attempts to capture the faces of today's fiction writers by characterizing them as "The New Fab Four": " 'I think we're all white males between 30 and 40, as far as I know,' is how Wallace coyly describes the group" (Sheppard 90). The article's author goes on to find affinities of influence and of

subject matter, and even more personal ties—Antrim and Franzen talk sometimes! Wallace and Moody have the same editor!—as a means of defusing the
suggestion that the "group" is a fabrication produced by critics who are seeking the new canon. Similarly, in response to a question about the group from
Salon's Laura Miller, Wallace demurs: "There's the whole 'great white male'
deal. I think there are about five of us under 40 who are white and over 6 feet
and wear glasses" (Miller). In the transition to "New White Guys" from these
comments that ostensibly intend to point out the meaninglessness of such
labels, the potential complexity of Wallace's commentary has been reduced to
a sound bite, an uncritically applied label.

Second, and more importantly: Wallace's original comments, both of
which not only acknowledge the whiteness and maleness of the "group" but
also suggest that these are superficial criteria for claiming its existence (as would
be a description of literary schools based around height or eyesight), attempt
to defuse the canon-building impulse by pointing directly to the social intent
behind such groupings. By suggesting that the group's particular groupness
is not only based on characteristics over which its members had no control,
characteristics that have nothing to do with their writing, but also based on
characteristics that in U.S. culture are the very absences that define the locus
of power—to be white is to have no race; to be male is to have no gender;
to be unraced and ungendered is to be the universal—Wallace attempts to
undermine the critical determination to center the literary future in these few
individuals. Transforming the " 'great white male' deal" into the "New White
Guys" shifts Wallace's evident discomfort with canonization, and above all
with the privilege that allows for canonization, into a hip irony, a cool suggestion that "white guys" can become, in their newness, not the center of power
but a marginalized special-interest group. In claiming such marginality for the
center, in marking the unmarked white male for both race and gender, this
reduction of Wallace's thought enacts precisely the centering I believe Wallace
sought to avoid.

That said, the argument that Wallace is seeking to avoid the recentering of
the white male viewpoint by defusing the claims of marginality that the "New
White Guys" moniker effects must be complicated by acknowledging a rather
difficult comment of Wallace's quoted in Jonathan Franzen's essay "Perhaps to
Dream." In an unspecified missive to Franzen, Wallace writes:

> Just about everybody with any sensitivity feels like there's a party going on
> that they haven't been invited to—we're all alienated. I think the guys who
> write directly about and at the present culture tend to be writers who find
> their artistic invalidation especially painful. . . . And it's not an accident that

so many of the writers in the shadows are straight white males. Tribal writers can feel the loneliness and anger and identify themselves with their subculture and can write to and for their subculture about how the mainstream culture's alienated them. White males are the mainstream culture. So why shouldn't we be angry, confused, lonely white males who write at and against the culture? (51).

The difficulties with this statement, even beyond the questionable labeling of nonwhite, nonmale writers as "tribal," are painfully obvious. First, equating white straight male "loneliness and anger" at not being invited to the party with the harassments and exclusions perpetuated by the dominant culture against the marginalized has the effect, whether intentionally or not, of invalidating the political claims of oppressed groups. Second, Wallace's statement lends itself to the same kinds of misappropriation that resulted in the "New White Guys" label, giving Franzen the freedom to claim, in the very next paragraph, that "[w]hite men are a tribe, too" (52). That this passage falls within an extended essay in which Franzen relates his own writerly struggles with his cultural irrelevance, at one moment in which he confesses to having begun writing, and "abandoned . . . in midsentence" (41), an essay called "My Obsolescence," should not come as a surprise. It is to the point, then, that this generation's writerly anxiety about exclusion from "the culture" seems to circulate around their whiteness and maleness; in their unmarkedness, in finding themselves the New White Guys, these writers feel themselves excluded from a culture of exclusion, marginalized by a culture that is finally paying attention to the voices originating on the margins.

The main difference between this perception of exclusion and that demonstrated by the novelists of obsolescence, however, is that these concerns are not masked by anxieties that declare themselves to be about medial shifts in contemporary culture. Thus, to read a bit further: among the problems presented by the ironizing of Wallace's rather complex, conflicted position into "the New White Guys" lies the deep contradiction between this hip knowingness and his own perhaps futile attempts to deactivate irony as the primary mode of work done by the contemporary U.S. novel. In "*E Unibus Pluram*: Television and U.S. Fiction," Wallace argues that irony, while originally a rhetorical stance that challenged the status quo through its refusal to be taken at face value, or to take the status quo with a straight face, has in the late age of television become one with the status quo as the primary mode of consumer discourse (i.e., advertising) and popular entertainment (i.e., the sitcom). In this shift, irony loses its politically critical edge and instead becomes reactionary, a means of avoiding change through avoiding the serious and painful exploration of sensitive human issues. "[I]rony and ridicule," Wallace suggests, "are entertaining and effective, and . . . at the same time they are agents of a great despair and stasis in U.S. culture"; moreover, because of this stasis and despair, irony poses "especially terrible problems" for young novelists, who must escape stasis in order to challenge the culture within which they write (49). Irony is, in its effects, dehumanizing, in no small part because its refusal to take contemporary problems seriously makes their amelioration and the formation of solutions impossible. In the ironic mode of discourse, the political status quo is held up to ridicule, not without justification; but by extension, all political problems—and actions—become ridiculous.

It is of course important to note that, for Wallace, irony's debilitating transformation into a U.S. cultural norm is connected to television not simply in the sense that television is the prime locus of such mainstreamed, commercialized irony but in the sense that television made irony possible in the first place. As he argues: "by offering young, overeducated fiction writers a comprehensive view of how hypocritically the U.S.A. saw itself circa 1960, early television helped legitimate absurdism and irony as not just literary devices but sensible responses to a ridiculous world" ("Pluram" 65). Television, in its whole-hearted early embrace of the traditional U.S. values embodied by such programs as *Leave It to Beaver* and *Father Knows Best*—values both hypocritical and oppressive in their assumptions of universal whiteness and middle-classness, in their support for the patriarchal nuclear family, and in the shield they form between that family and the rest of the world—set the stage for the rise to prominence of irony as a mode of critical reading. But according to Wallace, and as any viewer of the intensive media soul-searching surrounding scandals like the Bill Clinton/Monica Lewinsky revelations can agree, television is a ruthless incorporator and defuser of the criticism leveled at it. In this case, television absorbed ironic readings of its hypocrisies and, instead of altering the values that it espoused, altered the tone in which they were delivered, preemptively ironizing its own representations. In this manner, irony was both transformed into the dominant cultural mode of discourse and rendered useless as a critical tool; as Wallace suggests, irony is in the contemporary scene "not liberating, but enfeebling" (67), functioning as it does to dismantle old oppressive systems of values without being able—in fact, making it impossible—to build new ones to take their place.

Thus television forms a point of cultural concern for Wallace, as it does for both Pynchon and DeLillo. But with this exploration of the relationship between television and irony, Wallace proposes a different focus for that concern, one perhaps born out of his dramatically different relationship to television.

In "*E Unibus Pluram*," Wallace does the thing that numerous authors and interviewers have prodded him to do: consider himself and his work in its generational affiliation. Without naming the group of which he may (or may not) be considered a part, and without naming the members of that group, Wallace nonetheless distinguishes it from its predecessors in one crucial regard:

> Pynchon and DeLillo were ahead of their time. Today, the belief that pop images are basically just mimetic devices is one of the attitudes that separates most U.S. fiction writers under c. forty from the writerly generation that precedes us, reviews us, and designs our grad-school curricula. This generation gap in conceptions of realism is, again, TV-dependent. The U.S. generation born after 1950 is the first for whom television was something to be lived with instead of just looked at. Our elders tend to regard the set rather as the flapper did the automobile: a curiosity turned treat turned seduction. For younger writers, TV's as much a part of reality as Toyotas and gridlock. We literally cannot imagine life without it. (43)

Younger writers—a term that must be distinguished from the "New White Guys" in both its generality and its refusal to select a canon from the larger group—by this argument bear a substantively different relationship to the medium than do the novelists of obsolescence this study has been concerned with. Despite being "ahead of their time," Pynchon and DeLillo both treat television with the wariness with which the established approach new entries on the cultural scene; by contrast, younger writers understand television to be both no more and no less than a part of the cultural landscape, the backdrop against which all action and understanding take place.

But to suggest that the relationship of this new generation of writers to television is different is not necessarily to suggest that it is easy; in fact, as Wallace suggests, these writers born since 1950 bear a particularly challenged relationship to the irony that television has cultivated. Those raised in intimacy with the tube cannot consider life without it, and yet they cannot take it seriously; they view television with knowing skepticism, but that skepticism is itself evidence of television's deep influence, so incorporated into its modes of representation has such skepticism become. The danger for these younger writers is not that television will make their work obsolete, not that television will dehumanize or distract or deindividualize the potential audience for the novel, making it impossible for them to read with passion or conviction, but rather that proximity to the medium will dehumanize the writer himself,[1] making it impossible for him to look in a sustained fashion at a painful, intractable problem without flinching away with a reflexively ironic joke. This kind of protracted serious attention is of course necessary to writing anything meaningful, and thus, while the novel is still under threat from television in Wallace's view, the danger is one visited not primarily upon the great unwashed masses who take pleasure in television but upon the writer, who must struggle to escape its influence.

In fact, Wallace's reading of the dangers of television is at great pains not to suggest that television is inherently bad, or that its programmers operate under some evil intent, or that television viewers are either stupid or gullible. "Though I'm convinced that television lies," he writes, "with a potency somewhere between symptom and synecdoche, behind a genuine crisis for U.S. culture and literature, I do not agree with reactionaries who regard TV as some malignancy visited on an innocent populace, sapping IQs and compromising SAT scores while we all sit there on ever fatter bottoms with little mesmerized spirals revolving in our eyes" ("*Pluram*" 36). That television's role in such a cultural crisis, in the view of the younger generation, rather than being the problem, instead lies between being mere evidence of a problem and being a part of the problem to which the whole is reduced indicates a second distinction to be drawn between the novels of obsolescence with which this study has been concerned and more recent fiction: the problem with television, in this view, is not what it does to us—its powers of dehumanization, derealization, deindividualization—but rather what it signifies, or why we are attracted to it in the first place. For Wallace, television's power over the contemporary imagination reveals a profound sense of loneliness and disconnection in U.S. life; viewers are drawn to the tube by an unfulfilled desire for human contact, for human understanding. The danger this reliance upon television for such contact presents may be usefully contrasted with the representations of the network discussed in Chapter 4; where the network, in the novel of obsolescence, threatens the destruction of individuality by binding the audience into one mass, here instead television promises interconnection but fails to deliver, and in so doing more fully isolates viewers from the actual human interaction they seek. Television, for Wallace, exacerbates passivity in contemporary culture both by defusing, through irony, the potential of any kind of action and by presenting the fantasy of human contact without effort; however, it is key to note that, both in "*E Unibus Pluram*" and in his fiction, the root of television's danger, and thus the crisis that television presents, is created not by the medium itself but by failures in the larger culture, failures that encourage viewers to seek solutions to basic human anguish in representations rather than realities, in things rather than people.

Infinite Jest is the most useful example of Wallace's own fiction in exploring his representations of television; it is, however, logistically impossible to do the novel justice in one small part of one section of a chapter in a book focused on other writers. I want nonetheless to suggest, however incompletely, a few things about the novel's uses of television that distinguish it from the work of writers such as Pynchon and DeLillo. By the time of *Infinite Jest*'s present, television has long since been replaced by the teleputer, a single appliance that combines the functions of television, VCR, computer, and videophone. This digital device allows for video on demand, as well as for more interpersonal communications, rendering television itself obsolete; nonetheless, some concerns about the teleputer rightly remain. In a long digression in which Hal recreates the argument he'd developed in a paper on the demise of television advertising (for a course entitled "Intro to Entertainment Studies" [411]), the novel relates the history of this machine's rise to dominance, beginning with the changes wrought in the television industry by the spread of cable:

> Mounting an aggressive hearts-and-minds campaign that derided the 'passivity' of hundreds of millions of viewers forced to choose nightly between only four statistically pussified Network broadcasters, then extolled the "empoweringly American choice" of 500-plus esoteric cable options, the American Council of Disseminators of Cable was attacking the Four right at the ideological root, the psychic matrix where viewers had been conditioned (conditioned, rather deliciously, by the Big Four Networks and their advertisers themselves, Hal notes) to associate the Freedom to Choose and the Right to Be Entertained with all that was U.S. and true. (412)

Of course, the poverty of this vision of U.S. liberty leads not to genuine activity but to a new kind of passivity, used by a newly reorganized and consolidated Big Four to undermine cable's popularity:

> What matter whether your "choices" are 4 or 104, or 504? Veals's campaign argued. Because here you were—assuming of course you were even cable-ready or dish-equipped and able to afford monthly fees that applied no matter what you "chose" each month—here you were, sitting here accepting only what was pumped by distant A.C.D.C. fiat into your entertainment-ken. Here you were consoling yourself about your dependence and passivity with rapid-fire zapping and surfing that were starting to be suspected to cause rather nasty types of epilepsy over the longish term. The cable kabal's promise of "empowerment," the campaign argued, was still just the invitation to choose which of 504 visual spoon-feedings you'd sit there and open wide for. And so but *what if*, their campaign's appeal basically ran, what if, instead of sitting still for choosing the least of 504 infantile evils, the vox- and digitus-

populi could choose to make its home entertainment literally and essentially *adult*? I.e. what if—according to InterLace—what if a viewer could more or less *100 percent choose what's on at any given time* . . . ? What if, Veals's spokeswoman ruminated aloud, what if the viewer could become her/his *own* programming director; what if s/he could *define* the very entertainment-happiness it was her/his right to pursue? (*IJ* 416)

The result is the replacement of the TV with the TP, a double entendre that suggests the true value this appliance holds for the user's happiness. The pursuit, after all, is still for greater levels of entertainment, rather than for any higher form of enlightenment or personal satisfaction; moreover, the result is not a reduction in passivity but an increase, as suggested by the specifications of the present-day TP included earlier in the novel:

> Year of the Depend Adult Undergarment: InterLace Telentertainment, 932/1864 R.I.S.C. power-TPs w/ or w/o console, Pink$_2$, post-Primestar D.S.S. dissemination, menus and icons, pixel-free Internet Fax, tri- and quad-modems w/ adjustable baud, Dissemination-Grids, screens so high-def you might as well be there, cost-effective videophonic conferencing, internal Froxx CD-ROM, electronic *couture*, all-in-one consoles, Yushityu nanoprocessors, laser chromatography, Virtual-capable media-cards, fiber-optic pulse, digital encoding, killer apps; carpal neuralgia, phosphenic migraine, gluteal hypera-diposity, lumbar stressae. (*IJ* 60)

And thus, despite the ostensible interactivity of the TP and the arguable activity of its user, the teleputer nonetheless results in that future of "ever fatter bottoms" and other damage to the human organism.

The major interests of *Infinite Jest*, however, suggest that the viewers themselves are not to be held wholly responsible for the damage these systems inflict on them. Nor is television in this novel, as it is in *Vineland*, suspected to be one more tool of an oppressive political system designed to keep its subjects passive and benumbed, the better to manipulate them. Rather, as *Infinite Jest's* overall focus is on passivity and addiction in a larger sense, as the result of systemic national failures—the failure to fulfill the promises made of genuine liberty and actual happiness, resulting in extreme human suffering, as well as the crucial failure to provide any mode of escape from that suffering that is not more damaging than the problems it originated in—the teleputer becomes in this novel not a threatening tool of subjection but a symptom of larger cultural and interpersonal damage. This sense of television as symptom surfaces despite the fact that the novel's title is drawn from the ultimate piece of entertainment (referred to throughout, appropriately, as "The Entertainment"), a film by Hal's father made so perfectly entertaining that, having laid eyes upon it, its viewers are incapable of turning it off, becoming glued to the teleputer at the expense of their own physical needs, resulting finally in acute psychosis or even in death. The danger of this particular TP cartridge, it must be noted, does not originate in the technology itself or in the motives of its producer or in the malignancy of the systems of which it is a part or in the mindlessness of its consumers. Rather, its danger arises from the confluence of two circumstances: the desperation of a U.S. public conditioned to believe that entertainment is the highest level of happiness it can achieve, and the desperation of a doubly oppressed minority (the separatist Quebeçois, marginalized in the novel by the Anglo-Canadian majority and by the dominance of the former United States in the Organization of North American Nations) that seeks to exploit the U.S. desperation in order to alleviate their own.

The novel thus draws an analogy between television and drugs, two modes of escape from human pain that seem to result not in the promised amelioration of that pain but in its exacerbation, leading to addictions for which the sufferers cannot be wholly held responsible. This comparison of television watching and drug addiction, however, is hardly unique to Wallace; Marie Winn's 1977 *The Plug-in Drug: Television, Children, and the Family* popularized the metaphor by arguing that television diminished children's abilities to function in the "real" world. The tenor of Winn's critique, however, often strikes the "paranoid" tone of so many "reactionary adults' vision of TV" that Wallace suggests in "*E Unibus Pluram*" he strives to avoid. In fact, one of the key differences between Winn's and Wallace's depictions of televisual entertainment is their widely varying responses to the notion that television is like a drug. Wallace does not echo Winn's "just say no" line but examines in detail the despair that has driven the U.S. populace to crave such forms of escape as television and drugs in the first place. Television, in this view, is not the evil; the evil is that which makes television necessary in the first place.

Wallace is not alone among contemporary fiction writers in this assessment of television. Rick Moody, in *The Ice Storm*, gives brief consideration to one of its characters' television-watching habits as evidence not of her degradation but of the loneliness of suburban adolescence: "More about television. From *Sunrise Semester* to *Love, American Style*, from *Banacek* to *The New Price Is Right*, television served as the structured time, the safe harbor for Wendy Hood" (130). Television's safety, which allows Wendy to "[give] herself back to her childhood, to some part of herself that had never passed beyond that demographic category" (130), reveals that the locus of the threats to her well-being, to her interactions with "reality," lies not in the escape provided by the tube but in that which she is escaping from, a world alternately sexually charged and Puritanically repressed, a world that makes impossible genuine human contact other than the physical. What Wendy longs for most is "some association with the people of her town, some sense of community that stuck deeper than the country club stuff" (133), but all her environment will give her is television, and "[m]ostly she watched television alone" (131). Wendy, as an avid watcher of television, is not imagined to have failed but to have been failed by the generation ostensibly raising her.

What I mean to suggest through these dangerously incomplete readings of two novels among a myriad of contemporary possibilities is not that no younger writers have anxieties about television that are comparable to those expressed by Pynchon and DeLillo, nor even that Wallace and Moody are wholly free from such concerns. In fact, the suggestion that television-watching is evidence of cultural damage implies a hierarchy of media forms in which the novel itself is proposed to be sufficiently edifying to allow its escape from the category of entertainment, thus creating, in a fashion similar to that of the novel of obsolescence, a protected space outside contemporary culture's corruptions in which the novel can continue to flourish. This same perspective can easily mutate, as can be seen in Dave Eggers's *A Heartbreaking Tale of Staggering Genius*, or just as easily in Jonathan Franzen's *The Corrections*, into a kind of ironic sneer at mass culture, in which Eggers, for instance, holding television in extreme disdain, nonetheless embarks (though with a knowing affectlessness) on the project of becoming a cast member of the San Francisco edition of MTV's *The Real World*, or in which Franzen lumps television together with all the other aspects of life in the Midwest that he viciously caricatures. But even in those writers among the "New White Guys" whose work struggles to avoid the pitfalls of an impotent irony, concerns about television remain—fears, as Wallace suggests, about the problems in contemporary life that transform entertainment into an object of need, and particularly about television's effect on the writer himself, threatening as it does to trap him and his work in a state of terminal nonseriousness in which there are no problems that can't be treated with sarcastic detachment.

Insofar as there is a solution to such writerly anxieties, it is not, as it was for John Barth, simply to write a novel about them but, as Wallace suggests, a risky return to affect, in which problems—and not necessarily just the problems of the novelist, but the problems that alternately bind and divide contemporary U.S. culture at large—are taken seriously: "The next real literary 'rebels' in this country," Wallace argues, "might well emerge as some weird bunch of *anti*-rebels, born oglers who dare somehow to back away from ironic watching, who have the childish gall actually to endorse and instantiate single-entendre principles. Who treat of plain old untrendy human troubles and emotions in U.S. life with reverence and conviction. Who eschew self-consciousness and fatigue" ("Pluram" 81). In this kind of honest and in-depth confrontation of the range of human problems—which could easily be mistaken for a reactionary return to liberal humanism—the contemporary novel might genuinely stake its claim to territory that television either cannot or will not explore.

Writing from the Margins

Of course such writing—writing that takes human problems seriously, writing that confronts emotions and values without postmodernism's special sneer—has been produced all along during the postmodern era in the United States. Like postmodernist theory, however, which sought in part to restore relevance to the white male critics whose Marxist beliefs and arguments had been undone by the ironies of multinational capitalism, and who had been made obsolete by the passion and conviction of the Sixties' identity-based political movements, the hip ironies of postmodern fiction have functioned to provide continued relevance to a group of writers who felt themselves decentered at precisely the moment that previously marginalized writers—women, African Americans, Asian Americans, gays, and lesbians, among others—found a voice. In this manner, the double-edged notion of the "New White Guys" becomes particularly apt, as this group of white male writers imagines itself to have rediscovered affect after its long absence from favor. Alongside the mainstream of postmodern ironizing, however, marginalized writers continued writing, often using the same kinds of formal experimentation as their white male counterparts, but continuing at the same time to take dangerous human emotions, and the sociopolitical problems experienced by disenfranchised groups and individuals, seriously. Jane Elliott, in fact, in a review of Jonathan Franzen's *The Corrections* that cites Franzen's citation of Wallace's "tribal writers" comments, argues that the appropriation by mainstream white male writers of the personal and emotional material usually explored by the Oprah-style books that have been ghettoized as "chick lit" serves to accentuate the supposedly marginal status of white men in contemporary culture while simultaneously denigrating the texts produced by those women and "minority" writers who traditionally espouse such forms. "In other words," Elliott suggests, with reference to Franzen's "Perchance to Dream," "by dint of his mainstream status, Franzen was able to spend a 20-page article reinventing the same wheel tribal writers had been using, all the while arguing that theirs wasn't really a wheel anyway" (73).

The implication that postmodern irony has functioned over the last decades to preserve the relevance of white masculinity in a political and literary environment focused on otherness—and, in fact, to shut down the concerns of marginalized writers through an inability or refusal to take such problems seriously—suggests that postmodernism, for all its putative rebellion against the various oppressions of the modern, including mimesis, rationality, teleology, and hierarchy, is in part that political oxymoron, the conservative revolution. As I suggested in the first chapter, postmodernist theory came to prominence in the contemporary academy to some degree as a reaction to the identity-based political and intellectual movements of the 1960s and 1970s, reevaluating concepts of individual sovereignty just as some marginalized groups gained the political sway necessary to assert and give voice to their individuality, declaring the death of the master narrative in the wake of the articulation and critique of the master narratives of patriarchy, white supremacy, and colonial power. In this way, postmodernist theory functioned to return a group of predominantly white male thinkers to the center of intellectual inquiry while masking the social implications of both the theory's evacuation of individual identity and the particular identities of its practitioners. One might likewise begin to question whether postmodernist fiction—that too-slippery category—has been similarly marked from the outset by its escape from considerations of the social uses and misuses of power with regard to human difference, and its return instead to the universalized cultural problems of contemporary whiteness, maleness, Americanness.

Molly Hite's work on the postmodern novel suggests this possibility, even as she attempts to undermine the category's apparent restrictions. So, however inadvertently, do a number of the critics of obsolescence. As a pathway into the problem, let us consider briefly a passage from Neil Postman's *Amusing Ourselves to Death*; in arguing for the degrading effects on contemporary culture of both the sensationalism of television and the suggestibility of the viewing audience, Postman points to the following example: "In New Bedford, Massachusetts, a rape trial was televised, to the delight of audiences who could barely tell the difference between the trial and their favorite mid-day soap opera" (94). One can begin unpacking this comment's condescension by noting Postman's use of "audiences," a term John Fiske argues is ideologically loaded, implying passive consumption by "cultural dopes" (*Television* 16). Moreover, in positing that the form of entertainment from which these "audiences" can "barely" distinguish the trial is a soap opera, Postman inadvertently reveals the true target of his ire, the feminization of U.S. culture under the influence of television. Part of what is shocking about this slip is that it seems never to have occurred to Postman that women in New Bedford might have had some specific interest in watching a rape trial other than as an escape into lurid "soap opera" fantasy. But beyond this refusal to understand the stakes of such a trial for certain of its viewers, Postman's ill-submerged concerns about the feminization of contemporary culture through its adoption of modes of discourse accessible to the masses are in keeping with modernist anxieties about mass culture. As Andreas Huyssen writes in "Mass Culture as Woman":

> the nightmare of being devoured by mass culture through co-option, commodification, and the "wrong" kind of success is the constant fear of the modernist artist, who tries to stake out his territory by fortifying the boundaries between genuine art and inauthentic mass culture. Again, the problem is not the desire to differentiate between forms of high art and depraved forms of mass culture and its co-options. The problem is rather the persistent gendering as feminine of that which is devalued. (53)

Though for Huyssen, the "desire to differentiate" between high and low matters less than the assumption that the low exists in a feminized state, I would argue that the two points are inseparable. In a culture in which the "high" is considered the provenance of an elite, overwhelmingly masculine few, while the "low" belongs to the feminine mass, the act of distinguishing high from low is always an act of gendering and thus is always politically charged. Moreover, though Huyssen argues, along with numerous other postmodern theorists, that these boundaries between high and low, between art and mass culture, have dissolved in the contemporary era, one must ask for whom such boundaries have fallen, if indeed they have. Though it is now clearly possible for "high" artists such as Jonathan Franzen to appropriate the forms of mass culture formerly stigmatized as "chick lit," is it similarly possible for participants in the "mass"—watchers of television; readers of chick-lit—to partake of the objects of "high" art? As I noted in Franzen's conflict with Oprah, such popularization appears to represent a threat to the privilege of the elite cultural producer, and as Postman's concerns further suggest, what Huyssen calls the "anxiety of contamination," or the concern of the artist and intellectual with "stak[ing] out his territory" by shoring up these crumbling barriers against an infiltrating, infecting mass culture has not diminished. Canonical postmodernist fiction, through its relentless ironizing, works to distance itself from the contaminating otherness of the masses and to retreat into the purity of universal white masculinity.

One might then question whether novelists working outside the primary trajectories of modernism and postmodernism are similarly stalked by the anxieties of contamination and obsolescence that writers like Pynchon and DeLillo, as well as some of their younger counterparts, seem to exhibit. In defining the anxiety of obsolescence in the introduction to this volume, I connected the postmodern novelist's anxious reaction to the electronic media to an inversion of Bloom's "anxiety of influence," an Oedipal model in which the poet's anxiety about his predecessors undergirds his poem. The overwhelming masculinism of this model, in which the poet must "battle" his poetic "father" for the right to possess the Muse and thus full artistic maturity, is almost commonplace.[2] I would suggest, however, that it is precisely this masculinism that most closely binds the anxiety of influence to the anxiety of obsolescence. Bloom argues that "[w]hen a poet experiences incarnation *qua* poet, he experiences anxiety necessarily towards any danger that might *end him* as a poet" (58). In the novel of obsolescence, this danger is in part connected to a threatening televisual culture whose overpowering machinery, whose attraction to spectacle, and whose inescapable networks make the humanist, linguistic, individualist technologies of the novel appear hopelessly dated, if not downright obsolete. But the danger is equally the other writers who participate in the novel's technologies without succumbing to the universalizing pressures of humanism, those whose attention to human hierarchies and their effects on marginalized subjects aligns them with a socially activated postmodern politics. For this reason, it is important to note that, returning to Bloom's phrase, the poet must first have experienced "incarnation" as a poet, must have been granted a voice, before such threats to his position become effective. This perhaps begins to explain what appears to be a general absence of anxiety on the part of emergent or "minority" writers about the electronic media; television does not represent a threat from the outside to some guarded position for these writers, nor does the popularization that the medium might bring suggest the contamination of an elite preserve. Rather, insofar as contemporary culture holds a threat for marginalized writers, that threat lies in the culture's failure to take their voices seriously, or even to hear them in the first place. To put it plainly, only a culture that has experienced some form of dominance need fear its obsolescence.

In this sense, postmodernism generally, and the novel of obsolescence more specifically, contains within its rebellion a deeply conservative impulse, an attempt to preserve a position of centrality by dismissing the social interests of writers previously marginalized by the modernist project, and by further claiming that position of marginality or "decenteredness" for itself through its focus on the cultural, and particularly the mediated, aspects of postmodernism.[3] By way of contrast, I want briefly to consider the work of a contemporary of Pynchon and DeLillo whose novels are frequently included on the canon-revising lists of postmodern texts, but who was nowhere included in the originary lists: Toni Morrison.[4] Morrison has an extended, complex, and not untroubled relationship with television and related forms of popular media, briefly represented within her fiction and considered at greater length in her nonfiction writing, but it is important to note that she expresses no anxiety about these media forms as competitors with the novel. Instead, Morrison's concerns with the media focus primarily on their content, and particularly on the relationship of the mainstream media to the perpetuation of racism in the United States: "Popular culture," she argued in a 1993 *Time Magazine* article, "shaped by film, theater, advertising, the press, television and literature, is heavily engaged in race talk. It participates freely in this most enduring and efficient rite of passage [of recent immigrants] into U.S. culture: negative appraisals of the native-born black population" ("Backs" 60). In this fashion, television—accompanied by the mainstream literature of the United States— serves through its representations not to threaten women writers or writers of color with obsolescence but to reinforce the already-existing exclusion of disenfranchised groups from full participation in the culture. Where Morrison's writing evidences anxiety about television, then, that anxiety stems not from the changes it has wrought within U.S. culture but from its sustenance of that culture, and the ways that television supports a racist, patriarchal status quo.

Perhaps for this reason, Morrison's writings about television tend to have little to do with her role as a novelist, and more to do with her affective connections to the African American community. This can be seen in her public responses to the Anita Hill/Clarence Thomas hearings and the O.J. Simpson trial, the sources of Morrison's most direct comments about the medium. Here again, television is but one form in a widespread cultural complex that serves to perpetuate the exclusions and marginalizations effected by a racially hierarchized society. In the case of the former, television takes its place as one among many media forms consulted by those interested in the events:

> Everyone interested in the outcome of this nomination, regardless of race, class, gender, religion, or profession, turns to as many forms of media as are available. They read the *Washington Post* for verification of their dread or their hope, read the *New York Times* as though it were *Pravda*, searching

between the lines of the official story for one that most nearly approximates what might really be happening. They read local papers to see if the reaction among their neighbors is similar to their own, or they try to figure out on what information their own response should be based. They have listened to newscasters and anchor people for the bits and bites that pointed to, or deflected attention from, the machinery of campaigns to reject or accept the nominee. They have watched television screens that seem to watch back, that dismiss viewers or call upon them for flavor, reinforcement, or routine dissent. ("Introduction" viii)

Certain aspects of this description of the media's role in the Anita Hill/Clarence Thomas hearings echo the terms of the anxiety of obsolescence: "everyone interested" comes together as a sort of networked mass; the television screen, like that watching Oedipa Maas, seems to possess greater agency than do its ostensible viewers; the news seems to deflect rather than describe the truth. However, there are key differences as well, most notably that "everyone interested" turns to many forms of media, not just the television, in an active search not just for *the* story but for "their own response" to that story. Television's mediation of this story does not, for Morrison, necessarily result in uniformity of opinion, or passivity in the face of a technologized culture, in no small part because of the multiplicity of media forms available to the interested, and because, she goes on to note, "most of all, people talked to one another" (viii). The relations among individuals in U.S. culture, she seems to suggest, have not been wholly subsumed by their mediated forms.

Those relations, of course, are heavily inflected (or infected) by the racist legacy of slavery in the United States, a legacy that manifests in the forms of communication and entertainment that dominate contemporary culture. As Morrison writes of the massively popular drama that the media constructed out of the O.J. Simpson trial: "In a culture dominated by images, Mr. Simpson is ideal—already an entertainer with a surfeit of the talents successful entertainers have. Also, he is black. When race culpability or pathology is added to this market brew, profits soar and the narrative coalesces quickly, takes on another form and moves from commodity to lore" ("Official" xvii). While Morrison invokes the terms of the spectacle—the "culture dominated by images"—the crucial element in this particular spectacle is not the images themselves but the national history of race prejudice into which those images play. In this fashion, the media in general, and television in particular, *facilitate* the coalescing of what Morrison refers to as "a national narrative, an official story" (xv), but the elements of that narrative have circulated throughout the culture in various forms for centuries.

In these readings of both the Clarence Thomas and the O.J. Simpson affairs, Morrison suggests that television is not the *cause* of U.S. cultural decline but rather one of the *sites* at which representations of the damage wrought by racism may be found. For this reason, because television becomes in these readings a conduit rather than a force, Morrison seems to maintain some optimism about the medium, suggesting by her relationship with it (a relationship markedly different from those of Pynchon and DeLillo) that the conduit can be used to carry counterhegemonic ideas as well. This optimism bears out in Morrison's relationship with media other than print; not only has she personally read and recorded abridged versions of her novels for sale as books on tape, but also her novel *Beloved* has been produced for film and *Paradise*, arguably her most difficult novel, is reportedly being adapted for a television miniseries, both by Oprah Winfrey's Harpo Productions. Those productions further indicate Morrison's significance for this chapter's reconsideration of the Franzen/Oprah brouhaha, as she was the novelist whose work was most frequently included during the run of the original Oprah's Book Club. Three of her novels—*The Bluest Eye*, *Song of Solomon*, and *Paradise*—were official selections of the show, and a fourth, *Beloved*, was the object of a special discussion on an episode of the show that focused on the film.[5] As the *Independent* points out, in its review of Morrison's most recent novel, *Love*:

> Unlike Jonathan Franzen, who thumbed his nose at Oprah and her viewers when *The Corrections* was chosen for her club, Morrison, who teaches literature at Princeton University, was entirely open to selection, never felt like it compromised the seriousness of her work. She is most impressed by Oprah's transformation of a downmarket show into America's most powerful bookselling tool. "I think her impact has been positive, really powerfully positive, just lassoing people," she says. "It's just amazing to me that here's a television personality who says, in effect, turn off the television and read a book." (Freeman)

Morrison, as the article slyly indicates, has all the high-culture status one could hope for—a professor of literature at an Ivy League university, no less!—but nonetheless feels her work is uncorrupted by its brush with the popular. In fact, as John Young demonstrates, her work both as a novelist and, earlier, as an editor at Random House, has been driven in no small part by an "open desire for the market—for there to be 'such a thing as popular black women's literature . . . Popular!'" (187, quoting Morrison). The idea of such popularity is, quite evidently, not perceived to be a threat to the quality of her writing, to her readerly reception, or to her critical reputation; it presents, instead, the possibility of one's voice being heard, the necessary precondition for a readership and a critical reputation in the first place. It is perhaps only, as Young argues, for "white-male canonical authors" that some opposition between " 'integrity' and *Oprah*," or between the literary and the popular, obtains (186).

Literature is thus, for Morrison, not under threat by television; on the contrary, television can be mobilized by the literary as a vehicle for its coming into being. If literature is endangered, if it dies in the future, Morrison further suggests, writers themselves will be responsible. In her Nobel Prize lecture, Morrison tells the story of an old, blind, wise woman who is taunted by young people, asked to answer the one question they're certain she cannot: "Old woman, I hold in my hand a bird. Tell me whether it is living or dead." Her response gives the appearance of a nonanswer but is in fact an accusation: "I don't know whether the bird you are holding is dead or alive, but what I do know is that it is in your hands. It is in your hands." Morrison makes the connection of this story to the novelist's responsibilities clear:

> I choose to read the bird as language and the woman as a practiced writer. . . . Being a writer she thinks of language partly as a system, partly as a living thing over which one has control, but most as agency—an act with consequences. So the question the children put to her: "Is it living or dead?" is not unreal because she thinks of language as susceptible to death, erasure; certainly imperiled and salvageable only by an effort of the will. She believes that if the bird in the hands of her visitors is dead the custodians are responsible for the corpse. ("Nobel Lecture")

Those who have been given the greatest powers over language, then—and in this group one must include contemporary canonical novelists—bear direct responsibility for its fate. That language is for Morrison equated with agency—and that the old woman of the story comes to "trust" the young people, at lecture's end, only once they are able to tell her a story in return—suggests not only Morrison's belief in the continued importance of writing, despite the presence on the scene of new media forms, but also the kinds of empowerment that storytelling can produce.

Furthermore, Morrison suggests that her particular subjectivity enables the novel's future in a way that makes plain her distinctness as a writer from the main thread of postmodern ironizing. As a recent magazine article puts it:

> Emerging in an era when black writing was seen as a predominantly male endeavor and women writers were perceived as predominantly white, she redefined the role of a "black woman writer."

"I didn't want to be an honorary male or an honorary white person,"
Morrison says. "When people complimented me, saying, by implication,
'You're better than a black or a woman writer,' I would always counter with 'I
am a black woman writer,' and that was not a narrow field. Because of those
two modifiers ["black" and "woman"], I felt my imaginative world was wider
and deeper, that I had access to and some sensibilities about worlds that may
not have been available to white men." (Langer 46)

Because of this affective, imaginative engagement with the world—with the
multiple worlds—of the marginalized, and because of her conviction that the
agency that language provides is not a right but a responsibility, Morrison
demonstrates a sense of contemporary literature's continued significance, and
particularly of the significance of the voices of the marginalized within it.

As her Nobel lecture suggests, the affective spaces to which Morrison, as a
black woman writer, has a deepened access include the vital, and vitally communal, importance of story. Throughout Morrison's novels one can see the
double-edged effect of stories, particularly stories as the oral history of African
American culture. On the one hand, the anxiety revealed in these novels revolves around the burden that history places on the novels' characters and the
cultural damage that history can inflict. On the other hand, and at the same
time, Morrison's novels are filled with the insistence that history—in the form
of stories—must be transmitted, for it is in their telling that community is
built. But what is most important with regard to the anxiety of obsolescence
is that these histories are not, and cannot be, captured by the media. The electronic media, and their attendant technologies, exist almost wholly outside
the realm of the stories with which Morrison is concerned. As the mysterious
narrator of *Jazz* insists at the novel's end, speaking of the characters she has just
lovingly brought to rest: "When I see them now they are not sepia, still, losing
their edges to the light of a future afternoon. Caught midway between was and
will be. For me they are real. Sharply in focus and clicking" (226). The people
who inhabit these stories are not photographs, not trapped in the chronic past
or future tense of recorded images and the electronic media. Instead, they live;
they are present tense—and it is particularly notable that they live within and
for the novel, as it is the novel itself that is finally revealed to be its own narrator.[6] It is in the presentness of the stories told throughout Morrison's novels
that the focus on characters is created, and it is because these stories are so
present, so real, and so lived that they produce such anxiety about how they
could possibly end, about the continuing damage they can inflict.

Where the media does appear in Morrison, it is frequently depicted, as it is in Pynchon and DeLillo, as an illusion, a trap. Thus, part of the tragedy that befalls Dorcas in *Jazz* occurs because "[e]verything was like a picture show to her, and she was the one on the railroad track, or the one trapped in the sheik's tent when it caught on fire" (202). But there is in this statement little sense of indictment of film itself; rather this is an accusation leveled at Dorcas, a young girl who allows herself to get caught up in fantasies that do not belong to her. She is not, and cannot be, the damsel in distress, the woman bound to the tracks, the prisoner in the sheik's tent, at least in part because the damsel is always white. In these melodramatic films, in fact, when people of color are depicted, they are invariably the villains, not the heroes or the ladies waiting to be saved.

This, it seems, is the sole lesson that Morrison presents about the electronic media: it does not, and cannot, belong to the African American communities with which she is concerned. And the reasons behind this disconnection from the machineries of communication are not bound up in the lies told by images, or the alienating nature of mechanicity, or the destruction of the individual by the network. The separation between Morrison's characters and the media is instead directly related to the history of racism that structures their society. Television in Morrison becomes a commodity, a luxury whose price closes many black men and women out: "Guitar smiled at the sun, and talked lovingly of televisions, brass beds, and week-long card games, but his mind was on the wonders of TNT" (*SS* 181). Guitar's dreams of money, in *Song of Solomon*, involve television sets, but only as one among many possible luxuries, and the reality of Guitar's life is far too concerned with the murderous relationship between black and white to be very involved with the fantasy world of television at all.

It is unlikely, in fact, that television would have anything to offer these characters, as its near absence from Morrison's novels would seem to indicate. The purpose of the media that do exist in these novels is nothing more nor less than the communication of racism, both the reporting of racist acts and the general dissemination of racist ideology. Thus we find the men of Guitar's town gathered in the barbershop, listening to radio reports of Emmett Till's murder, each disbelieving that they've gotten the whole story.

> "It'll be in the morning paper."
> "Maybe it will, and maybe it won't," said Porter.
> "It was on the radio! Got to be in the paper!" said Freddie.
> "They don't put that kind of news in no white newspaper. Not unless he raped somebody." (*SS* 81)

As in the disappointing reality of the movie melodramas that create Dorcas's fantasies, African Americans appear in the white press only as villains, never as innocent victims. And thus the history that so binds the black community in Morrison, the history of slavery and racism, is closed out of nearly all media representations.

Where these stories do sneak in, they create divisions rather than build the communities forged by oral storytelling. Such is the case for Felice's father in *Jazz*, who religiously reads the newspapers even though it "worries his blood" (199), enjoying the arguments he has over the stories they report.

> "Once I thought if I read the papers we'd saved I could argue with him. But I picked wrong. I read about the white policemen who were arrested for killing some Negroes and said I was glad they were arrested, that it was about time.
>
> "He looked at me and shouted, 'The story hit the paper because it was news, girl, news!'
>
> "I didn't know how to answer him and started to cry so my grandmother said, 'Sonny, go somewhere and sit down,' and my mother said, 'Walter, shut up about all that to her.'
>
> "She explained to me what he meant: that for the everyday killings cops did of Negroes, nobody was arrested at all. . . ." (199)

Felice misses, in her innocent acceptance of the importance of what the newspaper prints, the real social relations that the newsprint serves to replicate. The black and white of the press renders the complex stories told in African American culture too apparently simple, too cut-and-dried. What becomes important, as Felice's father understands and Felice has yet to learn, is that an African American encountering the white media must become especially adept at reading not simply what is printed, but the ideologies that lurk between the lines. And thus Morrison repeatedly suggests that an essential relationship to text—a relationship that Pynchon and DeLillo seem to claim has been consistently undermined by the twentieth-century media—is at the heart of the African American community's successful negotiation of the world. As Macon Dead says about his father, the first Macon Dead: "Everything bad that ever happened to him happened because he couldn't read" (*SS* 53). The anxiety revealed here is not, then, that of a turn away from text, a lack of concern in the community for the writer, but rather that of being closed out of textual power in the first place.

The centrality of reading is the lesson acknowledged by Guitar before the role of killer into which he is driven by white racial violence begins to undermine the connections to his own community he is fighting to maintain.

He has come to understand the impossibly ingrained nature of U.S. racism through reading, insisting to Milkman that all whites would lynch a black man, given the right set of circumstances:

> I listen. I read. And now I know that they know it too. They know they are unnatural. Their writers and artists have been saying it for years. Telling them they are unnatural, telling them they are depraved. They call it tragedy. In the movies they call it adventure. It's just depravity that they try to make glorious, natural. (*SS* 157)

Guitar is able to find this depravity, to read this racism, only by getting underneath the media's—and, notably, the artist's—representations of "tragedy" and "adventure" and seeing what gets left out, who doesn't get represented.

But this racism so indelibly written into the media in the twentieth century seems to take account only of the "white" media, forms of communication and entertainment created, distributed, and imposed by the white in a top-down model of "mass" culture, a form of cultural production and distribution that should be read, according to Fiske's model, in opposition to the "popular," which has its origins in the people who create and use it.[7] Morrison reveals in *Jazz* a decidedly different relationship to the elements of this "popular" culture than that seen in much of Pynchon and DeLillo. Jazz itself, much reviled by the arbiters of high culture—see, for instance, Horkheimer and Adorno, who lump jazz in amongst the products of the "culture industry," disparaging it in relation to classical music for its "packaged" quality, a reading of this music that suggests a complete misconstrual of the relationship between the mass and the popular—becomes in Morrison, as in other writers such as James Baldwin and Ralph Ellison, the vivid, passionate musical embodiment of that storytelling community.[8] The only threat suggested in the jazz and blues of Harlem in the 1920s is that sensed by the Christian women who connect the music's passion to a general moral decline:

> When Alice Manfred collected the little girl from the Miller sisters, on those evenings following the days her fine stitching was solicited, the three women sat down in the kitchen to hum and sigh over cups of Postum at the signs of Imminent Demise: such as not just ankles but knees in full view; lip rouge red as hellfire; burnt matchsticks rubbed on eyebrows; fingernails tipped with blood—you couldn't tell the streetwalkers from the mothers. And the men, you know, the things they thought nothing of saying out loud to any woman who passed by could not be repeated before children. They did not know for sure, but they suspected that the dances were beyond nasty because the

music was getting worse and worse with each passing season the Lord waited to make himself known. Songs that used to start in the head and fill the heart had dropped on down to places below the sash and the buckled belts. Lower and lower, until the music was so lowdown you had to shut your windows and just suffer the summer sweat when the men in shirtsleeves propped themselves in window frames, or clustered on rooftops, in alleyways, on stoops and in the apartments of relatives playing the lowdown stuff that signaled Imminent Demise. (55–56)

These women, in their evocation of the evil being done by this music, are on the one hand mocked by the narrator for their concerns with "Imminent Demise" and on the other hand revealed by the intensity and physicality of their descriptions to be drawn to the music at the same time they fear its effects. But it should be pointed out as well that these fears are a far cry from the fears about jazz expressed by the (white) protectors of the high-cultural estate: this music is not the threatening sign of the rise of an uncontrollable mass that threatens the preserve of the cultural and intellectual elite, or the equally dangerous manifestation of the control of those mindless masses by a fascistic culture industry, but is here rather an expression of the sensuality, the vitality, the lifeblood of African American culture. This music is the voice of the men in shirtsleeves, a voice that threatens these Christian women through its raw sexuality but that threatens the dominant white culture through its uncontrollable otherness. It is because of this otherness to the dominant mass culture that jazz, like storytelling, is able to fully express the real social experience of Morrison's characters—something that neither the newspapers nor the radio, movies, or television could accomplish.

Morrison, then, reveals in the various types of writing she has produced across her career concerns about the mass media, including television, but these concerns do not circulate around anxieties about the health of the older literary forms they seem to be displacing; in fact, she repeatedly indicates the power that literature and other modes of storytelling still have within the African American community. On the contrary, where Morrison expresses dissatisfaction with the electronic media, she focuses upon the media's relationship to the endemic racism of U.S. culture, and the media's failure to represent and contend with the specific histories of such marginalized groups within U.S. culture. Where those media forms can be co-opted to the retelling of such narratives, however, whether through the adaptation of her novels for film and television or through the inclusion of her novels in Oprah's Book Club, her career suggests that the contemporary media can be a tool for the promotion of the novelist's voice rather than a threat to that voice. It is precisely to the point that the writers who most sense a threat from television—whether the threat of being silenced or the threat of being popularized—are members of the very group to and for whom the mass media have always spoken.

Melodramas of Beset (White) Manhood

Thus, the novelist of obsolescence turns a concern about the possibilities for the novel's future into fodder for its continuance, representing and interpreting the functions of the media that appear to threaten him with obsolescence in the manner that will best support the novel's claims to edification, humanism, and individuality. In so doing, he not only produces new novels but also, and not inadvertently, produces a new rationale for the continuing valorization of the novel as a form, ensuring its privileged position in the pantheon of cultural objects. However, in the process of representing the dangers he perceives in the media, he at times reveals another locus of anxiety—not television itself, but the television audience. In these moments, concerns about technology bleed into concerns about race and gender, about the otherness in U.S. culture that threatens to displace not just the novelist's productions but the novelist himself from centrality. Television thus serves both as a representation of what has gone wrong with U.S. culture and as a more comfortable site for the displacement of anxieties about human difference. Television provides an easy scapegoat, a safe target for the finger the novelist points at the causes of his marginalization; television makes a safe enemy because it exists at the intersection of a substantive range of cultural discourses already in motion that provide an ongoing dissection of the medium's deleterious effects. Among those discourses, as I have explored throughout this volume, are the discourses of television as machine, which point to the medium's dehumanizing effects; of television as spectacle, which point to the medium's destruction of the power of representation; and of television as network, which point to the medium's displacement of the individual. This combination of destructions and displacements reveals an anxiety about the role of the novelist in contemporary culture.

But underneath all this lies a concern about the continuing role of the white male subject in contemporary society. It is this underlying fear that John Kucich indicates is responsible for "the single greatest failure of Don DeLillo's work":

> it alternates between a suspicion that legitimation through social identity is a problem inherent in postmodern assumptions about language and culture,

and an insipid, compulsive whining about the fact that white males are out of fashion. Unfortunately, the whining is often much more obvious and persistent than the analysis. (340)[9]

This whining—a form of complaint that can be read across the postmodernist novel from Mailer to Barth, Nabokov to Barthelme—is part of what has led to the common criticism of the genre as the province of white men, as Molly Hite has indicated. More than simply calling it an insular boy's club, in fact, "[s]ome feminist critics have gone on to claim that the postmodern novel is essentially masculinist or misogynist, inasmuch as a number of the most famous works, especially those produced in the 1950s and 1960s, are preoccupied with aggressive, often violent male sexual behavior and the denigration of female characters" (Hite 698). But even where the canonical postmodern novel does not demonstrate so baldly its ethnocentric and sexist basis, it reveals ill-concealed anxieties about race, ethnicity, and gender. And even where the anxiety of obsolescence does not serve to mask inadequately repressed fears of the social other, it nonetheless provides the novelist with not only an assortment of writing strategies in the form of the intersecting cultural discourses of the machine, the spectacle, and the network, but also one overwhelming cultural theme, which may appropriately be called, after Nina Baym, a melodrama of beset white manhood.

Baym explores, as the subtitle of her landmark 1981 article indicates, "how theories of American fiction exclude women authors." Looking at a wide variety of critical texts that key the "American novel" to an exploration of specific definitions of "Americanness," and in particular response to two writers who set "serious literature" in opposition to the sentimental fiction that they refer to as "the ubiquitous melodramas of beset womanhood," Baym develops her own theory of U.S. fiction:

> I would like to suggest that the theoretical model of a story which may become the vehicle of cultural essence is: "a melodrama of beset manhood." This melodrama is presented in a fiction which, as we'll later see, can be taken as representative of the author's literary experience, his struggle for integrity and livelihood against flagrantly bad best-sellers written by women. Personally beset in a way that epitomizes the tensions of our culture, the male author produces his melodramatic testimony to our culture's essence—so the theory goes. (130)

That "the author's literary experience" is in Baym's model linked specifically to an encroaching femininity is precisely what makes the model adaptable to the anxiety of obsolescence, for the novelist's perception of his struggle against obsolescence is unquestionably connected to these earlier authors' struggles for "integrity and livelihood." The slippage comes in the shift from "flagrantly bad best-sellers written by women" to television as the mass medium that male authors must struggle against, but, as Huyssen's exploration of the gendering of mass culture as female and Postman's inadvertent revelation of his fears about the feminization of U.S. culture through television make clear, the otherness of the electronic media to the "higher" art of the novel parallels the otherness of women and racial and ethnic minorities to the experience of white men.

But what is most interesting about the novelistic representations of these two related forms of otherness is that the relationship of center and margins is inverted; the white male somehow becomes "other" to the "mainstream" now composed of women and "minorities," and the novel becomes "other" in a culture ruled so pervasively by television. It is in this light that I'd like to return, here at the close, to a comment by Don DeLillo in "The Power of History," published within weeks of the release of *Underworld*:

> Ultimately the writer will reconfigure things the way his own history demands. He has his themes and biases and limitations. He has the small crushed pearl of his anger. He has his teaching job, his middling reputation and the one radical idea he has been waiting for all his life. The other thing he has is a flat surface that he will decorate with words.
>
> Language can be a form of counterhistory. The writer wants to construct a language that will be the book's life-giving force. He wants to submit to it. Let language shape the world. Let it break the faith of conventional re-creation.
>
> Language lives in everything it touches and can be an agent of redemption, the thing that delivers us, paradoxically, from history's flat, thin, tight and relentless designs, its arrangement of stark pages, and that allows us to find an unconstraining otherness, a free veer from time and place and fate. (63)

I originally introduced this passage in Chapter 3 in connection with DeLillo's project of "reclaiming" language from the power of the spectacle. What I'd like to look at now is, first, the picture DeLillo paints of himself: "the writer," who can be no one but DeLillo in an article so relentlessly self-examinatory, becomes a man with a "teaching job," a man with a "middling reputation," a man with "one radical idea." DeLillo, of course, has never been required to hold a teaching job; his claim to "middling reputation" is spurious at best. But the notion of his having one—and no more than one—radical idea makes clear the article's polemical-political purpose. The novelist is in fact creating "counterhistory," attempting to use language not only to undo the effects of "conventional re-creation"—for which one must read the most mainstream representational form, television—but also to "redeem" the white male from his historical role as the dominant and to enable his search for "an unconstraining otherness," a more comfortable sense of himself as the marginalized.

This is, at its root level, the function of the anxiety of obsolescence: the release of the white male author from responsibility through an at times histrionic concern for his own imminent demise, a conversion of the forms and gestures of oppressed cultures to his own project of maintaining his cultural (and social) centrality. Phillip Brian Harper has argued that "the easy appropriability of the signifiers of certain forms of social marginality makes them prime commodities in the mass-cultural drive to market the effects of disenfranchisement for the social cachet that can paradoxically attach to it" (188). Marginality thus becomes, in a literary culture obsessed with fragmentation and decentering, a paradoxical source of return to dominance, a melodrama of beset white manhood. If, as Kucich has claimed, "one need not have suffered to sing the postmodern blues" (332), so one need not be disenfranchised to claim the position of the excluded. And, finally, one need not be dead to benefit from the pomp of an ongoing funeral.

Notes

Introduction

1. The distinction that I am implying between typography and screen fonts may suggest a rather unimaginative notion of what might constitute a "book" in the future; my intent in drawing this distinction is to focus attention on the cultural objects as they exist today. I will, however, encounter the possibilities presented by the e-book in Chapter 1.
2. On the battle over HDTV, see Joel Brinkley, *Defining Vision*. One must of course note the irony in the fact that these very references will themselves shortly be obsolete.
3. On these battles between media, see Green-Lewis; Stephens; Boorstin; Daniel J. Czitrom, *Media and the American Mind*; Postman, *Amusing*; Owen.
4. See Ken Auletta: "Since the time when the book industry started calling itself an 'industry,' it has been in a state of 'crisis.' And yet, whatever the crisis, there have always been people prepared not only to buy books but to buy more books than anyone had ever bought before" (Auletta 50). But in *The Death of Literature* Alvin Kernan argues—presumably without irony—that the sheer quantity of books published is in part responsible for reading's demise (138). I consider this point further in Chapter 1.

Chapter 1

1. See, on the history of death discourses, Mann, and on the history of technological obsolescence: McLuhan; Stephens; Levinson; Jay David Bolter and Richard Grusin, *Remediation*.
2. See Foucault, *Archaeology*, in which the author argues for the uncovering of "[r]elations between statements (even if the author is unaware of them; even if the statements do not have the same author; even if the authors were unaware of each other's existence); relations between groups of statements thus established (even if these groups do not concern the same, or even adjacent fields; even if they do not possess the same formal level; even if they are not the locus of assignable exchanges); relations between statements and groups of statements and events of a quite different kind (technical, economic, social, political)" (29).
3. See ibid., in which Foucault argues that discursive formations "define not the dumb existence of a reality nor the canonical use of a vocabulary, but the ordering of objects" (49).
4. In fact, this letter, while plausible, does not appear to exist; I have been unable to uncover the original. See Barth, *LETTERS* 439.
5. Moreover, Watt's and Armstrong's narratives both focus exclusively on the birth of the *English* novel; the novel's end point looks quite radically different if one takes Murasaki Shikibu's eleventh-century *Tale of Genji* as its origin.
6. "The novel was the subject of heated popular debate in the late eighteenth century and, in many ways, was to the early national period what television was to the 1950s or MTV

and video games to the 1980s. It was condemned as escapist, anti-intellectual, violent, pornographic; since it was a 'fiction' it was a lie and therefore evil. Since it often portrayed characters of low social station and even lower morals—foreigners, orphans, fallen women, beggar girls, women cross-dressing as soldiers, soldiers acting as seducers—it fomented social unrest by making the lower classes dissatisfied with their lot. The novel ostensibly contributed to the demise of community values, the rise in licentiousness and illegitimacy, the failure of education, the disintegration of the family; in short, the ubiquity of the novel . . . most assuredly meant the decline of Western civilization as it had previously been known" (Davidson, "Introduction" 3).

7. "To [its critics], the novel resembled a coquette who lured readers into a claustrophobic world of desire and self-indulgence, the antithesis of the public domain of rationality and men" (Gilmore 621).

8. On the purposeful exclusion of female authors from the canon of U.S. fiction, see Baym.

9. Temporarily: even aside from the standard postmodernist argument about the effacement of the difference between high and low, one can see a similar shift into the arena of respectability on the part of film since the 1970s introduction of film studies to the college curriculum. Once film became an object worthy of study, concerns devolved onto television. Now that the Birmingham school and its U.S. relatives have begun the process of recuperating television, one must wonder whether it will be able to make a similar migration across the great divide. Writing about much recent television (see, for instance, critical work on *Buffy the Vampire Slayer* and *The Sopranos*) would seem to indicate the possibility (see McGrath). Incidentally, a relatively new "death of film" discourse has recently surfaced (see Schickel).

10. As Cecelia Tichi suggests in *Electronic Hearth*, the loss of print's primacy in U.S. culture is "illusory, because the power and relevance of print never existed at the strength perceived. Most people did not read newspapers, especially in the 1800s. The whole notion that television intervened in the journalist's (and the larger print world's) relevance and timeliness to the vast populace is largely apocryphal, but an effective ideological base for the print world from which to argue against television" (180).

11. That such concerns may well be warranted can be seen in the locus of an *actual* crisis the book currently faces: academic publishing. Had there been time and space enough, and had the subject been less personally fraught than it is at the moment, I'd have liked to include in this volume some consideration of the contested future of the scholarly book.

12. Robert Coover likewise points out that "the very proliferation of books and other print-based media, so prevalent in this forest-harvesting, paper-wasting age, is held to be a sign of its feverish moribundity, the last futile gasp of a once vital form before it finally passes away forever, dead as God" (1). Coover's article "The End of Books" has often been misread in ways that suggest that Coover himself, in relating his adventures with hypertext, is advocating the retirement of the novel. Hardly so; Coover is here relating the conventional wisdom about the novel's death, a wisdom he finds useful in his novelistic deconstructions of the novel's presuppositions, but a wisdom he does not necessarily share.

13. From a New York University Graduate School of Arts and Science alumni mailing, June 1999. George Steiner reads this relationship of competition and co-optation between the novel and the media as producing a sort of "brain drain": "Talent is going into the competing media of television, film and their allied arts" (32).

14. That the anxiety is a pose is made manifest in "The Literature of Replenishment," in which Barth suggests that the previous essay has been chronically misread and rather petulantly insists that all he intended was to point to the rise of postmodernism all along.

15. George Steiner echoes this shrug-shoulderedness: "We are getting very tired in our novel-

writing; that makes perfect sense, there is nothing apocalyptic about it. Genres rise, genres fall, the epic, the verse epic, the formal verse tragedy, all have great moments, then they ebb" (33).

16. I consider the retrograde aspects of Barth's work in much greater detail in Fitzpatrick, "Exhaustion."

17. See Plato 78–82; Stephens 18–23; Postman, *Technopoly* 3–4.

18. For celebration of print combined with criticism of television, see Postman, *Amusing*; Birkerts. On the negative reactions to the rise of printing, see Stephens 33–34.

19. See, for instance, a page devoted to Postman's writing (preservenet.com/theory/Postman), a page of links related to his work (netaccess.on.ca/~glambos/neil_postman_stuff.htm), and even a page dedicated to the online discussion of *Technopoly* (charon.sfsu.edu/POSTMAN/Postmanmenu.html.)

20. Richard Dienst uses strikingly similar terms: "I offer here a map of television's possible economies organized between two conceptual poles called—in highly compressed shorthand—'machine' and 'image.' Any specific analysis of television must address the problems named by 'machine' and 'image,' and our positioning of these terms determines the definition of that other inescapable term always in play and at stake here—capitalism" (36). It is interesting that Dienst conceives of these terms as "poles" or opposites; I position them rather as two among many possible nonlinear concepts put into play in texts about the media. Further, dealing with these two concepts begs the question of their connection, a question perhaps resolved in my consideration of the network. Finally, rather than mobilizing these terms as a means of theorizing the political economy of television, I use them here as a means of focusing upon the circulation of discourses *about* television, Dienst's included.

21. See Tichi's *Shifting Gears*, in which she argues that new technologies "displaced the dominant Romantic view of a holistic, spiritual world of vegetative and bodily being" (xiii) into an inanimate world of machines and structures, and "fostered a conception of the human being as a machine for the consumption and production of energy" (xii).

22. See Green-Lewis: "A photograph is concerned with the way things are but will not remain, or perhaps the way we wish they were, or the way we wish they might have been. The perceived threat that this state will be lost is inherent in the act of photographing" (17).

23. See also Lynne Kirby's *Parallel Tracks,* in which, following Schivelbusch, she argues for the railroad as an "important *protocinematic* phenomenon" whose function was "training audiences for film" (2, 6).

24. See ibid.: "The 'paradigm' of the railroad prepared a path for the institutionalization of a certain kind of subject or spectator that cinema would claim as its own, a subject molded in relation to new forms of perception, leisure, temporality, and modern technology" (24).

25. R. W. Emerson, "Ode, Inscribed to W. H. Channing," 11. 50–51, qtd. in Marx 178.

26. See the National Railroad Museum Web site (nationalrrmuseum.org). The site is quick to qualify this comment, of course, by acknowledging that gender and race distinctions were scrupulously maintained through separate accommodations.

27. Ibid.

28. W. A. McKeever, "Motion Pictures: A Primary School for Criminals," qtd. in Levinson 56.

29. See Reid, particularly in his discussion of Marc Andreessen and Netscape.

30. For instance, the fall 1997 ads for a quickly cancelled Tony Danza sitcom featured Tony warily approaching his new PC, saying, "You look like a TV, but you're not a TV. You're an evil TV." This is perhaps television's anxiety of obsolescence about the Internet speaking:

computers pose as televisions, but with "evil" intent. On the battle between television and the computer, see Owen.

31. From WebTV promotional material (webtv.com/ns/tune/index.html). Note that WebTV, now effectively a dead technology, was no more than a temporary culmination, and not at all the real end point of these lines of development. A more recent convergence model might be found in TiVo.

32. Gilder in fact refers to early stabs at interactive television as "a convergence of corpses" (11).

33. "The moral for the evolution of media is very profound: when a new medium triumphs over an older medium in a given function, that does not mean the old medium will shrivel up and die. Rather, the old medium may be pushed into a niche in which it can perform better than the new medium, and where it will therefore survive, albeit as something different from what it was before the new medium arrived" (Levinson 48). See also Levinson 91–103.

34. See Connor: "Critical debates about postmodernism constitute postmodernism itself" (20).

35. See, particularly, Anderson. See also Hutcheon; Connor; Harper.

36. None of this is to suggest that no adequate work has been done on the conjunction of postmodernism and these other more socially contingent discourses. One immediately thinks of Harper's admirable model, along with those of bell hooks, Jennifer Wicke, Homi Bhabha, and many others. It is revealing to consider, however, that many of these scholars self-identify with the more socially mobilized discourses of African American studies, feminism, postcolonialism, and so on, rather than with postmodernism.

37. See, most pertinently, bell hooks's "Postmodern Blackness": "We should indeed [be] suspicious of postmodern critiques of the 'subject' when they surface at a historical moment when many subjugated people feel themselves coming to voice for the first time" (para. 9).

38. For a full reading of the Rushdie connection, see Scanlan.

39. In connection with these passages in the novel, see the text of a PEN America pamphlet written by DeLillo and Paul Auster. In reconsidering Salman Rushdie's five years of confinement, DeLillo and Auster speculate on the role other writers should play in this crisis: "What can we do? We can think about him. Try to imagine his life. Write it in our minds as if it were the most unlikely fiction" (Auster and DeLillo).

40. Their uses of the electronic media in conjunction with the 1997 releases of *Mason & Dixon* and *Underworld* equally give the lie to the death of the novelist. Of course, DeLillo was far more visible—attending numerous awards banquets, giving dozens of interviews, going on a limited reading tour, and even, most surprisingly, appearing on television—but Pynchon made shocking excursions from his retreat, including a recorded telephone call to CNN played in part over the air, in which he defended his privacy, claiming that "reclusive" is a code word for "doesn't like to talk to the media" ("Where's Thomas Pynchon?").

41. "Avant-garde discourse employs death-theory to terrorize artists and writers who must find some way to work despite these endlessly reflected deaths and resurrections, this ever-tightening cycle of differentiation and recuperation; who must produce new work in a climate where the new is simultaneously mandated and proscribed, where everything must always be new and nothing can ever be new again" (Mann 73).

Chapter 2

1. The entire line of contemporary cultural studies is aimed at overturning this belief in the passivity of participants in popular culture, Here is a representative notion from John Fiske's *Television Culture*: "Pleasure for the subordinate is produced by the assertion of one's social identity in resistance to, in independence of, or in negotiation with, the structure of domination. There is no pleasure in being a 'cultural dope' " (19).

2. On the relationship between reading and democracy, see Davidson, Introduction; and Cathy N. Davidson, ed., *Reading in America*.

3. On the frontier myth, see Turner; Santayana.

4. On the gendered nature of early film spectatorship and the anxieties it produced, see Hansen; on the threat to conventional gender roles posed by early television, see Spigel.

5. Similarly, these values betray hierarchical interests that correspond to categories of race, class, nationality, and sexuality; I am largely restricting my focus in this chapter to gender and sexuality in the interests of space and coherence.

6. See, most notably, Kurzweil, *Intelligent* and *Spiritual*; Moravec.

7. See of course Foucault, *Archaeology*, for an exploration of the ties between discourse and material existence. Postman's take on this relationship—as well as on the connection between changes in communications medium and changes in epistemology—is mostly clearly seen in *Technopoly*: "Surrounding every new technology are institutions whose organization—not to mention their entire reason for being—reflects the world-view promoted by the technology. Therefore, when an old technology is assaulted by a new one, institutions are threatened. When institutions are threatened, a culture finds itself in crisis" (18).

8. On the relationship between the posthuman and posthumanism, particularly as misread in contemporary novels about computers, see Fitzpatrick, "Exhaustion."

9. More deeply, of course, those origins can be traced back to the Cartesian dualism.

10. See Postman, *Technopoly* xii; Pynchon, "Is It OK" 1.

11. For instance: "in the most dramatic terms, the accusation can be made that the uncontrolled growth of technology destroys the vital sources of our humanity" (*Technopoly* xii).

12. Given the role of gender in this shattering of categories, it is extremely to the point that Pynchon's historical Badass is described as "usually male, and while sometimes earning the quizzical tolerance of women, is almost universally admired by men" ("Is It OK" 40). Pynchon's action-hero Badass reaffirms rather than undermines gender boundaries.

13. See, most notably, Lehman. For a reading of the machine in the antitheory discourse, see Liu: "Machines can always be read as uncanny doubles of our own inanimation, but more important, for Benjamin the nature of experience itself under high capitalism is forged in the crucible of mass production, mass reproducibility, and homogenization. The rise of economic forces whose rationalization of the everyday has an increasingly insidious effect on everyday life, but the enslavement to the machine is an image that emerges for a generalized sense of powerlessness before invisible forces, paternalistic in nature, whose unrepresentability, except as an infernal principle of the machine, is only one figure of the complex nature of capital's power. In the study of literature, however, it becomes obvious that a need to denigrate or repudiate machines becomes one symptom of the way in which the questions of mechanical reproduction are repressed. For many critics, it remains a scandal to think of the text as a thing that works, and even more scandalous to think of a reading as participating in mass production" (22).

14. I am, in what follows, interested solely in Deleuze and Guattari's representations of the machine in relationship to those representations in Pynchon and DeLillo. For a more thorough

reading of Deleuze and Guattari, as well as an extended Deleuzian reading of both authors, particularly in their mobilizations of the assemblage as a writing machine, see Johnston.

15. One should note, of course, that the notion that such magazines could "show" their readers that this disruption of desire "would" take place is, as noted earlier, based in one of the key fallacies about the medium: its audience's helplessness before its manipulations. As John Fiske argues, actual television viewers are less passive than their popular depictions would make them appear; television "does not 'cause' identifiable effects in individuals; it does, however, work ideologically to promote and prefer certain meanings of the world, to circulate some meanings rather than others, and to serve some social interests better than others" (*Television* 20). Just as television's representations "promote and prefer" particular ideological positions, so do representations of television. One of the social interests served by the representation of television's libidinal danger is precisely the traditional family, which reasserts its control in the face of danger.

16. To state that the coupling of television with the Deleuzian desiring-machine of the unconscious frees desire from its societal regulation is not to suggest that Deleuze and Guattari themselves read the medium as revolutionary, or even benign; as they argue in *A Thousand Plateaus*, the televisual machine is ultimately a machine of societal capture, rather than release: "one is subjected to TV insofar as one uses and consumes it, in the very particular situation of a subject of the statement that more or less mistakes itself for a subject of enunciation ('you, dear television viewers, who make TV what it is . . .'); the technical machine is the medium between two subjects. But one is enslaved by TV as a human machine insofar as the television viewers are no longer consumers or users, nor even subjects who supposedly 'make' it, but intrinsic component pieces, 'input' and 'output,' feedback or recurrences that are no longer connected to the machine in such a way as to produce or use it. In machinic enslavement, there is nothing but transformations and exchanges of information, some of which are mechanical, others human" (458).

17. Brian Massumi acknowledges that the position of "becoming woman" is "sexist," as "the burden of change is placed on women, since it is their cliché that is singled out" (89).

18. On the role of the fetish in *V.*, see Hanjo Berressem: "In *V.* this Law-of-the-Machine takes over both the individual and the cultural field, annexing the body in both dimensions. The fetish, all workforce or all sign, is the signifier by which the culturally determined, sexual economy is inscribed onto the body via the semiotic code. It is the relay by which Baudrillard's 'symbolic ambivalence' is replaced by a digital, phallic economy. The fetish as a signifier finally comes to designate the desire of the semiotic code itself" (71–72).

19. This array of parts may be opposed to the Deleuzian "body without organs" in its hyper-organization, rather than the dis-organization of the body without organs.

20. Postman borrows the term from Stanley Milgram's *Obedience to Authority*. See *Technopoly* 114.

21. The question nonetheless remains whether the map is actually an accurate representation of Slothrop's conquests, or whether it is fictionalized; as the investigation proceeds, certain of the women on the map are found not to exist, and Slothrop himself admits to fabricating some of the stories he tells his office mate, Tantivy. Whether the map is in fact mimetic in its relationship to Slothrop's reality does not obviate its importance, however, as fictionalized desire (or the desire of fiction) would thus be represented as having an equal force in the world as fact, a notion that would suit the novel just fine.

22. See Stephen Dodson-Truck's musical number, "The Penis He Thought Was His Own," which ostensibly refers to his own impotence but nonetheless attempts to convey to Slothrop "a terrible secret, a fatal confidence" (Pynchon, *GR* 216).

23. See Jameson, ix. It should also of course be noted that certain aspects of Stencil's investigation decidedly predate the postmodern, particularly his game of *cherchez la femme.*

24. Numerous critics explore this tie between the political and the mechanical in Pynchon, including Bruce Herzberg, who argues that the "imperial power struggles" in *V.* "exemplify the institutional belief that mechanical order is an appropriate model for the conduct of human affairs" (87), and Lance Schachterle, who acknowledges that "Pynchon sees technology as rules for manipulating more than just material objects; technology extends as well to principles for organizing whole societies along certain lines" (257).

25. This intimate tie between democracy and weapons of mass destruction is suggested in Marcuse's *One-Dimensional Man*, in which, in the fully technologized society, "even the existing liberties and escapes fall in place within the organized whole. At this stage of the regimented market, is competition alleviating or intensifying the race for bigger and faster turnover and obsolescence? Are the political parties competing for pacification or for a stronger and more costly armament industry? Is the production of 'affluence' promoting or delaying the satisfaction of still unfulfilled vital needs? If the first alternatives are true, the contemporary form of pluralism would strengthen the potential for the containment of qualitative change, and thus prevent rather than impel the 'catastrophe' of self-determination. Democracy would appear to be the most efficient form of domination" (52).

26. For an in-depth Heideggerian reading of Pynchon's representations of technology, see Schachterle.

27. For a full reading of this episode, which unpacks the fetish and the desire for the object therein, see again Hanjo Berressem.

28. See Kurzweil, *Spiritual*; Moravec; Gibson; Sterling; Rucker, *Software, Wetware,* and *Freeware.*

29. On Vaucanson, the duck, and the digestive debates, see Liu 83–85.

30. This scene of course literalizes the popular anxieties analyzed by Lynn Spigel, in which the television set was imbued with the qualities of the "other woman" (see Spigel 119).

Chapter 3

1. In the preceding, I have left "imaginary," "real," and "symbolic" in lowercase type, hoping to signify that, while these concepts owe an inescapable debt to Lacan, my analysis is not to be taken as Lacanian, in the least. To point out one among many distinctions between the use of these concepts within the novel of obsolescence and within Lacanian-inspired theory: while the Symbolic is in Lacan primarily considered to be the realm of ideology, of the Name of the Father through which the subject is disciplined and constrained, the symbolic in the novel of obsolescence is rather the realm of a verbal communication that *escapes* the ideological pressures of the image. Similarly, while in Lacanian theory the subject has no access to the Real, in the novel of obsolescence, the symbolic/verbal is imagined to provide an unmediated (or a more *truthfully* mediated) access to the real.

2. Hence, as Ferraro goes on to point out, Wilder's hysteria at the disappearance of Babette's image when the set is turned off; the disappearance of the image enacts for him the literal disappearance of his mother.

3. This of course begs the question of the visuality of print itself; I'll address this issue shortly in discussing the work of W.J.T. Mitchell.

4. Not to mention, of course, the resources that were, at the same time, being poured into the *Times*'s website. If newspapers were to go the way of the horse and carriage, the *Times* would not be left behind.

5. The following sources represent a mere smattering of such commentary: Duvall 140; Lentricchia, "Tales from the Electronic Tribe," 88–90; Lentricchia, "*Libra* as Postmodern Critique," 196; Frow 180–81; Keesey 136; Yehnert 359–60.

6. "Moving images use our senses much more effectively than do black lines of type stacked on white pages. In a video there is so much more to see, not to mention hear. Moving images can cut in, cut away, dance around, superimpose, switch tone, or otherwise change perspective, without losing their audience's attention; they can encompass computerized graphics, even words. Seeing, consequently, can become a more complex activity; we might see from more perspectives" (Stephens xi). This question of perspective is extremely important; as I'll argue later in the chapter, much of the novel of obsolescence's desire to contain the image is determined by a desire to reinforce the traditional hierarchies of watcher and watched.

7. For an exploration of the implications of history's textuality as it pertains to the postmodern novel, see Hutcheon. For a slightly counterreading of the relationship of history, textuality, and baseball in *Underworld*, see Fitzpatrick, "Unmaking."

8. See, for example, Daniel Boorstin, who feared that "image-thinking," which relies upon an "artificial imitation or representation of the external form of any object, especially of a person" (197), would triumph at the expense of "ideal-thinking."

9. This condensation of all communication into advertising may be seen in the examples that were frequently given during the late 1990s for ways that television could be made interactive in the future, in which it was suggested, for instance, that a viewer of *Friends* who liked Jennifer Aniston's dress could click on her for purchase information.

10. Whether this reification of intellectual life is directly ascribable to image-culture, however, is debatable. Mark Poster, in *The Mode of Information*, attributes the capitalist exchange of "objects" previously thought communal and inalienable to network culture; see Chapter 4 here.

11. It is worth noting that this rhetoric of the image as a tool of ideology resonates with echoes of the rationale for verbal representation's colonization of the provinces of visuality; in envisioning the threat of images that can look back, the novelist of obsolescence creates the terms of his own marginalization as object of an oppressive gaze. In this appropriation of the mantle of the oppressed, the novelist is able to mask his reinstatement of the traditional hierarchies of looking.

12. Let me hasten to add, in case I haven't made it clear enough: I consider my own project to be of a piece with cultural studies and heavily informed by cultural theory. Any hint of "pseudo" attached to those fields, any sense of decadence in the contemporary university's interest in image-culture, should be attributed to the texts under consideration, and not to the author of this study.

13. For more on entropy and the closed system in connection with the network, see Chapter 4.

14. Thus the irony that, while DeLillo attributes this redemption of the power of history to a writer with "a teaching job [and a] middling reputation" ("Power" 63), he nonetheless prides himself on never having been required to hold such a university position.

15. That this near disaster is not literally covered by the media is due only to an accident of geography; as it turns out, "[t]here is no media in Iron City." Jack's daughter expresses the indignation that the novel seems to expect the passengers to feel, the sense that this was clearly a media-driven event from the outset, whether or not the media actually showed up: "They went through all that for nothing?" (DeLillo, *WN.* 92).

16. See Lentricchia, "Tales" 106–7 and Keesey 144–45 on the implications of this movement to scientific euphemism.

17. John Fiske sees the "question at issue" here as "whether the mass media and popular culture debase our language or revitalize it" (*Understanding* 106), arguing the case for revitalization by pointing particularly to puns and coinages. DeLillo seems to suggest otherwise.

18. As Jack thinks, "We'd become part of the public stuff of media disaster" (DeLillo, *WN* 146). All such disasters are in themselves media by-products (just as the billowing black cloud is the by-product of insecticide manufacture), despite the fact that, once again, the lack of "media" in Iron City means that the disaster itself gets only minimal news attention (see 161–62).

19. See also Roland Barthes: "It is the advent of the Photograph—and not, as has been said, of the cinema—which divides the history of the world" (*Camera Lucida* 88).

20. See Green for an expanded reading of the Benjaminian moment.

21. John Duvall reads this disingenuousness as a sign that Murray is in fact a malevolent force within the novel (Duvall).

22. On this accusation of the political corruption of academia, one might also see *Mao II*'s George Haddad, the Lebanese-born political scientist (about whom Margaret Scanlan says that "the resemblance to Edward Said as he might be imagined by George Will is striking" [240]) who lures Bill Gray toward his eventual demise.

23. See Tabbi, *Postmodern* 199–201 for a different reading of this "redemption." Tabbi argues that Scott acts as a figure for the literary critic throughout the novel, and thus that Gray's literal death is a blessing for Scott, the critic having longed for—and even announced—the death of the author for some time. For, as Tabbi writes: "[t]o extend Roland Barthes's well-known formulation, the author's death has served as the condition of birth not only of the reader but of the photographer, the social scientist, the terrorist, and the literary critic" (197).

24. I elaborate on these cross-fertilizations, with particular attention to their effects on the development of television as a cultural form, in Fitzpatrick, "*Network*."

25. Interestingly, most of the recent criticism of *Underworld* that explores its media content focuses on this murder's aftermath, the playing of the tape on cable news programs and the on-air phone interview between Sue Ann Corcoran and the Texas Highway Killer, but leaves aside this originating moment of the image. See, for instance, Green 593; Walker 460.

26. On this dissociation and the fracturing of the narrative voice in the criminal moment, see Walker.

27. See also DeLillo's *White Noise*: "All plots tend to move deathward. This is the nature of plots" (26); and "every plot is a murder in effect. To plot is to die, whether we know it or not" (291).

28. These are, interestingly enough, the images literally reproduced on the section-title pages throughout the novel; for a discussion of these images and their role in the novel, see Osteen, "Becoming."

29. Thus Mitchell Stephens's suggestion that the image might allow us to "see from more perspectives" (xi).

30. It is of course arguable that the critique that follows of the link between concerns about the visual and ethnocentrism is part of the novel's satirical point, rather than evidence of its own racist underpinnings. However, satire, much like Linda Hutcheon's sense of parody, is always double coded, politically speaking: "it both legitimizes and subverts that which it parodies" (101).

31. Or, as Tim Engles suggests, in one of the few critical texts beginning to take on such questions: "Don DeLillo's *White Noise* can be read as a novel about the noise that white people make" (755).

32. John Kucich reads this move on Gladney's part in the context of other, similar moves by later DeLillo protagonists, suggesting it is symptomatic of the political "problem" with DeLillo's novels: "When not appropriating the gestures of other social groups, DeLillo's men desperately and outrageously attempt to transform white male cultural figures into acceptable models of protest" (338).

33. See, for instance, the violence unleashed by Brita's attempt to photograph Rashid's son: the narrative is quite conscious of his violence against her—he has "a violence in the eye that shows how hate and rage repair the soul"; he "hits her hard in the forearm"—while her violence against him is made to seem purely defensive: she "slaps him across the face" in retaliation for his hitting her (*MII* 237). The narration betrays little concern for her violent appropriation of his image in the first place, which requires first unmasking him: "On an impulse she walks over to the boy at the door and removes his hood. Lifts it off his head and drops it on the floor. Doesn't lift it very gently either. She is smiling all the time. And takes two steps back and snaps his picture" (236). This colonialist assumption that the boy's picture is there to be taken literally objectifies him, inspiring the violence that ensues.

34. Interestingly, the image on the final section-title page is of three young boys in a bunker, one of whom, as Mark Osteen points out, is "aiming a camera or a gun" ("Becoming" 645). It seems not to matter which.

35. This reading is indebted to Douglas Keesey's *Don DeLillo*, particularly 14–16.

36. See Keesey 143–44; Lentricchia, "Tales" 91–92; Duvall 138; and Johnston 184, among other possible sources.

37. As Michael Valdez Moses suggests, this is "the underlying promise of postmodern culture: Nature is on tap, on cable, readily available to any American viewer who possesses access to subscriber television. The sequence promises a complete and godlike control of the human 'environment'; health, weather, news, nature itself, all are at the disposal of the consumer" (64).

38. Similarly, Eugene Goodheart argues that the commodities sold in *White Noise*'s ubiquitous supermarket scenes are not food items but the representations of food; in the words of John Frow: "The world is so saturated with representations that it becomes increasingly difficult to separate primary actions from imitations of actions" (183).

Chapter 4

1. See, among other possible citations, McLuhan 247.

2. "The electric light is pure information. It is a medium without a message, as it were, unless it is used to spell out some verbal ad or name. This fact, characteristic of all media, means that the 'content' of any medium is always another medium" (McLuhan 8).

3. On the history of cybernetics, see Hayles; Johnston.

4. See Joseph Slade, "Thomas Pynchon, Postindustrial Humanist," in which Slade argues that cybernetics has "metamorphosed into systems theory on the assumption that the mechanical, electrical, biological, economic, industrial, ecological—all observable systems—belong to a single class. As technology has phased our period into postindustrialism, the word 'machine' has yielded to the term 'systems.' Cybernetics/systems theory studies the interactions and relationships between parts of systems. . . . The focus is now on organization" (57).

5. See of course *Gravity's Rainbow*, in which Pynchon suggests while there is "something com-

forting—religious, if you want," about paranoia, its opposite is the terror of "anti-paranoia, where nothing is connected to anything, a condition not many of us can bear for long" (434).

6. See Timothy Melley, who argues that paranoia is an "interpretive disorder" (16) that is inseparable at its root from "normal" processes of interpretation.

7. See Don DeLillo, *Libra*, 181. In DeLillo's rendering, these "men in small rooms" are the subjects equally of the novel and of history; the gender-specific nature of the comment is, I believe, entirely to the point.

8. See Pynchon's acknowledgment of this influence in his introduction to *Slow Learner* (13).

9. See Hayles's account of the Macy Conferences on Cybernetics, at which researchers including Wiener, John von Neumann, Claude Shannon, and Warren McCulloch gathered to develop the guiding principles of the emerging field. "To succeed," Hayles argues, "they needed a theory of information (Shannon's bailiwick), a model of neural functioning that showed how neurons worked as information-processing systems (McCulloch's lifework), computers that processed binary code and that could conceivably reproduce themselves, thus reinforcing the analogy with biological systems (von Neumann's specialty), and a visionary who could articulate the larger implications of the cybernetic paradigm and make clear its cosmic significance (Wiener's contribution)" (7).

10. See Shannon: "Frequently the messages have *meaning*; that is they refer to or are correlated according to some system with certain physical or conceptual entities. These semantic aspects of communication are irrelevant to the engineering problem. The significant aspect is that the actual message is one *selected from a set* of possible messages" (31).

11. "Audience," according to Fiske, "implies that television reaches a homogenous mass of people who are all essentially identical, who receive the same messages, meanings, and ideologies from the same programs and who are essentially passive" (*Television* 16). This suggestion of the viewing audience's homogeneity arises in part from Horkheimer and Adorno's musings on the "culture industry," in which they suggest that the "iron system" of mass communication has made individuation impossible, creating instead a fascistic mass: "What is individual is no more than the generality's power to stamp the accidental detail so firmly that it is accepted as such" (154).

12. In the case of television, however, Hall's model makes a couple of significant omissions: the feedback loop that connects audience back to producers via the ratings system, and the vast quantity of secondary publicity (reviews, interviews, "behind the scenes" pseudodocumentaries, etc.) that works to determine viewer interpretations. While the "culture industry" can never fully control reader response, and thus can never wholly avoid subversion, the industry attempts to incorporate and defuse such subversion through the feedback loops operating around television itself. It is not surprising, perhaps, that Wiener's primary contribution to the development of cybernetics is the concept of feedback, without which no system can be adequately controlled.

13. On "agency panic," see Melley.

14. We should again, as in the interaction between Benny Profane and SHROUD, remember that this description of the TV's eye as "dead" may be inapt, as "death" is not the opposite of "life" but contained within life as a boundary, a defining factor.

15. See Pynchon, *V.* 55.

16. On the connections between the uses of information, the wiring of the networks, and paranoia, see Leo Bersani: "Technology can collect the information necessary to draw connecting lines among the most disparate data, and the drawing of those lines depends on what might be called a conspiratorial interconnectedness among those interested in data

collection" (102). This drawing of "connecting lines" is an apt metaphor for the networking of the United States.

17. See also Postman's earlier but similar argument in *Amusing Ourselves to Death* about the degeneration of print culture resulting from the marriage of the newspaper and the telegraph.

18. On entropy and Pynchon, see Abernethy; Stark; Tanner; and of course the classic text, Anne Mangel's.

19. Heisenberg famously declared in 1927 that "[t]he more precisely the position [of a sub-atomic particle] is determined, the less precisely the momentum is known in this instant, and vice versa" (Heisenberg 64).

20. For a slightly different take on the matter, see Hanjo Berressem: "To complicate matters even more, there is a third, social form of entropy that intervenes in these dynamics, an entropy concerning the information that *has* been generated out of chaos. In a simulatory society in which information is everywhere, information itself becomes entropic, a realization on which Baudrillard rests his *reversal* of the second law of thermodynamics" (103).

21. Thus, while Keesey and Osteen both make convincing arguments that the product triads invoked throughout the novel do in fact signify within the contexts of the scenes in which they appear, I would counter that the novel suggests that the work of seeking such interpretations is likewise hastening signification toward its entropic end—a suggestion in keeping with the previous chapter's reading of the novel's less-than-stellar opinion of the contemporary academic project. See Keesey 141; Osteen, *Magic* 163–91.

22. See Osteen, *Magic*: "Everything is connected in the novel and in the society it portrays—but only in the underworld" (215).

23. On the fears that television's origins in surveillance and reconnaissance produced in its early consumers, see Spigel, esp. 47.

24. See also Raymond Williams, whose profound anti-McLuhanism—seen in his arguments against "technological determinism" (7)—contributes much to Barnouw's readings of the ideologically driven development of the medium. Despite my desire to avoid the pitfalls of technological determinism, I do not read Williams and McLuhan as diametrically opposed. In fact, their arguments seem to me two sides of the same coin: the ideological purposes behind the development of the technology determined that technology's structure; the ideologically-determined structure of that technology, once in place, itself delimits what messages it can send.

25. See also Postman on the distinction between Orwell's and Huxley's visions of dystopian oppression: "Orwell warns that we will be overcome by an externally imposed oppression. But in Huxley's vision, no Big Brother is required to deprive people of their autonomy, maturity and history. As he saw it, people will come to love their oppression, to adore the technologies that undo their capacities to think" (*Amusing* vii). The argument, of course, is that television is an equivalent of the feelies—which has nice resonances in conjunction with the scene of Metzger's seduction of Oedipa.

26. See, for another view, Deleuze and Guattari's conception, explored throughout *Anti-Oedipus*, of the territorializing force of paranoid desire, corresponding loosely to fascism, and its opposite, the deterritorializing force of schizophrenia, which is linked to revolution.

27. See Lynn Spigel's *Make Room for Television*, in which she uncovers multiple sources in the popular discourse surrounding the medium's introduction into the U.S. home that treat television as a window not simply *on* the world, but *open to* the world, most notably an article entitled "Be Good! Television's Watching" (118).

28. One should, of course, hear echoes of a much later president making the same blur out of

the distinction between his "filmic" and "real" experiences. This isn't exactly what Horkheimer and Adorno meant when they claimed that "[r]eal life is becoming indistinguishable from the movies" (126), but it's a telling development nonetheless in thinking about the connection between the various state apparatuses, ideological and otherwise.

29. See again Deleuze and Guattari, and particularly the link they draw between *délire* and "desire." The literal meaning of "delirium" is "to unfurrow"; thus perhaps Oedipa's only chance of remaining somehow important to "the legacy America" is to remove herself from both paranoid and schizophrenic desire. This doesn't solve the puzzle of this sentence but adds something nonetheless. See Berressem 105.

30. The term "superorganism" arises from the work of William Wheeler, who first began to conceive of emergent behavior by studying ant colonies as wholes rather than as massive numbers of individuals. See Kelly 11–13 on Wheeler's contributions to contemporary theories of emergence.

31. See again Melley, who reads such assumptions about the singularity of intelligence in conspiracy theory as a means of perpetuating liberal individualism: "To understand the organization as enemy, one must first make two tacit assumptions. First, one must conceive of the organization not as a system of complex relationships and structures, but as a unified *totality*. Second, one must imagine it as an active, living agency, against whose *will* to subdue and incorporate one must struggle. In order to save the imperiled liberal agent from incorporation into a larger controlling body, in other words, that social body must itself be imagined *as a liberal individual*, as an agent with a coherence and identity of its own, a sort of superindividual" (58).

32. Spigel also points out a dystopian underside to this electrical purity, in which such "cleansing" backfires: "television's antiseptic spaces were themselves subject to pollution as new social diseases spread through the wires and into the citizen's home" (113). I return to these fears of ethnic and sexual "otherness" and their connections to mass-mediated society in the concluding chapter.

33. See the discussion in Chapter 3 of the effects in *White Noise* of Dylar, which opens the individual so completely to the products of the mass media that identity becomes inseparable from it. Along these lines, it is useful to remember that Dylar's purpose is alleviating the fear of death, and that in *Vineland* Mucho will reminisce, along with Zoyd, about the knowledge LSD gave him that he would never die.

34. Thus David Foster Wallace, in the title of his essay "*E Unibus Pluram*: Television and U.S. Fiction," reverses the expectations for the novel of obsolescence. See Chapter 5.

35. See DeLillo's suggestion in Vince Passaro's "Dangerous Don DeLillo" that *Mao II* explores the conflict between "the arch individualist and the mass mind" (76).

36. Even more ironically, with the release of *Underworld*, DeLillo emerged from his own "seclusion" to give numerous interviews and embark upon a limited reading tour. The ironies of this emergence are epitomized by his appearance at the National Book Awards dinner (see Atlas).

37. John Fiske, in *Television Culture*, thinks interestingly about the reincorporation of the oppositional into the dominant, particularly in terms of what has been called "inoculation theory," in which a small amount of opposition is "allowed" by the dominant culture as protection against real opposition. One may perhaps see a case of the real-life emergence and incorporation of the writer in the summer 1997 example of DeLillo's ostensible model for Bill Gray, Thomas Pynchon. With the publication of *Mason & Dixon,* Pynchon moved into the public spotlight in ways thought unimaginable mere months earlier; his reclusiveness was in fact incorporated by the media as "yet another cultural narrative." During the

buildup to the novel's release, Nancy Jo Sales's "Meet Your Neighbor, Thomas Pynchon," ran in *New York* magazine, and once the book was out, "Where's Thomas Pynchon?" aired on CNN and James Bone's "Mystery Writer" appeared in the London *Times Magazine*, including a photograph Bone obtained by stalking Pynchon outside his son's preschool.

38. One might also see Michael Bérubé's assessment of Pynchon's attempts at progressive racial politics, which he argues "too often rely on a liberal sentimentalism indistinguishable from exoticization, and whose denunciations of racists and racism are welcome but sometimes cartoonish" (36).

39. Admittedly, the conclusion that Kelly draws from this argument—"This is why the network is nearly synonymous with democracy or the market" (27)—is more aligned with the libertarian ethos of the dot-com "revolution" than with any genuine social change, but the implications of such connection between the network and diversity are revealing nonetheless.

Chapter 5

1. Despite my assertion in the preceding paragraph that "younger writers" is not the intentionally gendered term that "New White Guys" unquestionably is, I nonetheless leave my pronouns in the exclusive masculine here in part because Wallace's examples in "*E Unibus Pluram*" of writers who suffer from this malady—the ironic inability to take anything seriously—are themselves male.

2. See, for instance, Nina Baym's characterization of Bloom's theory as "defining literature as a struggle between fathers and sons" (139).

3. On the mobilizations of "marginality" by canonical authors (including Thomas Pynchon), see Bérubé.

4. For a full-length comparative study of the postmodernisms represented by Pynchon and Morrison, see Patell, *Negative Liberties*.

5. For an extended reading of the relationship between Oprah's Book Club and Morrison's work, as well as of Morrison's audiobook releases, see Young.

6. See Young 198.

7. See Fiske, *Understanding*. Fiske is perhaps overly dismissive of the power of the dominant to determine mass culture but nonetheless argues interestingly for a reception theory–inflected reading of all culture, including that we label "mass," as contained via its uses and pleasures within the popular: "There is no mass culture, there are only alarmist and pessimistic theories of mass culture that, at their best, can shed light only on the industrial and ideological imperatives of the power-bloc" (177).

8. It should of course be acknowledged that, in their particular references, Horkheimer and Adorno focus upon a "whitened" derivative of jazz, but they nonetheless betray profoundly elitist attitudes in their lumping together of all nonclassical music.

9. It must be pointed out here that Kucich believes the "suspicion" of the first half of this statement to be not simply real but useful, a stand against identity politics that attempts to return white males to the center of political discourse in potentially troubling ways: "The most useful complaint of the novels is that the postmodern discourse of political opposition is dangerously built on a shallow mythology about social origins that limits its own political possibilities. Certainly, within such a discourse, the white male writer who seeks to discover his own political voice will necessarily find his desire for opposition to be unspeakable" (341).

Bibliography

Aaron, Daniel. "How to Read Don DeLillo." In *Introducing Don DeLillo*, ed. Frank
   Lentricchia. Durham, N.C.: Duke University Press, 1991. 67–81.

Abernethy, Peter. "Entropy in Pynchon's *The Crying of Lot 49*." *Critique* 14.2 (1972): 18–33.

Althusser, Louis. "Ideology and Ideological State Apparatuses." In *Lenin and Philosophy*, trans.
   Ben Brewster. New York: Monthly Review Press, 1971.

Anderson, Perry. *The Origins of Postmodernity*. London: Verso, 1998.

Armstrong, Nancy. *Desire and Domestic Fiction: A Political History of the Novel*. New York:
   Oxford University Press, 1987.

Atlas, James. "Ink." *New Yorker* (1 December 1997): 39.

Auletta, Ken. "The Impossible Business." *New Yorker* (6 October 1997): 50–63.

Auster, Paul. *The New York Trilogy*. New York: Penguin, 1990.

Auster, Paul, and Don DeLillo. "Salman Rushdie Defense Pamphlet." Rushdie Defense
   Committee USA, 1994. Accessed 3 November 1996, *haas.berkeley.edu/~gardner/rushdie_
   defense.html.*

Balsamo, Anne. *Technologies of the Gendered Body: Reading Cyborg Women*. Durham, N.C.:
   Duke University Press, 1996.

Barnouw, Eric. *Tube of Plenty: The Evolution of American Television*. 2nd rev. ed. New York:
   Oxford University Press, 1990.

Barth, John. *LETTERS* (1979). Normal, Ill.: Dalkey Archive Press, 1994.

———. "The Literature of Exhaustion." *Atlantic* 220 (August 1967): 29–34.

———. "The Literature of Replenishment: Postmodernist Fiction." *Atlantic* 245 (January
   1980): 65–71.

Barthes, Roland. *Camera Lucida: Reflections on Photography*. New York: Hill and Wang, 1981.

———. "The Death of the Author" (1968). In *The Rustle of Language,* trans. Richard Howard.
   New York: Hill and Wang, 1986. 49–55.

Baudrillard, Jean. *For a Critique of the Political Economy of the Sign* (1972). Trans. Charles
   Levin. St. Louis: Telos Press, 1981.

———. *The Gulf War Did Not Take Place*. Trans. Paul Patton. Bloomington: Indiana
   University Press, 1995.

———. *The Mirror of Production*. Trans. Mark Poster. St. Louis: Telos Press, 1975.

———. *Simulacra and Simulation* (1981). Ann Arbor: University of Michigan Press, 1994.

Baym, Nina. "Melodramas of Beset Manhood: How Theories of American Fiction Exclude
   Women Authors." *American Quarterly* 33 (Summer 1981): 123–39.

Begley, Adam. "In DeLillo's Hands, Waste Is a Beautiful Thing." Review of *Underworld* by
   Don DeLillo. *New York Observer* (15 September 1997): 38.

Benjamin, Walter. "The Work of Art in the Age of Mechanical Reproduction" (1936). In
   Illuminations, ed. Hannah Arendt. New York: Schocken Books, 1969. 217–51.

Berger, John. *Ways of Seeing* (1972). New York: Penguin, 1981.

Berressem, Hanjo. *Pynchon's Poetics: Interfacing Theory and Text*. Chicago: University of Illinois
   Press, 1993.

Bersani, Leo. "Pynchon, Paranoia, and Literature." *Representations* 25 (1989): 99–118.

Bérubé, Michael. *Marginal Forces/Cultural Centers: Tolson, Pynchon, and the Politics of the Canon.* Ithaca, N.Y.: Cornell University Press, 1992.

Birkerts, Sven. *The Gutenberg Elegies: The Fate of Reading in an Electronic Age.* New York: Random House, 1994.

Bloom, Harold. *The Anxiety of Influence: A Theory of Poetry.* London: Oxford University Press, 1975.

Bolter, Jay David, and Richard Grusin. *Remediation: Understanding New Media.* Cambridge: MIT Press, 1999.

Bonca, Cornell. "The Ineluctable Modality of the Marginal." *Orange Country Weekly* 6.28 (16 March 2001). Accessed 24 November 2002, *ocweekly.com/ink/01/28/books-bonca.php.*

Bone, James. "Mystery Writer." *London Times Magazine* (14 June 1997): 26–29.

Boorstin, Daniel. *The Image: A Guide to Pseudo-Events in America* (1964). New York: Vintage, 1992.

Boucher, Geoff. "What Will Be the Net Effect?" *Los Angeles Times* (4 July 1999): Calendar 7–9, 67.

Brinkley, Joel. *Defining Vision: The Batlle for the Future of Television.* New York: Harcourt Brace, 1997.

Connor, Stephen. *Postmodernist Culture: An Introduction to Theories of the Contemporary.* 2nd. ed. Oxford: Blackwell, 1997.

Coover, Robert. "The End of Books." *New York Times Book Review* (21 June 1992): 1, 23–25.

Czitrom, Daniel J. *Media and the American Mind: From Morse to McLuhan.* Chapel Hill: University of North Carolina Press, 1982.

Davidson, Cathy. Introduction to *The Columbia History of the American Novel*, Ed. Emory Elliott. New York: Columbia University Press, 1991. 3–5.

Davidson, Cathy, ed. *Reading in America: Literature and Social History.* Baltimore, Md: Johns Hopkins University Press, 1989.

Davies, Duncan, Diana Brathurst, and Robin Brathurst. *The Telling Image: The Changing Balance between Pictures and Words in a Technological Age.* Oxford: Clarendon Press, 1990.

Debord, Guy. *The Society of the Spectacle* (1967). Trans. Donald Nicholson-Smith. New York: Zone Books, 1994.

DeCurtis, Anthony. " 'An Outsider in This Society': An Interview with Don DeLillo." In *Introducing Don DeLillo*, ed. Frank Lentricchia. Durham, N.C.: Duke University Press, 1991. 43–66.

Deleuze, Gilles, and Felix Guattari. *Anti-Oedipus: Capitalism and Schizophrenia* (1977). Minneapolis: University of Minnesota Press, 1983.

———. *A Thousand Plateaus: Capitalism and Schizophrenia* (1980). Minneapolis: University of Minnesota Press, 1987.

DeLillo, Don. *Americana* (1971). New York: Penguin, 1989.

———. *Great Jones Street* (1973). New York: Penguin, 1994.

———. *Libra* (1988). New York: Penguin, 1991.

———. *Mao II* (1991). New York: Penguin, 1992.

———. *The Names* (1982). New York: Vintage, 1989.

———. *Players* (1977). New York: Vintage, 1989.

———. "The Power of History." *New York Times Magazine* (7 September 1997): 60–63.

———. *Ratner's Star* (1976). New York, Vintage, 1989.

———. *Running Dog* (1978). New York: Vintage, 1989.

———. *Underworld.* New York: Scribner, 1997.

———. *White Noise* (1985). New York: Penguin, 1986.

Derrida, Jacques. "Signature Event Context." In *Limited Inc.* Evanston, Ill.: Northwestern University Press, 1988. 1–24.

Dienst, Richard. *Still Life in Real Time: Theory after Television.* Durham, N.C.: Duke University Press, 1994.

Dobrzynski, Judith H. "Glory Days for the Art Museum." *New York Times* (5 October 1997).

Duvall, John N. "The (Super)Marketplace of Images: Television as Unmediated Mediation in DeLillo's *White Noise.*" *Arizona Quarterly* 50.3 (Autumn 1994): 127–53.

Eggers, Dave. *A Heartbreaking Work of Staggering Genius.* New York: Simon and Schuster, 2000.

Elliott, Jane. "O Is for the Other Things She Gave Me: Jonathan Franzen's *The Corrections* and Contemporary Women's Fiction." *Bitch Magazine* 16 (Spring 2002): 70–74.

Emerson, R. W. "Ode, Inscribed to W. H. Channing." *The Norton Anthology of American Literature.* Vol. 1. 4th ed. New York: W.W. Norton, 1994. 1141.

Engles, Tim. " 'Who Are You, Literally?': Fantasies of the White Self in White Noise." *Modern Fiction Studies* 45.3 (1999): 755–87.

Epstein, Joseph. "Who Killed Poetry?" *AWP Chronicle* 21.4 (1989): 1.

Ferraro, Thomas. "Whole Families Shopping at Night!" In *New Essays on White Noise,* ed. Frank Lentricchia. New York: Cambridge University Press, 1991. 15–38.

Fiedler, Leslie. "Cross the Border, Close the Gap." In *The Collected Essays of Leslie Fiedler.* Vol. 2. New York: Stein and Day, 1971. 461–85.

Fiske, John. *Television Culture.* New York: Routledge, 1994.

———. *Understanding Popular Culture.* New York: Routledge, 1989.

Fitzpatrick, Kathleen. "The Exhaustion of Literature: Novels, Computers, and the Threat of Obsolescence." *Contemporary Literature* 43.4 (Fall 2002): 518–59.

———. "*Network*: The Other Cold War." *Film and History* 31.2 (2001): 33–39.

———. "The Unmaking of History: Baseball, Cold War, *Underworld.*" In *UnderWords: Perspectives on Don DeLillo's* Underworld, ed. Joseph Dewey and Steven Kellman. Newark: University of Delaware Press, 2002. 144–60.

Foucault, Michel. *The Archaeology of Knowledge and the Discourse on Language.* Trans. A. M. Sheridan Smith. New York: Pantheon, 1972.

———. "What Is an Author?" In *Language, Counter-memory, Practice: Selected Essays and Interviews,* ed. Donald F. Bouchard. Ithaca, N.Y.: Cornell University Press, 1977. 113–38.

Francese, Joseph. *Narrating Postmodern Time and Space.* Albany: State University of New York Press, 1997.

Franzen, Jonathan. *The Corrections.* New York: Farrar, Straus and Giroux, 2001.

———. "Perchance to Dream." *Harpers* 292 (April 1996): 35–54.

Freeman, John. "Toni Morrison: Love at the Last Resort." *The Independent* (21 November 2003). *enjoyment.independent.co.uk/books/interviews/story.jsp?story=465925.*

Frow, John. "The Last Things before the Last: Notes on *White Noise.*" In *Introducing Don DeLillo,* ed. Frank Lentricchia. Durham, N.C.: Duke University Press, 1991. 175–91.

Garrison, Deborah. "On Reading and Writing." In "Dean's Day Extra," a mailing from the Graduate School of Arts and Sciences, New York University. N.d. (2000?).

Gass, William. "The Medium of Fiction." In *Fiction and the Figures of Life.* New York: Knopf, 1971. 27–33.

Gates, Henry Louis, Jr. *Loose Canons: Notes on the Culture Wars.* New York: Oxford University Press, 1993.

Gibson, William. *Neuromancer*. New York: Ace Books, 1984.

Gilder, George. *Life after Television: The Coming Transformation of Media and American Life*. New York: Norton, 1992.

Gilmore, Michael T. "The Literature of the Revolutionary and Early National Periods." In *The Cambridge History of American Literature: Volume 1, 1590–1820*, ed. Sacvan Bercovitch. New York: Cambridge University Press, 1994.

Gleick, James. *Chaos: Making a New Science*. New York: Viking, 1987.

Golden, Robert E. "Mass Man and Modernism: Violence in Pynchon's *V.*" *Critique* 14.2 (1972): 5–17.

Goodheart, Eugene. "Some Speculations on Don DeLillo and the Cinematic Real." In *Introducing Don DeLillo*, ed. Frank Lentricchia. Durham, N.C.: Duke University Press, 1991. 117–130.

Graff, Gerald. *Literature against Itself: Literary Ideas in Modern Society*. Chicago: University of Chicago Press, 1979.

Green, Jeremy. "Disaster Footage: Spectacles of Violence in DeLillo's Fiction." *Modern Fiction Studies* 45.3 (1999): 571–99.

Green-Lewis, Jennifer. *Framing the Victorians: Photography and the Culture of Realism*. Ithaca, N.Y.: Cornell University Press, 1996.

Habermas, Jurgen. "Modernity—An Incomplete Project" (1980). In *Modernism/Postmodernism*, ed. Peter Brooker. London: Longman, 1992. 125–38.

Halberstam, Judith, and Ira Livingston, eds. *Posthuman Bodies*. Bloomington: Indiana University Press, 1995.

Hall, Stuart. "Encoding/decoding." In *Culture, Media, Language: Working Papers in Cultural Studies, 1972–79*, ed. Stuart Hall, Dorothy Hobson, Andrew Lowe, and Paul Willis. New York: Routledge, 1992. 128–38.

Hansen, Miriam. *Babel and Babylon: Spectatorship in American Silent Film*. Cambridge: Harvard University Press, 1991.

Haraway, Donna. "A Cyborg Manifesto." In *Simians, Cyborgs, and Women: The Reinvention of Nature*. New York: Routledge, 1991. 149–81.

Harper, Phillip Brian. *Framing the Margins: The Social Logic of Postmodern Culture*. New York: Oxford University Press, 1994.

Hayles, N. Katherine. *How We Became Posthuman: Virtual Bodies in Cybernetics, Literature, and Informatics*. Chicago: University of Chicago Press, 1999.

Hassan, Ihab. "Toward a Concept of Postmodernism." In *The Postmodern Turn*. Columbus: Ohio State University Press, 1987. 84–96.

Heidegger, Martin. "The Question Concerning Technology." In *Basic Writings,* ed. David Farrell Krell. New York: HarperCollins, 1992. 307–41.

Heisenberg, Werner. "The Physical Content of Quantum Kinematics and Mechanics." In *Quantum Theory and Measurement*, ed. John Archibald Wheeler and Wojciek Hubert Zurek. Princeton Series in Physics. Princeton: Princeton University Press: 1983. 62–84.

Herzberg, Bruce. "Breakfast, Death, Feedback: Thomas Pynchon and the Technologies of Interpretation." *Bucknell Review* 27.2 (1983): 81–95.

Hite, Molly. "The Postmodern Novel." In *The Columbia History of the American Novel*, ed. Emory Elliott. New York: Columbia University Press, 1991. 697–725.

hooks, bell. "Postmodern Blackness." *Postmodern Culture* 1.1 (September 1990): paragraphs 1–15. *muse.jhu.edu/journals/postmodern_culture/v001/1.1hooks.html*.

Horkheimer, Max, and Theodor W. Adorno. "The Culture Industry: Enlightenment as Mass Deception" (1944). In *The Dialectic of Enlightenment,* trans. John Cumming. New York: Continuum, 1993. 120–67.

Hutcheon, Linda. *The Politics of Postmodernism.* New York: Routledge, 1989.

Huyssen, Andreas. *After the Great Divide: Modernism, Mass Culture, Postmodernism.* Bloomington: Illinois University Press, 1986.

Jacobs, Alexandra. "Clench Buttocks and Talk!" *New York Observer* (29 April 2002): 1.

Jameson, Fredric. *Postmodernism, or, the Cultural Logic of Late Capitalism.* Durham, N.C.: Duke University Press, 1991.

Johnson, Steven. *Emergence: The Connected Lives of Ants, Brains, Cities, and Software.* New York: Scribner, 2001.

Johnston, John. *Information Multiplicity: American Fiction in the Age of Media Saturation.* Baltimore, Md.: Johns Hopkins University Press, 1998.

Keesey, Douglas. *Don DeLillo.* Twayne's United States Authors Series 625. New York: Twayne, 1993.

Kelly, Kevin. *Out of Control: The New Biology of Machines, Social Systems, and the Economic World.* Cambridge, Mass.: Perseus Books, 1994.

Kernan, Alvin. *The Death of Literature.* New Haven: Yale University Press, 1990.

Kingston, Maxine Hong. *Tripmaster Monkey: His Fake Book.* New York: Vintage, 1990.

Kirby, Lynne. *Parallel Tracks: The Railroad and the Silent Cinema.* Durham, N.C.: Duke University Press, 1997.

Kittler, Friedrich. "Gramophone, Film, Typewriter." *October* 41 (Summer 1987): 101–18.

Klapp, Orrin. *Overload and Boredom: Essays on the Quality of Life in the Information Society.* New York: Greenwood Press, 1986.

Klinkowitz, Jerome. *Literary Disruptions: The Making of a Post-Contemporary American Fiction.* 2nd. ed. Urbana: University of Illinois Press, 1980.

Kucich, John. "Postmodern Politics: Don DeLillo and the Plight of the White Male Writer." *Michigan Quarterly Review* 27.2 (Spring 1988): 328–41.

Kurzweil, Ray. *The Age of Intelligent Machines.* Cambridge: MIT Press, 1990.

———. *The Age of Spiritual Machines: When Computers Exceed Human Intelligence.* New York: Viking, 1999.

Langer, Adam. "Star Power." *Book Magazine* 31 (November/December 2003): 40–46.

Lapham, Lewis. "The Eternal Now." Introduction to *Understanding Media: The Extensions of Man* by Marshall McLuhan. Cambridge: MIT Press, 1994. ix–xxiii.

Lawrence, D. H. "Surgery for the Novel—or a Bomb" (1923). In *Selected Literary Criticism.* New York: Viking, 1966. 102–8.

———. "Why the Novel Matters." In *Selected Literary Criticism.* New York: Viking, 1966. 114–18.

Leavis, F. R. *Two Cultures? The Significance of C. P. Snow.* New York: Pantheon, 1963.

LeClair, Tom. *In the Loop: Don DeLillo and the Systems Novel.* Urbana: University of Illinois Press, 1987.

Lehman, David. *Signs of the Times: Deconstruction and the Fall of Paul de Man.* New York: Poseidon Press, 1991.

Lentricchia, Frank. "*Libra* as Postmodern Critique." In *Introducing Don DeLillo,* ed. Frank Lentricchia. Durham, N.C.: Duke University Press, 1991. 193–215.

———. "Tales from the Electronic Tribe." In *New Essays on White Noise,* ed. Frank Lentricchia. New York: Cambridge University Press, 1991. 87–113.

Levinson, Paul. *The Soft Edge: A Natural History and Future of the Information Revolution.* New York: Routledge, 1997.

Liu, Catherine. *Copying Machines: Taking Notes for the Automaton.* Minneapolis: University of Minnesota Press, 2000.

Lyotard, Jean-François. *The Postmodern Condition: A Report on Knowledge*. Minneapolis: University of Minnesota Press, 1979.

Mangel, Anne. "Maxwell's Demon, Entropy, Information: *The Crying of Lot 49*." *Triquarterly* 20 (1971): 194–208.

Mann, Paul. *The Theory-Death of the Avant Garde*. Bloomington: Indiana University Press, 1991.

Marcuse, Herbert. *One-Dimensional Man: Studies in the Ideology of Advanced Industrial Society* (1964). Boston: Beacon Press, 1966.

Marx, Leo. *The Machine in the Garden: Technology and the Pastoral Ideal in America*. New York: Oxford University Press, 1964.

Massumi, Brian. *A User's Guide to Capitalism and Schizophrenia: Deviations from Deleuze and Guattari*. Cambridge: MIT Press, 1992.

McGrath, Charles. "The Triumph of the Prime-Time Novel." *New York Times Magazine* (22 October 1995): 52–59, 68, 76, 86.

McKeever, W. A. "The Moving Picture: A Primary School for Criminals." *Good Housekeeping* (19 August 1910): 184–86.

McLuhan, Marshall. *Understanding Media: The Extensions of Man* (1964). Cambridge: MIT Press, 1994.

Melley, Timothy. *Empire of Conspiracy: The Culture of Paranoia in Post-War America*. Ithaca, N.Y.: Cornell University Press, 2000.

Miller, Laura. "The *Salon* Interview: David Foster Wallace." *Salon*. *salon.com/09/features/wallace1.html*.

Mitchell, W. J. T. *Picture Theory: Essays on Verbal and Visual Representation*. Chicago: University of Chicago Press, 1994.

Moody, Rick. *The Ice Storm*. Boston: Little, Brown, 1994.

Moravec, Hans. *Robot: Mere Machine to Transcendent Mind*. New York: Oxford University Press, 1999.

Morrison, Toni. "Introduction: Friday on the Potomac." In *Race-ing Justice, En-gendering Power: Essays on Anita Hill, Clarence Thomas, and the Construction of Social Reality*. Ed. Toni Morrison. New York: Pantheon, 1992. vii–xxx.

———. *Jazz*. New York: Knopf, 1992.

———. "Nobel Lecture." 7 December 1993. *nobel.se/literature/laureates/1993/morrison-lecture.html*.

———. "The Official Story: Dead Man Golfing." Introduction to *Birth of a Nation'hood: Gaze, Script, and Spectacle in the O. J. Simpson Case*. Ed. Toni Morrison and Claudia Brodsky Lacour. New York: Pantheon, 1997.

———. "On the Backs of Blacks." *Time Magazine* (2 December 1993). Special Issue: "The New Face of America." *time.com/time/community/morrisonessay.html*.

———. *Song of Solomon*. New York: Knopf, 1978.

Moses, Michael Valdez. "Lust Removed from Nature." In *New Essays on White Noise,* ed. Frank Lentricchia. New York: Cambridge University Press, 1991. 63–86.

Moulthrop, Stuart. "No War Machine." In *Reading Matters: Narrative in the New Media Ecology*. ed. Joseph Tabbi and Michael Wutz. Ithaca, N.Y.: Cornell University Press, 1997. 269–92.

National Railroad Museum Web site. *nationalrrmuseum.org*.

Newman, Charles. *The Postmodern Aura: The Act of Fiction in an Age of Inflation*. Evanston, Ill.: Northwestern University Press, 1985.

Norris, Christopher. *What's Wrong with Postmodernism: Critical Theory and the Ends of Philosophy*. Baltimore, Md.: Johns Hopkins University Press, 1990.

Olster, Stacey. "When You're a (Nin)jette, You're a (Nin)jette All the Way—Or Are You? Female Filmmaking in *Vineland*." In *The Vineland Papers*, ed. Geoffrey Green, Donald T. Greiner, and Larry McCaffrey. Normal, Ill.: Dalkey Archive Press, 1994. 119–34.

Osteen, Mark. *American Magic and Dread: Don DeLillo's Dialogue with Culture*. Philadelphia: University of Pennsylvania Press, 2000.

———. "Becoming Incorporated: Spectacular Authorship and DeLillo's *Mao II*." *Modern Fiction Studies* 45.3 (Fall 1999): 643–74.

Owen, Bruce. *The Internet Challenge to Television*. Cambridge: Harvard University Press, 1999.

Passaro, Vince. "Dangerous Don DeLillo." *New York Times Magazine* (19 May 1991): 36, 38.

Patell, Cyrus. "The Hive Mind." In *Raizes e Rumos: perspectivas interdisciplaires em estudos americanos*, ed. Sonia Torres. Rio de Janiero: 7 Letras Press, 2001.

———. *Negative Liberties: Morrison, Pynchon, and the Problem of Liberal Ideology*. Durham, N.C.: Duke University Press, 1999.

Pattee, Howard. *Hierarchy Theory: The Challenge of Complex Systems*. New York: Braziller, 1973.

Percy, Walker. "The Loss of the Creature." In *The Message in the Bottle: How Queer Man Is, How Queer Language Is, and What One Has to Do with the Other*. New York: Farrar, Straus and Giroux, 1975. 46–63.

Plato. *Phaedrus*. Trans. Alexander Nehamas and Paul Woodruff. Indianapolis: Hackett, 1995.

Poster, Mark. Introduction to *The Mirror of Production* by Jean Baudrillard. St. Louis: Telos Press, 1975. 1–15.

———. *The Mode of Information: Poststructuralism and Social Context*. Chicago: University of Chicago Press, 1990.

Postman, Neil. *Amusing Ourselves to Death*. New York: Penguin, 1986.

———. *Technopoly: The Surrender of Culture to Technology*. New York: Vintage, 1993.

Powers, Richard. *Galatea 2.2*. New York: Farrar, Straus and Giroux, 1995.

Pynchon, Thomas. *The Crying of Lot 49* (1966). New York: Perennial, 1990.

———. *Gravity's Rainbow* (1973). New York: Penguin, 1995.

———. "Is It OK to Be a Luddite?" *New York Times Book Review* (28 October 1984): 1, 40–41.

———. "A Journey into the Mind of Watts." *New York Times Magazine* (12 June 1966): 34–35, 78, 80–82, 84.

———. *Mason & Dixon*. New York: Henry Holt, 1997.

———. *Slow Learner*. Boston: Little, Brown, 1984.

———. *V.* (1963). New York: Perennial, 1990.

———. *Vineland*. Boston: Little, Brown, 1990.

Reed, Walter. "*Don Quixote*: The Birth, Rise, and Death of the Novel." *IJHL: Indiana Journal of Hispanic Literatures* 5 (Fall 1994): 263–78.

Reid, Robert H. *Architects of the Web: 1,000 Days that Built the Future of Business*. New York: Wiley, 1997.

Remnick, David. "Exile on Main Street: Don DeLillo's Undisclosed Underworld." *New Yorker* (15 September 1997): 42–48.

Riesman, David, with Nathan Glazer and Reuel Denny. *The Lonely Crowd* (1950). New Haven: Yale University Press, 1969.

Rubin, Louis. *The Curious Death of the Novel: Essays in American Literature*. Baton Rouge: Louisiana State University Press, 1967.

Rucker, Rudy. *Freeware.* New York: Avon Books, 1997.

———. *Software.* New York: Avon Books, 1987.

———. *Wetware.* New York: Avon Books, 1988.

Sales, Nancy Jo. "Meet Your Neighbor, Thomas Pynchon." *New York Magazine* (11 November 1996): 60–64.

Santayana, George. "The Genteel Tradition in American Philosophy." In *The Genteel Tradition: Nine Essays.* Cambridge: Harvard University Press, 1967. 37–64.

Scanlan, Margaret. "Writers among Terrorists: Don DeLillo's *Mao II* and the Rushdie Affair." *Modern Fiction Studies* 40:2 (Summer 1994): 229–52.

Schachterle, Lance. "Pynchon and the Civil Wars of Technology." In *Literature and Technology,* ed. Mark Greenberg and Lance Schachterle. Bethlehem, Pa.: Lehigh University Press / Associated University Presses, 1992. 253–74.

Schickel, Richard. "Cinema Paradiso." *Wilson Quarterly* 23.3 (Summer 1999): 56–70.

Schivelbusch, Wolfgang. *The Railway Journey: The Industrialization of Time and Space in the Nineteenth Century.* Berkeley: University of California Press, 1986.

Seltzer, Mark. *Bodies and Machines.* New York: Routledge, 1992.

Shannon, Claude, and Warren Weaver. *The Mathematical Theory of Communication* (1949). Urbana: Illinois University Press, 1964.

Sheppard, R. Z. "Fiction's New Fab Four." *Time Magazine* (14 April 1997): 89–90.

Simpson, David. *The Academic Postmodern and the Rule of Literature: A Report on Half-Knowledge.* Chicago: University of Chicago Press, 1995.

Sklar, Robert. *Movie-Made America: A Cultural History of American Movies.* Rev. ed. New York: Vintage, 1994.

Slade, Joseph. "Communication, Group Theory, and Perception in *Vineland.*" In *The Vineland Papers,* ed. Geoffrey Green, Donald T. Greiner, and Larry McCaffrey. Normal, Ill.: Dalkey Archive Press, 1994. 68–88.

———. "Thomas Pynchon, Postindustrial Humanist." *Technology and Culture* 23.1 (1982): 53–72.

Snow, C. P. *The Two Cultures: And a Second Look.* New York: Cambridge University Press, 1963.

Sontag, Susan. "Against Interpretation." In *Against Interpretation.* New York: Anchor Books, 1990. 3–14.

Sorid, Daniel. "Team Links Brain Cells with a Robot." *New York Times* (15 June 2000).

Spigel, Lynn. *Make Room for TV: Television and the Family Ideal in Postwar America.* Chicago: University of Chicago Press, 1992.

Spilka, Mark, and Caroline McCracken-Flesher, eds. *Why the Novel Matters: A Postmodern Perplex.* Bloomington: Indiana University Press, 1990.

Stark, John. *Pynchon's Fictions: Thomas Pynchon and the Literature of Information.* Athens: Ohio University Press, 1980.

Steiner, George. "Talent and Technology." *Prospect* 8 (May 1996): 30–33.

Steiner, Wendy. "Postmodern Fictions, 1960–1990." In *The Cambridge History of American Literature: Volume 7, Prose Writing, 1940–1990,* ed. Sacvan Bercovitch. New York: Cambridge University Press, 1999. 425–538.

Stephens, Mitchell. *The Rise of the Image, the Fall of the Word.* New York: Oxford University Press, 1998.

Sterling, Bruce. *Schizmatrix Plus.* New York: Ace Books, 1996.

Tabbi, Joseph. *Postmodern Sublime: Technology and American Writing from Mailer to Cyberpunk.* Ithaca, N.Y.: Cornell University Press, 1995.